THE VOCAL VISION

VOICE & SPEECH TITLES FROM APPLAUSE

ACTING IN OPERA (Video) with Jonathan Miller

THE ACTOR AND THE TEXT by Cicely Berry

MY BREATH IN ART by Beatrice Manley

ON SINGING ONSTAGE by David Craig

A PERFORMER PREPARES by David Craig

SPEAK WITH DISTINCTION by Edith Skinner

    Edited by Lilene Mansell and Timothy Monich

    90-minute audiotape also available

A VOICE OF YOUR OWN (Video) with Patsy Rodenburg

THE VOCAL VISION

VIEWS ON VOICE
BY 24 LEADING TEACHERS, COACHES & DIRECTORS

EDITED BY

MARIAN HAMPTON
&
BARBARA ACKER

THE VOICE AND SPEECH TRAINERS ASSOCIATION

EDITORIAL ADVISORY BOARD
MARY CORRIGAN
DONNALEE DOX
DOROTHY RUNK MENNEN

APPLAUSE
NEW YORK • LONDON

AN APPLAUSE ORIGINAL

The Vocal Vision: Views on Voice by 24 Leading Teachers, Coaches &Directors
edited by Marian Hampton and Barbara Acker
Copyright © 1997 by: Marian Hampton and Barbara Acker

"I Charge Thee Speak": John Barrymore and His Voice Coach, Margaret Carrington
originally appeared in the Journal of American Drama and Theatre

A Consumer's Guide to Voice and Speech Training originally appeared in the New
England Theatre Journal

That Secret Voice reproduced by permission of The Agency (London) Ltd.
©1992 Cicely Berry.
First published in SHAKESPEARE COMES TO BROADMOOR,
Jessica Kingsley Publishers Ltd
All rights reserved and enquires to The Agency (London) Ltd., 24 Pottery Lane,
London, W11 4LZ fax 0171 727 9037

Library of Congress Cataloging-in-Publication Data

The vocal vision : voice in tomorrow's theatre / edited by Marian Hampton
    & Barbara Acker.
      p.   cm.
    ISBN 1-55783-282-X (pbk.)
      1. Voice culture. 2. Acting. 3. Speech. I. Hampton, Marian E.
  II. Acker, Barbara.
  PN2071.S65V63 1997
  808.5--dc21   97-13927
                                         CIP

British Library Cataloging-in-Publication Data

A catalog record for this book is available from the British Library

APPLAUSE BOOKS

211 West 71st Street
New York, NY 10023
Phone (212) 496-7511
Fax: (212) 721-2856

A&C BLACK

Howard Road, Eaton Socon
Huntington, Cambs PE19 3EZ
Phone 0171-242 0946
Fax 0171-831 8478

Distributed in the U.K. and European Union by A&C Black

CONTENTS

PREFACE

The book you are at this moment perusing grew out of a need to explain the work of voice and speech teachers to people in other walks of life and a deep desire to share the richness of experience and diversity of thought that is VASTA, the Voice and Speech Trainers Association. The book has been several years in the making, but it had its beginnings when I asked Donna Aronson, Head of the Theatre Program at Incarnate Word College, to help me brainstorm a table of contents for a new book that would express the ideas and issues, the hopes and dreams, and the deeply held thoughts and beliefs of our VASTA colleagues. It was Donna who came up with the title, *The Vocal Vision*, and it seemed to me that her title perfectly expressed the necessity of being heard in a world which is rapidly becoming more and more visually oriented, as well as pointing out that voice professionals are indeed, possessed of a rare sort of vision. We are visionaries of the intangibles of tone, quality, inflection, breath, and phoneme, of sound and sense, of attributes which may sometimes be scientifically measured but which are nonetheless ephemeral in nature. The human voice is the most truly of-the-moment of all the senses, for it pierces the silence of the universe with an invisible yet undeniable power, and its power may be remembered as if indelible in the mind's ear. Who among us can forget a particular word or tone of voice, spoken at just the right—or just the wrong—moment?

The prospective Table of Contents contained the names of some of the "stars" of voice work whom you will see represented in this volume: Arthur Lessac, Kristin Linklater, Cicely Berry, Bonnie Raphael, Lucille Rubin, Dorothy Mennen, Sue Ann Park, Patsy Rodenburg, Mary Corrigan, names which have become the equivalent of household words in the theatre voice profession. Also contained were the names of other stars, such as Evangeline Machlin, the great voice teacher and text writer, who served on the founding Board of Directors of VASTA; and Clyde Vinson, present for the founding of VASTA in 1986, but now passed on. We had hoped for both of these VASTA pioneers to be represented in this book and regret that they are present only in spirit on these pages.

As the volume progressed, other "stars" began to emerge, such as Kittie Verdolini, our brilliant voice scientist; Frankie Armstrong, the inspired British folk singer/teacher, better known in Britain, but loved by all of those VASTA members who participated in her workshop at an Annual Conference; Dudley Knight, the elegantly articulate professor at the University of California, Irvine; Catherine Fitzmaurice, passionate theorist and teacher of teachers; and many others whose thoughts you will find between the covers of this book.

No attempt has been made to shape the essays/articles contained herein into a common style. Each writer speaks from his or her own heart and experience, and in her/his own voice. This seemed appropriate for a compendium of the writings of voice teachers. Thus, subjects range from factual to speculative, from historic to prophetic, from intimate personal reflections to thoughtful consideration of issues to meditative philosophical musings. There is something here for everyone interested in the field of vocal training.

Barbara Acker, as co-editor of this book, has contributed a great deal of creative thought and energy to its realization. Without her efforts, it might never have been realized. Other contributors of time and talent were our editorial board, Mary Corrigan, Dorothy Mennen, and Donnalee Dox. Thanks are due also to those who helped in the final preparation of the manuscript: Caroline Cox, Jamie Axtell, and Tricia McDermott; and to Glenn Young, our publisher, and Rachel Reiss, his editorial associate, for their guidance and patience.

VASTA intends this book as a document of the ten years of our organization's history, of the history which led up to the founding of VASTA, and of our best thinking about where we are headed. We are grateful to all of those who work tirelessly in the field, to help actors, students, and people in all stations in life to fulfill their potential as speakers and communicators. It is to them that we dedicate this book.

Marian Hampton
April 1997

I

VOICE IN THEATRE AND SOCIETY

1

THOUGHTS ON THEATRE, THERAPY, AND THE ART OF VOICE

KRISTIN LINKLATER

Theatre, therapy, and the art of voice: it would be presumptuous of me to think that I can corral these three huge and restless subjects into a cohesive holding pen for long enough to separate, brand, and relocate them for classification, breeding, and sale, were these not cattle already grazing in my training pastures. I have to examine the art of voice training within the context of where theatre is headed next and what kind of healing power is generated by my work and the greater art it serves because these questions are daily present, not theoretically but practically, in my classroom.

At drama school in London where I trained and taught in the late fifties and the early sixties, teachers of actors considered themselves gardeners: planting, fertilizing, pruning, and grafting as they tended the budding and blossoming of each student actor. Metaphors of racehorse training came in now and then to help harness powerful imaginative energies in impulsive muscular bodies, but one way or another cultivation of preexisting talent was the order of the day. The sociological and psychological climate of the nineties is demanding animal husbandry, some experience in lion taming and the ability to recognize a rabid raccoon as part of the job description for actor trainers.

I remember students at the London Academy of Music and Dramatic Art sitting with their eyes obediently closed in Iris Warren's voice production class, looking inward and downward with their minds' eyes as they relaxed and breathed. When asked what they saw deep inside themselves they reported lovely visions of rose gardens or beds of lilies, forest pools or calm seashores. Recently, in response to a similar exercise at a workshop I was running, an actor gave a vivid description of looking down through a glass ceiling at a cageful of growling, slavering, enraged wild animals which would eat her alive were they to escape.

If, as many voice and acting teachers suggest, the voice that tells the truth comes from deep inside, forged on the anvil of emotion, and if, as seems evident, the theatre of tomorrow even more than today must reflect an increasingly violent society if it is to remain useful, the actors whom we train must be able to conjure up their own psychological monsters from the deeps, look them in the eye, tame them, and train them to leap through hoops of fiery texts telling tales of horror that lead to redemption, destruction, or transmutation. For catharsis is still the mission of the theatre. And catharsis originally meant shedding light into dark corners. Dark corners of kitchens or dark corners of the soul, the darkness, the dirt, must be illuminated before it can be cleansed. The human soul absorbs dirt from dusty psyches, grubby memories, and scrofulous experiences, and the actor must at least have knelt down on the floor of his or her own soul with the scrubbing brush before contemplating the illumination of the souls of others.

In my experience, the voice is a powerful scrubber, with words an excellent cleaning agent. The right words are alchemical touchstones that can turn the deadly, poisonous lead of an abused and wounded childhood into the life-restoring gold of art. A playwright forges the right words to expose a monstrous issue that society would rather ignore, and it is the actors who have found words to bring their own monstrous experiences out of the dark and into the light who can bring authenticity and the ring of truth to the playwright's words. The climate of our times has brought words that used to be taboo into the broad light of day and onto the airwaves. Experiences that used to be hidden in shame or not even known because not named can now be named easily. "Incest," "rape," "abuse" — with the naming comes the memory and the monsters emerge from their caves in the shape of stories we would rather not hear and emotions that shake the day loose from its moorings.

Theatre is alchemy and if theatre is to be potent the ingredients must not avoid the extremities of life. Unless the actor-alchemists are emotional warriors, the lead will turn to pablum that poisons as it soothes. If the actors are emotional warriors what must the teachers be? How do these bold words translate into classroom life?

These are some of the questions that are being asked with increasing urgency: what are the boundaries of teaching? Can I teach theatre and stay clear of involvement with my students' personal problems? What happens when a student comes face to face with an unresolved trauma in the middle of my class? Should I be able to draw a clear line between theatre and therapy?

A lively, three-hour panel discussion at the 1993 Association for Theatre in Higher Education Conference in Philadelphia centered on the subject of theatre and therapy, airing for the first time in public some of the anxieties that exist in the field. Acting teachers, voice teachers, and movement teachers are finding that exercises which they have used for years in successful pursuit of theatrical ends have, in the past five or ten years, been triggering responses in their students of an increasingly emotional nature, and sometimes stimulating memories of childhood traumas that may seem inappropriate to the training task at hand.

Here are some not uncommon events in theatre training classrooms: A voice teacher spends a couple of classes teaching relaxation, and gradually student belly muscles let go so that breath can enter a body fully for what seems like the first time in years, and the student begins to cry uncontrollably. When asked to say something about what is going on, the tears are articulated in memories of a) being told not to answer back by a parent or a teacher; b) holding his breath as his parents fought; c) hating her body so much that she became anorexic, bulimic, and/or suicidal; d) being sexually or physically abused in a variety of ways... the list goes on. A movement teacher notices a lack of coordination in a student's body; exercises for the legs and pelvic area provoke resistance — boredom, exaggeration, panic, or collapse. A student may say in response to an individual critique: "I don't understand" or "I'm frozen" or "I don't feel anything in my lower body; it feels numb." These days the movement teacher who has read any kind of psychophysical literature or even *Newsweek* will suspect sexual or physical abuse as the cause of this separation of mind from body. An acting teacher asks students to bring in a monologue. A student brings in something from *Extremities* (or one of a dozen other plays or monologues about rape). She cannot speak. A contemporary scene class includes scenes from *A Lie of the Mind* or *'night Mother*. One actor has a brother who is dying in hospital; another's sister committed suicide.

We ask for the truth on stage. We say that the actor's raw material is her/himself. The demands we make are time-honored and valid. Yet many teachers, myself included, are becoming alarmed by the responsibility they are faced with when these facts of theatrical life spark a personal horror story in the student actor, together with the threat of "going over the edge," "collapsing," "falling apart," "breaking down completely," "going crazy, killing myself." What are we supposed to do?

Those of us teachers who belong to the humanistic, psychophysical, "use yourself" genre find ourselves in a variety of classroom dilemmas:

a)   One student "goes" and they all "go": horror is as contagious as tears.

b)   Half the class is in tears and the other half is in angry resistance, furious that their time is being wasted in emotional indulgence.

c) We deal with the situation in the classroom; someone says, "This seems like therapy to me. Are you qualified?" If no one says it, someone is noisily thinking it.

d) We do not deal with this situation in the classroom and set up an appointment during office hours. The next thing we know is that we have taken on hours of personal commitment and bought into an unhealthy codependent scenario.

e) We tell the student we are not equipped to deal with such distress and suggest or insist that s/he gets counselling. The next thing we hear is that s/he cannot get an appointment until next month or that s/he would rather work it out in class because acting class is better than therapy.

These emotional incidents, I hasten to emphasize, are not the whole story but only, as it were, the highlights in a long semester's hard daily work. Focusing on the problems in this way is akin to presenting a two-hour performance of nothing but the climax scenes from all of Shakespeare's plays. Luckily in both the plays and the classes there are long stretches of calm exposition; sometimes there is a dull passage and often there is comic relief. The purpose of this examination is to isolate the emotional incidents and see where (or whether) they fit into the art of theatre. Are they just therapy? Just personal?

Of course, there is a whole other style of teaching that manages to avoid the personal, emotional problems altogether and I confess I often wish that I had adhered to the school that says: "Leave your personal life behind you when you come into the classroom (or rehearsal or the stage)." This approach says: "You become a character and for a brief moment on stage you escape from yourself." The notion of losing myself in a character implies that the character is bigger, more estimable, more exciting than I am while the idea of finding the character in myself suggests that I am multi-faceted and illimitable and that each character I play finds the roots of its truth in the fact that I am All as well as One; that from my wholeness I can create multiplicity; that I have the capacity to understand the natures of all people and can become any of them by expanding the seed of my understanding until it dislodges and rearranges the ingredients of my personality and a different part of me dominates. This temporarily dominant characteristic proceeds to rearrange my physical and vocal behavior as I develop a character that is rooted in truthful experience because rooted in me, and has blossomed into a flower or a tree or a poisonous plant — or a ravening beast or a purring kitten — that is unrecognizable to my familiar self.

The kind of teaching that we focused on at the ATHE conference and to which I clearly belong is this inside-out approach to training the actor. In fact, we are training the person who will become the actor and therefore we are inevitable inhabitants of therapeutic territory because we are restoring a lost sense of illimitability. It does not seem such a bad thing really; if we believe that one of the missions of theatre is healing we can accept the fact that healing goes on in the microcosms of theatre we call classrooms. The person who becomes the actor needs unblocked access to the fullest capacity of voice, body, emotions, intellect, and imagination. Very often one or more of these essential attributes is held hostage by past experience that says emotional expression is dangerous, impulse and spontaneity are dangerous, words are dangerous. Inner voices shout STOP at the moment a creative impulse yells GO and the resonance of these hidden voices flooding the inner ear deafens the sound of one's own true, individual voice. There is no authentic individual artistry until the reverberation of personal truth replaces the resonance of naysaying; until then derivative performance is inevitable and real art is elusive.

If real artistry depends on the authenticity of the artist's voice, and if we are talking about the real, physical voice, not a metaphorical one, then we must recondition real usage on a psychophysical level, by which I mean not just the discrete respiratory and laryngeal mechanisms but their deployment in the larger arsenal of emotional defenses. The emotions that are being defended are often huge and the order of the art they produce is seldom "recollected in tranquillity" but more often forged in a chaotic escape on the rehearsal floor or in the classroom when they are afforded relaxation and permission.

Nine times out of ten, magical performance results when a teacher and her student can channel undammed emotional energy into a scene or a monologue or a poem. We witness artistic transformation. But the tenth time, an enormous personal story presents itself that demands personal work right then and there. Such work can result in personal transformation or vocal transformation or breakdown. When either transformation or breakdown occurs at the very end of a class there is potentially some danger that the student will be left feeling out of control or disoriented if s/he is unused to intense experiences of this nature.

We are operating within a social climate that has changed radically in the past twenty years and many of us are looking for ways that expand the safety nets both for us and for our students without ducking the issues. At the ATHE conference we talked about ways of "cooling down" emotionally to balance the practice of "warming up," and shared techniques of "stepping out" of emotional hot spots. Panel member Robert Barton, who teaches acting at the University of Oregon, adamantly expressed the point of view that if we soft-pedal, sidestep, or soothe away the painful emotions that erupt from time to time in our classes we will produce actors fed on pablum who will in turn produce theatre that is pablum. We must be able to step into the fire. And we must avoid getting burned. We must build emotional muscle and exercise the passions, passions which are hottest at the core of the toughest personal ordeals. And we and our students must be able to step out of the core, cool down and go on with our days.

I remember saying to the actor with the glass-ceiling zoo in her belly that if she could learn the names of the raging beasts and find the keys to their respective cages, she could, over time, develop a relationship with her monsters. I suggested that if she let them out and exercised them on a leash they would learn to behave and might become useful guard and attack animals. They could also transform into fabulous engines of creativity when she needed them to be that and then go back under the glass and sleep peacefully. This is, of course, easier said then done, and I am grateful to Robert Barton and to Susanna Bloch, who was also on our ATHE panel, for offering us practical techniques for handling wild animals.

Susanna Bloch brings a background in neuroscience to her study of emotional effector patterns and her work is provoking considerable interest among actor trainers. From laboratory observations she found that specific emotional feelings were linked to specific patterns of breathing, facial expressions, degrees of muscular tension, and postural attitudes. Her experiments led her to develop a "step out" procedure which will restore neutrality to someone who is caught in an emotion and cannot shift the state.

The procedure is: take at least three slow, regular, and deep full breathing cycles; then totally relax the face muscles and change posture. Not only will this end the emotional state but it will obviate the "emotional hangovers."

Robert Barton pointed out that we seldom spend as much time on rituals to end classes or rehearsals as we do to start them off. "Ritual" might simply mean a warm-up or a circle but might be more elaborate. His suggestion was that we end each work session as we began, thus formally "taking off the mask" of our work and returning to our daily selves. He also has a "step out" process in which he as the teacher stands opposite the person who is emotionally trapped and asks to be mirrored as he stretches, massages his own face, and breathes slowly. He always sets up agreements with his students that give the option of disengagement from any exercise that may be emotionally demanding; he defines boundaries of safety and sets up ground rules of support and comfort. For example, students learn to ask for a hug if that is what they need. Unsolicited hugs are discouraged as they sometimes come from the wrong person even though with the right intention; sometimes they come from the wrong person with the wrong intention; sometimes they are counterproductive because an emotional condition that looks painful from the outside is thrilling from the inside and comfort is an unnecessary distraction from a long-desired and enlivening experience.

I myself sometimes ask a student who suddenly starts crying uncontrollably in the middle of a group relaxation to sit out for ten minutes and write in his or her journal until s/he feels better—it is important that s/he does not leave the room. This can work well for the more advanced student who understands what is happening on the personal level, does not really need help, and appreciates that the class cannot always stop its momentum to accommodate the rise of an emotion, but also wants to record and examine the details of a valuable spontaneous memory or insight. The student always rejoins the class in a good state. This solution honors emotions without letting them rule the day.

Students who have yet to learn the value of the sudden onset of emotion and who feel frightened when it happens must, of course, have personal attention. With careful planning, a light-hearted approach, and a modicum of luck, I try to postpone the possibility with new students until we have a shared experience of voice exercises that can be drawn on. At that point real emotion is a key ingredient in the true reconditioning of habitual defense patterns. Once the student knows how to keep the throat open and can choose where the breath goes in the body, vulnerability is experienced as strength, and emotions become a source of power as their owner is no longer incapacitated by them.

Quite recently I had a student who even after a semester of voice work still spoke in a breathy whisper most of the time. She was the survivor of all manner of childhood abuses, was in therapy, had attended violence workshops, and generally understood her state of mind and body well but could not yet risk a full voice. One day in class she became choked with fear as she was doing an exercise and whispered, "I'm scared I'm going to cry." I said, "Open your throat and say that on the vibrations of sound." She opened up her clenched throat and in a loud, clear voice said, "I'm scared I'm going to cry—oh! That's funny—now I don't want to cry any more!" When she went back to the whisper the emotion threatened to incapacitate her; when she found her voice the emotion receded.

The practice of setting up agreements with one's students is essential to the health and integrity of this kind of work. Without them we run the risk of abusing our positions of power. Students must know that they are in a collaborative relationship with their teacher; that they are working together towards the same goal. Ideally, "problems" are made explicit and "solutions" openly discussed. If the teacher diagnoses resistance (and worthwhile change nearly always meets some resistance) the student should accept the diagnosis and endorse the prescription before the teacher administers treatment.

This is not only healthful but twice as effective as the old authoritarian mode of teaching—so long as the partnership is genuine. The ultimate caveat about emotional work with acting students is that the teacher must be as psychologically healthy as possible.

The question of the emotional and mental health of theatre practitioners is obviously beyond the scope of this piece of writing and may properly belong in a standup comedy routine, but it should be equally obvious that there are serious ethics involved in stirring up the interface of the personal and the artistic experiences. Teaching that stays forever behind a locked classroom door is almost always unhealthy. The artistic worth of a method of teaching can and should be measured in an artistic product visible to all. Artistic output can provide some sort of guarantee of the competence of a teacher and the health of his or her methods; process and product can be assessed in a public product more objectively than in the classroom. But finally it is the teacher who should be his or her own severest judge. S/he must ask students for honest feedback on how the classroom culture and content is working and be willing to make changes where responses are negative. Honesty, openness, and courage in a teacher create an environment where students can be honest, open, and brave. They want to be; if they are not then we must take responsibility for having failed them.

For myself, I teach the same basic technical progression of voice production exercises that I inherited from Iris Warren between 1957 and 1963. But after thirty years of admittedly random consciousness raising and refining I see much more about my students now than I used to. Willy-nilly (often more nilly than willy) I have learned more and more about the causes of human dysfunction and I have read enough about psychological development to recognize not only the behavioral manifestations of traumatic childhood but the potential for huge expressive talent beneath the behavior. I have picked up basic principles from Stanley Keleman and many others that clarify how the body's intelligence develops survival habits that save a person's life but can at some point be exchanged for the energy of life itself. Dozens of books, seminars, and workshops are available to the searcher after truth, freedom, and creativity.

What I have learned reflects the psychophysical knowledge of this century in this very privileged country. We—we privileged few—have been relieved enough of our external survival needs to be free to focus on internal survival and something which has come to be called "human growth." (This is a term which should not deny the moral growth many humans experience in the face of external adversity.) The "human growth movement" of the past twenty years focuses on release from psychophysical adversity, emphasizing the benefits of emotional and psychological freedom in achieving a fully lived life. This goal would be immorally self-centered did it not include the notion that the purpose of growing as a human being must be to look at and listen to the whole human condition with increased understanding and compassion and, in the case of the artist, to shed an ever brighter light on the causes of humanity's more egregious errors. The theatre is home to both light and sound, and it is the sound of the actor's voice that is the ultimate instrument of catharsis. It penetrates like ultrasound to the hidden recesses of a listener's soul if its frequencies are begotten in true feeling and delivered free of distortion and effort.

The voice of a very good actor rings with authenticity whether in the wild poetic extensions of the classics of Western dramatic literature or the equally wild poetic extensions of language that express the contemporary soul *in extremis*, and although I know more and more about the workings of the psyches of my students and my intention is that they prosper as human beings, my objective is that they become very good, very exciting, very idiosyncratic actors. My super-objective is that they advance the art of theatre.

We often use as a challenge to take our discipline seriously the analogy of the musician or the dancer: talent is not enough — you must train. Does a talented musician (or dancer) go out and perform Beethoven (or *Swan Lake*) on the strength of talent alone? Invoking the years of scales and arpeggios, barre exercises and hard, slogging, self-sacrificial technical work that dedicated musicians and dancers undertake before inflicting themselves on an audience, we goad our students into voice and body work that, alas, often trains them out of authenticity and into a slick showcase of styles.

Musicians seldom have to perform Beethoven *and* hard rock, and ballet dancers are not required to do both *Swan Lake and* break-dancing, but actors must be able to deliver the authentic ring of the streets, the shelter, the prison, the hospice *and* Shakespeare, Restoration, Shaw, Chekhov, and Tennessee Williams. Today's high earners in film and television are often cast from real life. Training would have ruined their authentic look and sound. If they continue in the profession, however, they discover the need for training and often come to a moment when their artistic wings yearn for the spread of the classics. Do the classics represent the highest echelon of the art of theatre? Or is the art at its highest when it engages a community (or just one individual) and helps bring healing through reflection and transformation? Is it inevitable that "the classics" are distanced from the daily grind of real life? Or can they connect with current issues at least as graphically as a movie or a soap opera?

Those of us who train actors' voices cannot afford to make a choice between the classics and contemporary drama, nor do we have to make any such large distinction. We encounter contemporary drama daily in our contemporary students and when we listen carefully they already possess the stuff of the classics, only requiring access to some different forms of expression to gain entry and command. What sometimes seems like emotional chaos tearing us apart like an internal zoo full of rabid wild animals becomes the passion that authenticates King Lear on the heath, Medea, and Oedipus.

The miracle of the voice is that it connects both inwardly and outwardly, and the depth of the art with which the voice is deployed by the actor depends on the depth to which it plunges internally in the creative process and the scope of its outward journey. Voice is air and vibration; it is infinitely malleable, transformable, and expressive. It can communicate more intimate nuance over a greater distance than the body can. It is the bridge between souls. The art of the voice flourishes in the ground of a healthy psyche, and though in today's theatre it is an art not much heralded, I hope that if we can heal the rifts that society and upbringing have made between the souls and voices of the actor/artists that are our charges now, the voices of the next theatre generation will discover how to penetrate the inner worlds of their audience with harmonies of understanding, compassion, and true healing.

2

FROM BEYOND WILDNESS TO BODY WISDOM, VOCAL LIFE, AND HEALTHFUL FUNCTIONING:
A JOYOUS STRUGGLE FOR OUR DISCIPLINE'S FUTURE

ARTHUR LESSAC

A quick glance at the title of this discussion highlights four major, interrelated topics — Body Wisdom, Vocal Life, Healthful Functioning, and Joyous Struggle — and our essay begins with an advanced concept of Body Wisdom. In Lessac training, "Body Wisdom" may be characterized as representing and stressing a particular "kind" and "quality" of physicalized inner intelligence that beneficially and creatively affects one's behavior, attitudes, and actions. Within our frame of reference, *body* is synonymous with *inner*, and *wisdom* refers to *energy* and the *transmission of energy* within our personal environment — an inner world all its own.

When we relate to such vital instinctive body dynamics as the smile, spirit, rhythm and balance, resonance, synergy, imaging, and love, we really mean a physical and harmonic sensing of the *inner* smile, *inner* spirit, *inner* rhythm and balance, *inner* resonance, etc.

This is the calibre of body wisdom that liberates the gut-related drive to dissolve and diffuse habit patterns — patterns that needlessly put day-to-day (dis)stress and strain on the human organism — habit patterns that lead to loss of inner rhythm, inner equilibrium — patterns that inevitably obscure perception and conscious awareness of body wisdom qualities.

The inference that follows is that besides the obvious existence of our outer collective environment, there is the "not so obvious" existence of the individual *inner environment* wherein is harbored multifarious experiencing systems, and wherein there exists an ecology all its own. Thus, with such awareness, we are all personally offered a genuine *forward directive* towards developing a natural and vital "systems approach" to a fresh understanding of the ecology of the human body organism. Put another way, it represents the very essence and nature of a never-ceasing *gentle turbulence* and *kaleidoscopic motion* within each and every individual "body environment."

There was a time when there existed just one environment which, in and of itself, elicited a smooth-flowing response from the human organism; a time when the body and mind operated in consonance with one another and in accord with the rhythms of the immediate surroundings—a time when the environment was virginally "wild" and the human animal, in order to survive and survive better, actually had to function better.

Unlike the wild environment of "instinctive man," our current complicated and socially determined environment no longer demands complete health of the human instrument, just various prescribed terms of "social health." In exchange for the advances of civilization, technology, moral and ethical codes, systems of law and government, social and economic order, and the ascension over all other living beings, we have had to leave behind the instinctive, physically reactive human instrument. It seemed a small cost to pay for civilization, and in the past there has always been a balance between what was gained and what was lost.

Indeed, as long as the psychology of outside institutions remained constant, we could continue to somehow evolve self-images that made sense. But now, environmental frameworks are shifting. We experience immense changes within the space of a single lifetime. Our entire sense of time has shifted. Body time and social time are out of sync. The outside natural environment is polluted and is contagiously infecting our personal inner environments. Our institutions have become inconsistent. Worse, they are chaotic and contradictory. The "civilized constants" we have become accustomed to are no longer working. Societal frameworks and behavioral standards that allowed perception of ourselves within some outer uncompromising context are no longer trusted. Religious and moral constants no longer exist. Political and ideological constants have failed. And even sexual frameworks are in a state of rapid, uncertain transition. The more constants disappear, the more we lose our own sense of context.

In other words, the balance has been lost. As a result, we are still deteriorating physically and perceptually but no longer growing intellectually. We still accept as normal poor posture, poor breathing, tension, anxiety, the loss of musicianship in our voices, a lack of perceptual and physical responsiveness, and increasingly more frequent psychosomatic illnesses, disease, and weakened states of body and mind. Only the exchange rate has changed as the bottom dropped out of the justifying norm for these unhealthy compromises.

The chaos and constantly shifting currents of the outer environment have had a jarring effect upon the psycho-physical balance of the human organism. We have even adopted a common terminology around it; Alvin Toffler calls it "Future Shock." Properly understood, Future Shock is Culture Shock to the human body — at least to the body as it was designed to function in an environment that once was "wild." Because of Future Shock, psychological evolution is no longer a natural process generation to generation. Consequently, survival in the age of Future Shock is no longer a question of further "civilization."

What, then, are we looking for? What do we have left to hold on to? Where is the new context now that the "civilized constants" are no longer working? The fact of the matter is, within our own individual personal body environments, we represent the only possible remaining natural wildness; the only remaining natural environment that is potentially reclaimable. This is our context. As an adult species, we may not now function with the same health that was implicit in the human instrument when the environment was truly wild, nor would we, even if we could, return as knowing, communicating, intellectual beings to that environment.

But we certainly can rediscover and regain much of the instinctive body wisdom that we lost along the way and then some. It is constantly regenerated every time a child is born and grows naturally and healthfully, provided the child is truly prevented from becoming patterned and adulterated out of optimal function by the imitative standards (now shifting and inconsistent) of the outer environment. It is now eminently possible to understand ourselves as natural, instinctive, and primitive environments of our own, and to reconstruct self-images within the context of Body Wisdom awareness. If we reconstruct this awareness as a "body of knowledge" and allow it to become a complex source of our self-image-making, we may at least create for ourselves one persevering environment — one constant referent to which we can organically relate.

To do this means to move "beyond wildness," beyond that early discipline, to an occidental (western) Wisdom that takes its place proudly and operates co-laterally with oriental (eastern) Wisdom as beacons of future health and future light. It is now that we must find and engage the special, intrinsic energy qualities that will help us to redefine "terms," diffuse ingrained habit patterns, and seriously reassess the concept of "healthfulness." Now is the time to reacquaint ourselves with our own "inner wildness" as one of "nature's originals" that demands, first and foremost, total body health in order to survive. It is now that we must navigate and encourage our rediscovered "inner wildness" (and the elements of it we desperately need to reclaim) to live within quite another discipline. It is now that such elements must live and function as revitalized intelligence, knowledge, and awareness within a rejuvenated civilized discipline.

And so, in order to regain the body wisdom inherent within every single human organism (without going back to the cave), it is incumbent upon each of us to develop a still more profound intimacy with the ecology of our own body environment, relearn its secrets, and re-explore its fullest potential.

All human beings are constitutional beneficiaries of superb "Stradivarius" equipment, barring defect or accident. Many human beings manage to realize a proportion of this natural potential and place themselves on the path to mature and healthful functioning. Those who persevere could possibly become our great artists, our great talents, our great athletes. The danger, unfortunately, is that for too many the fullest genuine realization of Body Wisdom potential is becoming so rare that it is being perceived as something almost super-human.

A number of "destruct patterns" do have the power to force the attrition of body wisdom. Such destruct patterns might, for example, stem from 1) a loss of relationship and empathy with our body organism and a loss of qualitatively communicating with it; 2) the conditioned patterning of our perceptive capacity and general body functioning by outside constraints, inhibitions, and super-imposed standards; 3) the premature deterioration of the body's systems and Stradivarius talents due to misuse or non-use, which generally leads, unknowingly, to imitation, suppression, surface functioning, and extrinsically-ordered behavior.

Nevertheless, the fact remains that the capacity to rediscover, perceive, and coordinate all the body's inborn potential does remain a natural and primitively instinctive one. We all once had the potential and, to reiterate, it is still reclaimable. Once started, our multi-faceted body intelligence and body languages will establish a foundation of awareness that softens and melts away habit-conditioned patterns, making them more fluid and turning them once again into a freshly responsive awareness to the day-to-day need for growth, positive change, and healthful progress. We will relearn how to speak to ourselves: how to discover and explore the myriad number of body languages, how to interpret them, how to communicate with them, how to reclaim the body's natural genius.

We will be rediscovering "origin" all over again, upon recognition that this seemingly new form of organic communication is, in fact, an old intelligence rooted in non-linear language that organically instructs the body to do and to know what the body is doing through bio-neurally experiencing "the feel of it."

Because humanity all over our planet is immersed in chaos, it is essential now, more than ever, to learn and train ourselves how to gauge two very dominating opposites: 1) to learn how the body wants to function instinctively and naturally towards its optimal capacities, and 2) at the very same time, to continue to recognize and perceptualize how the present outer environmental and social influences can destructively condition, pollute, and erode our inner natural capacities and creative potential. When the former takes precedence, and influences, and "leads" the latter, we just may be able to approach the state of healthful equilibrium between the two environments.

Vocal Life

Body Wisdom encompasses all of Vocal Life and its verbal dynamics, as well as all the non-verbal communicating behaviors. "Vocal" relates to any and all phonated activity whether it be speaking, singing, calling, screaming, yodeling, laughing, crying, humming, etc. "Life" here implies vitality, energy, involvement, spirit, imaging, awareness, perception, etc., through the senses rather than through the intellect. In Lessac training it has become a "given" that vital (organic) voice training should always be preceded by *integrated body training* — just as speech training must be preceded by vital voice/music training.

We teach ourselves breathing through body posture, and posture through body breathing. We develop warm, rich, mellow, expressive, euphonious speech and singing tones through physical inner harmonic sensing, rather than through the ear. We learn perfect symmetrical pear-shaped vowels through kinesthetic facial posture dynamics, not through the outer ear. We teach ourselves smart, sensitive, concise, exciting, euphonic consonant articulatory skills and speech intelligibility through inner body harmonic music-sensing, rather than by imitation or through the ear from the outside. These are all *body jobs* — all body wisdom — all originating intrinsically, and organically — all experienced and applied realistically, qualitatively, creatively. I have learned more about "smooth utterance" and "speech rhythms" from our body energy "sit-up" explorations than from any other source.

Voice and speech training is body training and body training is language/communication training, as well as bio-neuro-psychic "heightened sensitivity" training. The eyes, the smile, the frown, laugh, vocal timbre, gestures, energy states, the sigh, gasp, pant, pause, interpretive breath, reflexive or aggressive body movements, and many more are all non-verbal body dynamics. It seems quite logical to postulate the "seeming contradiction" that "the body speaks *louder* than words." In our training we could very profitably consider *"words"* as empty symbols or receptacles that require and demand being filled up with a "quality essence" usually referred to as *inner feeling, inner experiencing, inner perceiving, inner involvement, inner subtext.* It is the essential "self-to-self" communicating that fuels and feeds the inter-related "self-to-other" communicating.

We might take note of the pair of "trinity configurations"at work here: Body/Voice/Speech; and Physical Life/Vocal Life/Emotional Life. Together they become a "holistic Gestalt constellation"—all of which is sensed, identified, and perceived through what I call *"kinesensic" inner harmonic intelligence.*[1] Inasmuch as our body organism is constantly in a state of gentle turbulence and kaleidoscopic motion, "kinsensics" becomes a "self-teaching" process to objectively experience the harmonic dynamics that will be applied as organic instructions. These organic instructions are experienced motor-image configurations which are powerful reducers of complexity and serve to evoke a conscious capacity to perceive and register the body's vital internal physicalized experience. It is a first step in the heuristic process of identifying sensations and promoting a new, fresh quality of awareness, that grows naturally into a "visceral awareness" and matures into "habitual awareness."

Such awareness, by the way, is not to be confused with judgment. It is, rather, a sensory reinforcement of the body's perceiving systems; such awareness is a form of "spirit energy" that becomes part of the fail-safe "servomechanism" helping the body stay "on-keel." It is a great teacher of organic balance, rhythm, and humor-sensing and provides for an ongoing flow of the "pleasure principle."

Also worth noting is the sibling relationship of the voice and the emotions. What is fascinating about the relationship is that, while the emotional experiencing system can and does function easily and well without vocal-verbal accompaniment, the vocal experiencing system is always in a "Siamese-twinned," one-to-one relationship with the emotional experiencing system. If we keep in mind that the first thing that "destructs" during frenzied anger or hysterical behavior is the voice, it should seem logical that a built-in physical control of our voice becomes "constitutionally bonded" with a built-in physical control of our "self." The inner physical control-valve of vocal energy production, naturally provides a *co-lateral organic control-valve* over our emotional behavioral effectiveness, so that as long as our bone-conducted voice remains salutary and liberated, so will our nerve

---

[1]   Kinesensic: *Kino*—for movement and motion; *enens*—for basic essence, nature, spirit, study of sensation; *sens* (or sensing)—for the actual identifying and dealing with internal cues, signals, codes, and other body intelligence/information; *sic*—for familiar occurrence.

conducted emotions remain healthy, sturdy, creative and equilibrated. Clearly, the healthful functioning of our natural human *potential* derives considerably from an organic contribution of physical/vocal, emotional, and perceptual relationships. The *physical* vital forces are the most tangible, and when experientially understood, are synergistically inter-mixed and naturally "joined-in" by the other two.

HEALTHFUL FUNCTIONING

Throughout this discourse of Body Wisdom and Vocal Life, I have been using the generic term "energy" (often contracted in my publications, to the phonetic pronunciation of its consonants as "NRG"). Let us examine this term a bit more specifically. When related to the human body, NRG too often appears to function quantitatively — too much NRG can cause fatigue, too little NRG brings on apathy. One person has a lot of NRG; another, none at all. This is all quantification, and I am interested in quality. I am interested in understanding NRG by translating it into "expression"!

We all know that universal NRG cannot be lost, that it does not get used up, and cannot be originally and additionally created. We also know that it *can* be converted into different forms of NRG — electrical, chemical, hydro, thermal, tidal, nuclear, wind, resonance, vibratory, neural, psychic, etc. We also know that all this, or most of it, takes place within the human organism, and that we could *qualitatively* feel it, experience it, perceive it, and use it. We could teach ourselves to see, hear, touch, taste, feel, perceive, and sense their attributes inside each of us as part of NRG states or specific NRG *qualities*, rather than as energy quantities. These belong primarily to the harmonic right brain rather than to the numeric left brain, and body wisdom NRG becomes a verb rather than a noun as it functions creatively, synergistically, and synesthesically, among and within the body's many experiencing systems. A good "motto" for this self-teaching modality might be: "The more heuristic the approach, the more holistic the process."

Presently, I am working with seven such body NRG* states, which I published in my text *Body Wisdom: The Use and Training of the Human Body*. Three of these are vocal NRG qualities, servicing the voice, speech, and singing talents, and four are non-vocal NRG qualities that serve the body as a whole. Their quality components and ingredients cover a spectrum involving the sensing or radiance, buoyancy, potency, inter-involvement NRG, tonal-resonance NRG, consonant-instrumental NRG, kinesthetic-yawning-structural NRG.

These components generate vital ingredients such as lightness, weightlessness, gracefulness, flowing motion — balance, equilibrium, inner

---

*   The symbol NRG is also an acronym for: Neurological Regenerative Growth.

rhythm—strength, power, vigor—agility, alertness, spark, pulse, spirit—inner-glee and eagerness, innocent vulnerability, fresh curiosity—body humor, body expressiveness—fear diffusion, fatigue diffusion, gut awareness—the "pleasure principle," self-trusting, the self-image complex.

I have been exploring a number of other NRG dynamics that are potential candidates for classification as "body NRG states." These are still unpublished and in varying degrees of investigation and experimentation. But I do want to emphasize that before earning the status of a "body NRG state" at least seven qualifications must be met. Each must be able to contribute meaningfully and productively to the following:

1st   Body Therapy: contributing to the art of healing;

2nd   Body Ecology: contributing to the art of health and wellness; to body de-pollution, and body feedback;

3rd   Body Esthetics: (as opposed to body anesthetics) contributing to habitual awareness, and conscious expanded sensitivity;

4th   Body Performing: contribute to the creative arts and skills and talents;

5th   Body Athletics: contribute to the creative arts in sports and physical education;

6th   Body Juvenation: contribute to the creative arts in living and growing young—right on through age ninety-nine;

7th   Body Synergy: contribute to the validating and activating of synergy and synesthesia in the human organism.

These body NRG states, both vocal and non-vocal, are complete languages. Each has its own art form, its own expressiveness, dance style, song style, speech quality. Each has its own sensitivity, character, personality—and, yes, its own inner "spiritus" or spirituality.

All these NRG qualities, plus such body dynamics as breathing, postures, laughter, imaging, relaxer/energizers, inner rhythm and balance, the inner "love" NRG, are not techniques—they are Stradivarius resources that we use to explore the human instrument in order to recapture it. Whether we use them singly or in combinations, we train ourselves to tune in to them, play them with creative sensibilities, and use them with healthful effectiveness.

Obviously I am talking about holistic health, about therapeutic living, about being selfishly committed and dedicated to healthful functioning, particularly as relating to our inner environment. Each of us can, and should, exert actual control over our private personal environment before attempting to bring healthfulness to our outer environments which include our outside institutions, our politics, our sense of history, our disciplines. If our ongoing quest is for "universal truths," then it must include "universal health," and that means a profoundly fierce appreciation of health as the opposite of disease or distress—a "universal health" that will stave off any pollution, whether in the air, in the human organism, in politics, in the education system, in the theatre/film discipline. For many centuries we have been repeating the axiom that "cleanliness is next to Godliness," but in today's social and political ecology, the word *cleanliness* is not essential enough to meet the realism of our tempestuous and chaotic outside environment. Since we live in an explosive era in which redefinition of many terms, phrases, mottos, and key words is absolutely mandatory, we need to redefine this maxim, from *cleanliness* to *"healthfulness* is next to Godliness"—and I care little whether that last word is spelled with one "o" or two; for me they carry the same meaning.

So I would like to define "health" as *an ongoing healing and "growing young" process.* And, as a "majority of one," I individually feel very strongly that I must be singularly selfish in acquiring that healing process, in nurturing it, in protecting it. When I opt for peace, for example, I do so selfishly, for my own personal health. When I eschew prejudice, I do not want to do it for the personal honor of morality, ethics, or principle. I want to do it because it is healthful, because it is good for my body's constitution, because prejudice is a deadly poison, and I, very selfishly, do not want to succumb to it. If I eschew prejudice in order to remain healthy, I find that health, then, is much more strongly binding than moral or ethical amenities. And besides, if I eschew prejudice solely for the sake of personal health, then morals, ethics, and principles will take care of themselves; they become built-in— they become part of instinct, and thus they become healthier all the time.

The finest and healthiest theatre ensembles, or string quartets, or basketball teams are created only by genuinely selfish artists and talents; they may not see a lot of each other on the outside, but they sure do "commune" with each other on stage, or in the concert hall, or on the basketball court. The very best preventive medicine against body poisons is a very healthy and generous supply of positive selfishness.

Of course, a major requirement in this process is the ability and the need to recognize what constitutes poisons and pollutions. If I become aware of tightening my muscles, or impoverishing my thinking, or find myself lying, and if I am ready to recognize and accept these as dangerous and potentially cancerous poisons swimming around in my body, then it is probably true that only my selfish desire and need for health would prompt me to get rid of them or totally neutralize them.

There are at least three different significant categories of poisons that invade or reside within the human organism: 1) the "people produced" outside toxic and radiation pestilence — these are the most difficult to eradicate or defend against due to socioeconomic and political conflicts; 2) substance abuses of tobacco, drugs, alcohol and their "follow-through" addictions; 3) the most dangerous of all — and at the same time (all opinions to the contrary notwithstanding) the easiest to overcome or conquer — the psychological and emotional poisons such as hate, inculcated fear, prejudice, wrathful anger, greed, dishonesty, lying, etc. These are the most dangerous poisons because the ego's vanity, itself a near-poison, is loathe to recognize greed or prejudice or lying as poisons; more dangerous, too, because, unless we deal with the emotional and psychological poisons first, we will have neither the will, nor the "guts," nor the motivation to tackle the others. They are, on the other hand, the easiest to overcome, only if one is sufficiently and strongly selfish enough about one's own quality and calibre of health.

To some extent it is a matter of choice — do we choose health, wellness, and organic body youth and freshness? If we do, it must be eminently clear that there is no room in our body environment for both the Body Wisdom NRG's and the polluting poisons — one or the other must go! The Body Wisdom NRG qualities cannot constitutionally or physically tolerate such natural predatory enemies. Any thought whatsoever of accommodating a compromising "double occupancy residence" in order to somehow turn the "poisons" into a "lesser evil," is false logic; for such wishful thinking will simply exacerbate the body condition into a "creeping paralysis."

I can think back to the days of Senator Joseph McCarthy and tell you that when thousands of fine Americans were ordered to lie about their friends, and were threatened with jail if they refused, it was quite easy to see how one might prefer to be healthy in jail and "keep one's healthy voice," rather than be unhealthy out of jail and "lose one's healthy voice." A healthy voice always needs a healthy body — and a healthy body demands a healthy voice — on all levels, including that of "healthfully" expressing oneself.

On quite another and different level of "voicing," I might as well suggest right here that any speech or voice exercise that encourages distortion, artificiality, phoniness, or habit patterning is, from the psychological and personal viewpoint, unhealthy and will not only lead to conflict in the communication process but to the communicating personality as well.

Health, then, on all levels could become our new barometer: our new standard for our voice, for our body, for our speech, for our soul, for our thoughts, for our creativity, for our art! If someone or some program is not fully healthy, that someone or program cannot be fully morally healthy, ethically healthy, or honesty-healthy. Heaven preserve us from the partially moral, partially ethical, and partially honest!

A Joyous Struggle!

In a sense, the word "struggle" refers to striving — to problem-solving — to a militant defense of principle and commitment.

It evokes experiencing a "spirit NRG quality" that belongs to a love of labor and a labor of love. In that sense we really do live in order to struggle — struggle in order to conquer both inner and outer poisons — struggle in order to function healthfully — struggle in order to grow, mature, and achieve.

I am convinced that in a primitive way our body NRG states and our inner harmonic sensing system contribute fundamentally and harmonically toward ongoing investigation and study in parapsychology, brain research, extrasensory perception, psychokinetic theories, and other bio-neuro-psychic research.

Today no problem exists in registering and measuring our heartbeat and pulse and brain waves, and tomorrow, some day, we will also know how to register and measure our "spirit beat," and our "soul pulse," and our "buoyancy weightlessness." It is, for me, a bone-marrow feeling that these body para-dynamics exist neuro-physically and synesthesically — and therefore, realistically somewhere in the still-mysterious wildness of our inner organismic environment. It is the perception of the mysterious that is the origin of discovery. There is certainly plenty of mystery in the infinitely vast reclaimed wilderness of our body's inner space — an inner space we can plumb, and teach ourselves to taste, feel, and perceive. This will surely become manifest if we develop the instinct and inclination, not only to wonder, but also to wander through that inner wilderness of ours; to wander and wonder with the ingenuousness and curiosity of "that child within us" — as well as with the inquisitive searching, questioning, and mature wisdom of the adult. This can be the "key" to learning how to cope individually and collectively with the mammoth, mostly impersonal, and often unfriendly, outside environment.

It is a joyous struggle, and also my dream to participate in the realization of a Bauhaus-like "center-clinic-creative-research" project, which could grow and function in part as a conduit to help bridge the many serious "gaps" created between the "runaway" high-tech puissance, and the plodding gasping, human high taste and high touch sensibilities. If a health-unfriendly and ecology-unfriendly high-tech culture puts too much distance between itself and a yearning, struggling human high touch/high taste culture, then that high-tech hierarchy can become criminally dangerous.

A successful "struggle" to organize and establish a Bauhaus-like "think and work tank" so that we might crack open some doors, and raise some windows a bit higher, where we could, first and foremost, inter-train with each

other...where we could enthusiastically separate the wheat from the chaff...
where we could bridge and consolidate our training procedures, resources,
and philosophies...where we could dedicate ourselves to the search for universal truths rather than chase after eclectic or pragmatic devices...

Where we could, by proper selection, blend oriental Wisdom with occidental Wisdom...where we could investigate body wisdom and vocal life,
not only for actors, singers, and dancers individually but also collectively,
for inter-disciplinary exploration and cross-cultural intelligence and understanding on the world stage...

That is my dream! And while (having reached age eighty-seven) I do
not have too much time to wait around, you may be sure I shall keep right
on dreaming.

3

THAT SECRET VOICE

CICELY BERRY

My work in the closed institutions of prisons and schools has been totally to do with exploring text, mostly Shakespeare, to experience how language goes through us and how we react to it as we speak it. It has been spasmodic, but at times quite wonderful.

Because I have arrived at certain methods of work by way of two different strands of experience, and because that work has always been to do with relating the secret self to the forming of words, I think it would be useful to give a brief outline of this experience, and how each form of work has informed the other.

THE VOICE IN ACTION

First, I will look at the work I have done with actors, as that has been my chief concern since I began teaching. As Voice Director for the Royal Shakespeare Company for the last twenty-five years, I have worked in depth with actors on most of the major productions during this time. When I began work with the Company, it was geared to "voice production": this meant training the voice to be clear and interesting, and the speech to be articulated "correctly" — i.e., acceptable to upper-class standards. But, as I worked more and more closely on the productions themselves, I became deeply aware of the physical connections between the making of the word and the emotional motive of the actor — in the terms of Stanislavski, the want/need of the character in the scene.

I then began to realize that the work had to be in two parts:

1. the technical facility, and
2. how this technical facility reached into, and fused with, the actor's

intentions. This has far-reaching consequences in that it could affect the presentation of the character.

To add to this complexity, I also realized that the perception we have of our own voice is almost totally subjective. For we arrive at our own voice through an intricate and private mixture of the following four factors:

1. what we hear — involving our early environment/accent, position in the family unit, etc.;
2. how we hear it — our "ear": in other words, how we interpret sound — always a subjective response;
3. our habit of speech — involving early speech patterns plus the physical make-up of the person and his/her muscular ability;
4. how we use our voice in the light of our personality and experience, and our self-image — in other words, how we want it to behave.

I have given a full account of this in my book, *Your Voice and How to Use it Successfully*. All this applies to the "ordinary" person in day-to-day communications. But the actor has to learn that how he/she delivers a text gives specific interpretations to the listener, and so he/she must begin to know the voice objectively, and must adjust it accordingly.

But — and this is the vital point — that adjustment may make the actor feel untruthful, and this is both unnerving and harmful to the performance. And so the actor has to match how he/she hears his/her own voice not only with performance technique and the needs of the character, but also with the needs of the audience who must be given the right message.

So, doubly, we ask — how necessary are words and how are those words tied up with reason and motive? When words are written down, the actor has to be both taken over by them and take them over. And this has many layers, for words have different associations for different people, and some are more confident with words than others.

Parallel with my work with actors, I have run countless workshops on the language of Shakespeare in schools, mainly with sixth-formers, in community groups, and also with English teachers — these over a number of years. I think without exception the first task was to break down some kind of received idea of how Shakespeare should be spoken, in order to get near what the words could hold for them: this was not necessarily to do with how they were taught, for so often the teachers wanted the time to do work with them that opened the speaking up; it was to do with the necessity of getting through exams. It is also to do with these facts:

1. we treat language that is written down differently; we make it "behave" and so strait-jacket it in some way; and
2. I believe we respect the written word more than the spoken word.

In Shakespeare's day there was a strong oral tradition which is not with us now.

And so I began to realize the value of working on the physical associations of language in Shakespeare, and how that work enabled the group to "apprehend/More than cool reason ever comprehends" (*A Midsummer Night's Dream* V,1,6). If, somehow, we can release the language from its literal/academic meaning, we allow our responses to fly.

To do this work in a group it is necessary to get them to do something physical, not directly related to the text in hand, and which to begin with may seem irrelevant. The purpose is to free the speaker from over-concentration and so release a subconscious response. The exercise also has to fit in the space in which we are working. My aim always has been to get them to feel something from speaking the words that enriched their understanding of them — one could hear this reaction immediately in their voices. And of course, once they found this internal response, they could see the point of the exercise, and were excited by it — and by working on language.

I remember working with a group of A Level students on *Othello.* They understood it all in a hidebound kind of way, and of course "appreciated" it, but I could not think of how to get them "in" to the language — to get them taken off-guard by it. We were looking at Act III, scene 3, the pivotal scene where Iago has worked so successfully on Othello's hidden doubts and jealousy that Othello finally believes Desdemona to be unfaithful. I got them all standing round in a circle, reading these lines:

OTHELLO: Never, Iago. Like to the Pontic Sea,
Whose icy current and compulsive course
Nev'r feels retiring ebb, but keeps due on
To the Propontic and the Hellespont,
Even so my bloody thoughts with violent pace
Shall nev'r look back, nev'r ebb to humble love,
Till that a capable and wide revenge
Swallow them up. Now, by yond marble heaven,
In the due reverence of a sacred vow
I here engage my words.

(*Othello* III, 3, 451)

We did this several times, and then quite simply I got them to link arms firmly and pull away from each other as hard as they could. It was fairly chaotic, though obviously I watched to see they did not go too far: the point was, for a few moments they were swinging round against each other, out of control. And one of them said, "I see what Othello feels; he is drowning in his feelings" — always in Shakespeare the sea holds an image of being out of control — it was a revelation. Having found that idea, we then looked at how the verse was built, and saw that there is one long sentence from "Like to the Pontic sea" down to "Swallow them up." If you try to do this on one breath the sense of desperation is there in the rhythm of the words and the music of the whole passage, and this relates both to the surge and current of the sea, and to the sense of panic when you are out of breath.

And that seems to me to be what we should be after: a sense that the words both define and release the feeling and are never separate from it. But also when you do an exercise like that, words take on different shapes and lengths, vowels become extended and consonants more muscular, the movement of the words becomes one with the movement of the inner self, and the word becomes active in every sense. It also becomes subversive in that language does not behave quite as you expect. Now these two strands of work have allowed me to see how text can be explored objectively, yet with a purpose to open up individuals to the possibility of defining themselves through language. I think that the majority of people have so little self-esteem when it comes to expressing their inner selves that they resort to accepted, clichéd responses: the thought crosses one's mind as to what extent we define ourselves through clichés. Perhaps our greatest fear is the fear of appearing ignorant.

So, in fact, language rules: the people who have a facility with language, who can manipulate it, can invade and inhibit our secret voice. In his excellent book, *Our Master's Voices*, Max Atkinson sets out a few simple rules of rhetoric which, if used by a politician, will win his/her audience over and be persuasive enough to ensure success. However, Atkinson also goes on to say that those forms of rhetoric evolved over centuries when oral culture was predominant; we just have to practice it. Also, the barrage of television advertising, etc., telling/selling us what we should need, what we should feel, what we should have, what we should "go for," all executed with wonderfully persuasive rhetoric — and some poetry — inhibits and confuses, and makes us lose faith in our own ability to put across what we feel. We are being taken over by technological indifference to the emotional roots of language. What chance then do the less well-educated have of defining themselves? But not just the under-educated, those who feel deeply, whose feelings perhaps are complex, who cannot compete/compute with those who have more facility with the language. So often the mental ability is way above the ability to express.

Having been at a point once in my life when I had an overwhelming sense of my speech being blocked so that I could not speak the words that I needed to, I realized in a very precise way the effort it takes to make words when they are felt at a particular level. Obviously, we do not and cannot live our lives at this level for long at a time, but how do we help people overcome some of this constraint when they need to? For when you cannot speak, what is left but violence?

I think by using good dramatic text we can manoeuvre people into wanting to talk:

1. first, quite simply to see that they can take pleasure in language, and that it is available to them: this involves some technical facility;
2. then, by using text which deals with feeling, the inner landscape, to realize that this can be put into words;
3. from this, to appreciate that feelings are frequently ambivalent and cannot be given concrete conclusions;
4. further, that there is a connection between what you are feeling and the body's response to what you are saying.

Now Shakespeare satisfies all these needs. I would not say his was the only text to use, but certainly I have found it quite the best in starting any work off, perhaps not the least because, if for a moment, the group has understood it, there is a great sense of achievement — such is his mystique. Also, because there is nothing didactic there, it is open to many individual responses, and nearly everyone in the group will find something which is personal. And lastly, there is something about its musicality that touches a core of recognition of "something other than the self." The aim of the work always should be to achieve some sort of involvement between the speaker and the words spoken — a private recognition.

Now to the practicalities. I have found that every session should start off with sensible, relaxed breathing exercises to get the breath as deep into the body as possible; this gives a sense of assurance. If you know the group, this can be done on the floor; the benefit of this is that we can feel the length and width of our bodies, the swing of the ribs, and any obvious tensions in the neck; also it helps to focus on the self. Initially, however, the exercises should be done in pairs, with one sitting on a chair and the partner feeling the movement of the ribs by putting his/her hands on the rib cage. This is good in that it gives an awareness of the whole breathing mechanism. It should then be taken into sound, an easy humming and then singing on vowels, which will give an understanding of how breath makes sound. What is important is that we feel our own vibrations, and, depending on the group, each other's.

To begin with in most groups there is usually a certain amount of embarrassment at this — it is curiously unnerving to listen to one's own sound, and perhaps we should ponder on this — but the embarrassment soon goes. Each one can then make sound on his/her own and begin to listen to his/her inner voice — a voice that is not trying to make an impression. The concentration of energy then becomes quite different.

One small point: It is particularly useful to work in pairs in that the person being "felt" has something to flex him/herself against, and the person who is "feeling" becomes more aware of his/her own body mechanism at the same time: but of course how one sets this up does depend on the group.

Having come so far, it is then right to go through some of the speech sounds — some consonants and vowels — in order to experience their energy and shape. This starts to take us into a different view of language — into the enjoyment of its physicality. For it seems to me that the most important thing we can do is give people a voice, the sense that they have a right to speak, and that speech can be enjoyed. And so my next stage is always to do with allowing the language to be subversive in some way, kicking it about — sometimes literally. And so we go on to text.

MOVING INTO A CUSTODIAL SETTING

So how can all this work in a prison or closed institution, and what are the differences? I will address these concerns in a moment, but what is so striking when you begin the work, once the members of the group have got over their initial shyness at speaking text aloud, is the very raw and immediate energy that is brought to the language. They are not afraid of its extremes, nor the sense of outrage that is so often there. Are they more in touch? I started to go into Her Majesty's Prison Long Lartin, the top security prison near Evesham, in about 1982. It came about because Sheila Hancock, at that time an actress with the Royal Shakespeare Company, was invited into the prison to do some kind of show.

At that time I was working on a poetry program called "Groupings — Gropings" in which Hancock was involved. It was a rather rich mixture of classical and modern poetry, plus bits of dialogue, a couple of Feiffer cartoons, and a Bob Dylan song — a bit "seventies," but I liked it a lot — (it has been performed recently in the US with Whoopi Goldberg). As Sheila Hancock had nothing of her own that was suitable, we decided that this would be a good program to take in: the theme was serious but had a good deal of comedy as well, and it had a small cast of only six — an ideal size. Basically, it was about how most people need to join a group, whether the group be a religious, political, or family one — we need to belong. We pursued this theme through all the stages of life, from childhood to a poem written by an elderly lady in a geriatric ward. There was some quite dense material such as one of Donne's religious sonnets, poems of Hopkins, Yeats, Ferlinghetti — a good mixture — plus a Feiffer cartoon which started off something like this:

> Once I belonged to a Group that really had the Word
> I worked like hell for them

> And then another Group came along and said that they had a
> very much better Word.
> So I left the first Group, and joined this second Group.
> I worked like hell for them, etc., etc.

And so it went on with the "voice" joining groups and leaving them until finally on his/her own, he/she asks someone with similar interests to join him/her and make a group. And so it posed questions about our need to belong.

From the reception we got, and the comments from the group afterwards, the program struck a number of chords. However, what amazed us about the whole evening was the quality of the listening: the absolute attention, the hunger, which is something one does not experience normally. We were all knocked out by this attention, by the sense of energy in the listening, and by the details that were picked up and responded to in a most perceptive way.

Out of this experience I came to know the Education Department at Long Lartin quite well, in particular Gill Ganner, who ran courses in English literature and, among other things, organized talks and lectures on poetry and so forth, by visiting writers, when these were possible.

I then started to go in fairly regularly for two-hour workshops. I worked nearly always on Shakespeare, though we had several sessions on Beckett and on T. S. Eliot. The sessions were arranged particularly well: Gill Ganner would prepare the group for the play we were going to look at by giving them things to read in it, and where possible they would have seen videos round the subject. This meant that they had some kind of view of the play before I came in to work, and we could get straight down to looking at the language and to working through scenes.

What never ceased to surprise me was the energy that seemed to come from the group as they walked into the room to work—like two World Cup teams—and that sense of expectancy.

My format was this: I always started with breathing exercises, exactly the same in principle as the ones I described. However, as with any group one gears the work to the particular needs of that group, so in Long Lartin I concentrated on simple stretching and relaxing, taking deep breaths, and taking breath into sound. I always did some work in pairs, so that they could feel the muscular activity of the ribs, but always did this quite briefly. For one thing, the Prison Officers would get anxious, and for another, it is just a very big thing for them to touch each other in that situation—and perhaps they do not want to touch, for there are tensions between different categories of prisoners, and so we have to leave that open. Yet I feel it is important to let it happen if possible.

I understand completely why the Prison Officers might get anxious. I think the exercises could not be readily understood, and they would appear to be perhaps too informal. We are, after all, doing things which are freeing and relaxing and which would seem to have no order; and this could release too much.

Next we would sit on the floor to go through some exercises. This is good in that not only is it unexpected, but it also takes away any kind of authority image, and I think perhaps makes one feel less threatened and more individual. For one must never forget that each one of the prisoners brings in a world we can never know about.

In this position you can, through exercise:

1. become aware of the channel of breath from the stomach;
2. lean back and feel your own weight, then sigh out and hear the breath coming through your body;
3. hum and sing out on vowels, and feel the resonance in your whole body, i.e., your chest, head, face, and, by bouncing on the floor, you feel that resonance even in your seat.

Getting this sense of one's own sound is absolutely crucial.

After a few vowel and consonant exercises to focus on the activity of language, we would start to look at the play. I want to take as an example one particular session when we were looking at *The Winter's Tale*. We all sat round the room on chairs to read the beginning — the first scene and a few pages of the second scene down to Leontes' first soliloquy. We read it once round in a circle as best we could, some more ably than others. We talked a little of the plot to get a general idea of what was happening. I then got volunteers to read it again taking the different parts. We read it this time with the characters speaking in the middle, and the rest of the group sitting round them in a circle, and asked the group to repeat the words which they had heard spoken which were to do with love — either in the sense of affection and admiration, or, as happens later in the scene, in the sense of sexual desire. In doing this they began to choose words for themselves and in a way to own them. They were surprised by the quality and texture there: how in the first scene Archidamus and Camillo openly compete with each other over the quality and richness of their hospitality. But they were even more surprised at the sexuality they found in these words of Hermione:

HERMIONE: What? Have I twice said well: When was't before?
          I prithee tell me. Cram's with praise, and make's
          As fat as tame things. One good deed dying tongueless
          Slaughters a thousand waiting upon that.
          Our praises are our wages. You may ride's
          With one soft kiss a thousand furlongs ere

With spur we heat an acre. But to th'goal:
My last good deed was to entreat his stay.
What was my first? It has an elder sister,
Or I mistake you. O, would her name were Grace!
But once before I spoke to th'purpose? When?
Nay, let me have't; I long.

(The Winter's Tale I, 2, 90)

Always the language takes us into the world of the play. There is an extremely good essay by Maynard Mack on *Hamlet* (1968) which elaborates on this theme.

We continued to work on the play in different ways. For instance, we took the speech of Leontes which begins "Inch-thick, knee-deep, o'er head and ears a fork'd one." We worked on it all together, and then I asked them to move round the room while speaking, and changing direction on each punctuation mark in order to find the emotional movement in the language and the sudden and violent turns of thought. We also look at the violence in the language by repeating the words that express/contain disgust in some way, such as contempt, cuckold, sluiced, bawdy, fished, and so forth — the list is long. Now, by doing simple things like banging your hand on the floor at these words, or kicking a chair, we become aware that the words themselves are letting us into the nature of the man, and further, they are self-feeding, for they lead him on to action. There are many ways of opening up the hidden agenda in the language, so that we realize the extent to which feelings are ambivalent and complex. And this is surely what is important: opening up to hidden feelings through formal, articulate language.

This was a particularly good session, I remember, for near the end of it one of the group was so excited that he said something like — "You see, they didn't need scenery in those days — it's all in the words." And that was a revelation for them.

Now, of course, one does not only work to release the violence in the language; it is simply that if we start with that area it is unexpected and, therefore, immediately awakens curiosity. It also makes a statement that one is open to these ideas.

Having found this response to the language, one can then go on to find a delicacy of feeling, a discovery of love perhaps, as in the scene between Perdita and Florizel later in the same play, Act IV, Scene 4, where Florizel discovers his feelings for Perdita:

FLORIZEL: What you do
                Still betters what is done. When you speak, sweet,
                I'd have you do it ever; when you sing,
                I'd have you buy and sell so; so give alms;

> Pray so; and, for the ord'ring your affairs,
> To sing them too. When you do dance, I wish you
> A wave 'th'sea, that you might ever do
> nothing but that; move still, still so,
> And own no other function. Each your doing,
> (So singular in each particular)
> Crowns what you are doing in the present deeds,
> That all your acts are queens.
> *(The Winter's Tale* IV, 4, 135)

The touching out of the words is very delicate: the play on the word "do," for instance.

There are a number of exercises that we can use to find this fineness of feeling between two people. One that I have found particularly useful is to get the two people reading the characters to speak to each other from different ends of the room, and to give them the objective of trying to get to each other while they speak. Without their realizing, I would then ask several members of the group to keep them apart, not by manhandling them, but simply by somehow preventing them from getting close. This opens up the most wonderful sense of the need/longing contained in the words, and brings home just how difficult it is to make real contact with another person — to get inside them almost.

This exercise has produced wonderful results for me, and I have used it on many scenes, such as the beginning of *A Midsummer Night's Dream* between Theseus and Hippolyta; also between the Ghost and Hamlet — it brings a sense of urgency and longing purely through the words.

All these exercises, and many more, can help take us deeper into the text. I have written about them at length in *The Actor and the Text* (1987). These exercises work for actors; they work for any group who wants to explore text, though obviously one modifies them according to capability of the group, and certainly one finds a way of working together to gain confidence before asking anyone to read on his/her own until he/she is ready.

These prison visits, for various reasons, stopped around 1986. However, I know they were extremely useful. A great deal of feedback about the sessions at the time came back to Gill Ganner, and I myself still, in roundabout ways, get feedback about them.

In 1984 I became involved with Blind Summit — Dartmoor. This amazingly interesting project was started by the filmmaker Paul Schoolman. His aim was to film the story of Julius Caesar inside HM Prison Dartmoor. In setting up this project, he arranged many workshops in Dartmoor on text, on acting, but chiefly on writing scripts. Obviously the project demanded a great deal of time and patience, and there were many difficulties attached, as you will imagine, but it had very warm support from Governor May. Governor May, I know, realized the enormous value of these sessions in terms of prison morale.

Though I did a number of workshops on Shakespeare in the prison, for me, the project culminated on the day I arranged for three film scripts to be read in the RSC Swan Theatre. The scripts were read by sixteen members of the RSC and two ex-cons who had been involved in the writing workshops.

These three scripts—*Nonce, The Stone Hotel*, and *Julius Caesar*—were extremely powerful pieces of writing. The audience numbered around 120, and nearly all stayed for the very valuable discussion at the end. Among those from the prison service who attended were Governor May, Governor Timms from Maidstone, and Mr. S. C. Handley who was deputizing for Judge Tumin. There was also one Deputy Governor and a number of Prison Officers.

The discussion afterwards was chaired by the film producer Rex Bloomstein and was really excellent in that it dealt with English attitudes to crime and punishment and how we should be preparing prisoners for life outside. Several members of the audience said that the day had altered their whole perspective on the prison system: they wanted to know how they could positively contribute to improving it. It seems to me crucial that this kind of work continues in order to prepare prisoners better for their re-entry into society.

I like to think that finding "that secret voice" is part of a liberating process for individuals and society.

4

RE-DISCOVERING LOST VOICES

Patsy Rodenburg

When I was a child I wanted to be an archaeologist. Consequently my parents' garden was riddled with excavation holes and my bedroom was cluttered with carefully cleaned fragments of pottery and glass.

Instead of pursuing my childhood dream, I became a voice teacher, and it occurs to me the two professions have similarities. Like archaeologists, voice teachers are constantly unearthing, cleaning, and then polishing lost voices, and in the process, uncovering many forgotten memories. The difference is that to find and release a voice is a living and transforming experience. A voice is not to be displayed in some glass case!

Most people arrive for a lesson with just a glint of their potential voice showing through years of encrusted clutter — habits. Most come because their voice has, in some way, failed them, and they want a repair job. They are always shocked to realize that their natural voice is lost and wonderful! The clutter has become their voice.

How many voice teachers have heard laments like:

"I feel more interesting than I sound."

"My creativity never comes through my voice."

"My voice is boring...ugly...bad."

So the first bit of spade work is to convince them that there are no boring, ugly, bad voices, only lost ones.

I start work on the shell, the outside of the voice — the body. Here all our emotional, intellectual, and spiritual secrets eventually embed themselves.

Shoulders, neck, jaw, spine, knees, feet, posture. As one area is released, another deeper tension might be revealed or, if we are lucky, righted. The body is an intriguing web of interconnected systems. Tension or an injury anywhere will ripple out and block the whole. If we are too tense, too loose, or misaligned, the voice will be masked.

Then the breath. The life force. In the breath is the imprint of every life experience. All our human energy is first manifested in how we breathe. Most people have long ago forgotten their natural breath. As the work continues and the breath begins to enter deeply into the body, becoming free, strong, and flexible, I have a vivid image of skins being shed, like a snake, as the natural breath is rediscovered!

The removal of each skin can reveal all sorts of memories and blocks. Alongside the joy and liberation of a free breath there are some monsters lying in wait. But, if the student is willing and has courage, the free breath always releases the monster.

It is always good for me to remember I had been teaching voice seventeen years before I had the emotional courage to really breathe. Although I had been doing practical voice work myself during that time, I had diligently refused to really free my breath. Emotionally I was not really ready to confront a ghost. When I did, I took my first free breath in years. A few years ago I had my first, and hopefully only, severe asthma attack and again, in order to live, I had to breathe ghosts away.

After breath I work on support and connecting that powerful column of air to the voice. Breath support is again the most natural thing we can do — dogs do not bark nor tigers roar without it — yet most people entering a voice studio have not used their support in years. Most have only vague memories of how powerful their voices really are and are amazed that this power can be constantly with them.

And then we move on to the voice — freeing and placing sound; releasing a full open, clear, and effortless voice; finding that the voice need not be trapped in the body, rumbling around inside. As blocks go, jewels are discovered. The voice can be fun. Words can leave the speaker to enter others in whatever way we choose: words piercing, stroking, informing, enchanting the listener. The next discovery is often the physical and sensual power of words. As we learn to own and reveal a word's power, we leave a mark on the world around us. Of course, there are many other vocal discoveries to make: resonators that need the cobwebs blown away, notes in a range that cannot be touched, muscles in the mouth that have not been worked for years.

Each discovery takes us deeper into ourselves. Layer after layer of our lost vocal potential is revealed. Sensations are unknown and yet strangely known until, one day, the realization that we have found our own voices, not the ones that we have been forced to use, but our lost ones. And it is always a voice that is compelling to the listener because the barriers are down, the mud and grime of all those years of fear and judgment washed away. It is now what it has always been, but dug up and cleaned.

Now, as life continues to try to contain the voice, we have enough technical knowledge to keep any invasion out of the body and the breath. In this way we can all keep our voices free from clutter, and life can then enrich the voice and never diminish it — experience will make the voice better.

This work is for everyone, and yet most voice coaches come to voice work through theatre. In fact, it is quite a new notion that we all need voice work. Actors and singers have always recognized the work, but it is only recently that other professions are seeking help. So I would like to dwell on the work connected to theatre.

Actors need voice work. To speak, for instance, in iambic pentameter to a thousand people requires vocal strength and flexibility that few of us naturally have. As athletes have to train their bodies, so actors have to train their voices so that vocal muscularity seems to be effortless. The audience should not be watching the process or noticing the technique but should be engaged in the text. This ease of vocal production demands a thorough training. But there is more than mere audibility in training a voice. The audience not only needs to hear but must be engaged with and drawn into a text. In order to do this an actor has to own the text — the voice should sound true, the words springing from the actors' own being, head, and heart.

Clarity, passion, and truth are the vocal springboards that will begin to hold an audience. There was no need for a voice coach in Shakespeare's day. He wrote in and for a society that cared about speaking, debating, and using words to explore inner and outer worlds of being and living. It was a society that went on all the important journeys of life with words and the right to speak them. His actors would have picked up his text and delivered it without all the fears that crowd our actors into dead-end streets of lost voices.

Voice coaches are in constant demand today in theatre because everything an actor has to do to release the great classical texts has been eroded by society. Through no fault of our own, we neither believe nor trust words, and we lack courage when we are asked to use our voices with joy and conviction. I have constant battles when facing actors with this lack of conviction. Many do not trust that truth can be large and clear or that we can all listen. Truth, to many actors, is found in mumbling or denying the word. They constantly want to cover a great oral text with the twentieth-century habits of non-communication. Yet these texts are about heightened states and come from a time when people spoke to each other. We all, even when bound by vocal clutter, begin to speak clearly when the need is great enough! And I find it always interesting to note that I have never worked with a modern playwright who has not asked me to "heighten" the actor. I have never been asked to make them smaller or more "real."

Of course, this enthusiasm in speaking has not been lost. There are societies all over the planet who are still excited by words and speaking; there are pockets in our own society that still need and care about truthful communication. It is often to do with survival. We reach for words as the last hope in clarifying a dangerous or changing world.

I have recently been teaching Shakespeare to black township actors in South Africa and I have worked in a top security prison on a production of *Hamlet*. Both groups of actors have no trouble with vocal passion and the power of words. They all understand a fundamental requirement in revealing Shakespeare's text; that is, you must speak it aloud and allow the physical and sensual quality of the language to release you. For many actors, this simple release fills them with fear. If they are frightened of their own voices, how can they begin to find the playwright's voice? Only by rediscovering their own free and flexible voices can they serve a text.

In this vein, these are the problems I encounter on a daily basis — there is no particular order to this list and no criticism of actors, who are trapped in a system that will smother them if they, for a moment, lose resilience.

Fear. So many fears — their own voices are not good enough, interesting enough, their accents are wrong. These are always fears that have been drilled into actors. There are very few bad voices. I have never met a bad voice, and every accent is valid. These fears lead to voices that never dare to experiment. Locked into the actors' minds is a sense that they have no choices.

Fear of judgment, be it by the director, audience, or critic. How can you play — and actors do "a play" — when judgment hangs over the process like a guillotine? Of course, we all have to face judgment at some point in any creative process, but surely we must have moments in rehearsal when there is no fear of judgment. The physical manifestations of fear are shoulders up, breath high, voice held, text rushed or falsely manufactured. The actor goes into denial or bluff.

The unworked voice. A voice that has not been used fully or imaginatively for a period of time — sometimes years. Perhaps the result of being out of work or too much TV or film work. The voice has to be stretched and strengthened in order to cope with space and a vigorous text. Craft has to be put into place so that the voice will be there on stage for the actor every night.

Band-Aid. This is the least ideal part of my work but one I have to face weekly: an actor going on stage unprepared, often an understudy.

The worst scenario can be a coach standing in the wings with a shaking individual, giving him/her survival techniques: breathe, support, do not rush, keep releasing the shoulders, do not rush... terrible but it happens.

And, at last, the **ideal situation.** The situation in which you can work organically with an actor on his/her voice and you can then marry that voice to a text. As the work proceeds the actor discovers not only his/her voice, but the text's true voice. To do this you need time to work, an actor willing to take a journey — this is not work for lazy actors who exist on their habits and are content with reducing the text — and a director who respects voice and text work.

The result is electrifying — a free, uncluttered, exciting voice connected to a text and, as this connection appears, time and space disappear. We are rewarded when we hear the writer's breath pattern and voice reborn after a silence of perhaps a thousand years. The actor has given words life, and yet the actor's own unique experience of those words has enriched the writer; and the audience hears words spoken as if for the first and only time. The triangle is complete — text, actor, audience — all is revealed and found.

5

FREEING OUR SINGING VOICE

FRANKIE ARMSTRONG

In English culture we have lost the sense that singing is a natural form of expression, but this was not always so. A. L. Lloyd, the British folklorist and singer (1908–1982), told me that in the seventeenth and eighteenth centuries, we English were known on the continent as the "singing English." My understanding of how this change came about has increasingly informed the way I have developed my Voice Workshops to encourage people to reclaim this natural and spontaneous form of expression.

In pre-industrial communities, singing and chanting are/were an integral part of every tribal and village person's life. Many activities from the cradle to the grave were accompanied by the melodic voice: lullabies, collective rhythmic working chants, hollas to bring in the cows, and soothing onomatopoeic croons to milk them by, spinning and weaving songs, ritual and devotional chants, songs to dance to, to walk to the next village to, to while away the hours behind the plow, to amuse and move family and friends of an evening, to tell the stories of the gods and the ancestors, to wail and grieve by the body of a loved one — people sang thus over thousands and thousands of years. Hence this cannot but fulfill a basic human need, one which I believe cannot have disappeared in two hundred years or less of industrialization.

Throughout most of human history, each child was born into a community that assumed they would sing, as we assume each child will learn to talk. Imagine the situation if, somehow, the idea had taken hold of parents and teachers that only a certain percentage of children would be able to speak and that we (adults) had to devise a method of "testing" whether a child was a speaker or not. What untold damage and suffering this would cause!

And yet, in relation to the singing/melodic voice, which, in individual development, and probably in terms of human evolution, predates conversational speech, some teachers and parents do just this: "I was told I was tone deaf so I needn't bother coming to the choir." "I was told to go to the back of the class and mime when we sang." "They said I was a growler so I had to pretend to sing but not let out any sound." "I was made to feel foolish/ashamed/I was hit over the knuckles with a ruler in front of the class for being out of tune." "I was told I had a horrid voice when I was seven — I remember the moment vividly, and I've never sung publicly since." "My mother/father/brother/sister was/were very musical — I was the unmusical one of the family." "I loved singing as a child but when my voice broke I was told to leave the choir and, somehow, I've never felt confident about my voice since."

These are samples of the oft-repeated tales from participants in my voice workshops. I have had hundreds, if not thousands, of such statements over twenty years of working with community groups, actors and dancers, people with special needs, the young, the old, disabled and able-bodied, and those only willing to sing in the bath or to their babies.

So when and why did this censorial attitude emerge, robbing so many of the power and delight of song? Here are some of my musings. At the time of Forster's Education Act in 1870, which brought in compulsory education for all, the dominant aesthetic among the upper and middle classes was excessively genteel. We have numerous wonderful descriptions from literature of musical soirees, with refinement and niceness oozing out of every descriptive word. These were the people who made up the ranks of teachers, and had the task of "civilizing" the massed ranks of the poor and illiterate children in country, town, and city. The bold "raucous" way in which such children would naturally sing did not suit the ideals of refinement and musicality of their educators, and hence the process of which we are heirs was set in motion. The style of singing that grew up in the courts, churches, parlors, and, later, concert and opera halls of Europe is, at its best, both sublime and dramatic and we would be spiritually and culturally impoverished without it. Yet the inappropriate dominance and imposition of this aesthetic on the majority (through the education system) still filters down to children today, though, I trust, less often than in the past.

Nowhere have I come across a more graphic description of this process than in Richard Llewellyn's marvelous novel *How Green Was My Valley* (1939). The story is set at the end of the last century and early in this, in South Wales (where I now live) — in a mining village. The narrator is a miner's son who describes the miner's choir:

And the crowd made little moves all the way from the top to the bottom, not in restlessness but to find room for arms to have ease, for feet to be firm, for chests to give good breaths, for chins to point and for room to sing...Now gather yourselves, O men of the valleys. Now open the throat, higher with the chin, loud, loud, as the trumpets of the hosts sound...Sing then! Sing indeed. Shoulders back and heads up, so that some of the song might go through the roof and beyond to the sky. Mass on mass of tone with a hard edge and rich with quality, every single note a carpet of color woven from basso profundo, basso, baritone and alto and tenor and soprano and alto and mezzo and contralto singing and singing until life and all things living become a song.[1]

Not long after this enthralling description, the storyteller is sent off to the English school over the mountain. He is punished for speaking his own native language and is forced to speak and sing in English. The singing is thin, reedy, and tremulous, the children standing timid and shrunken, rather than with the proud, open stance of the village choir:

> "O," sang Mr. Motrill, in a couple of keys, and then sliding down to find the note, "Ah. Take your note, Ah."
>
> "Ah," sang the boys and girls, with mouths like button-holes, no tone, no depth and no heart![2]

They have been robbed of their voice and cultural inheritance. Their natural voices are deemed uncouth and they must inhibit these to be acceptable to the new class of elders and betters — their teachers. In Wales, as with Ireland and very large parts of Scotland, this process was exaggerated because their very language was forbidden, but I believe the essence of the process to be true for all children who came from the poor majority (in England as well) — their voices were unacceptable. Out of this came the concept that lingers on as received wisdom — some could sing and some could not. A related issue is that of style — the artistry of the best traditional singers calls on a distinctive and different aesthetic from that of the classical singer. In the 1950s David Attenborough produced a series on BBC Radio called "As I Roved Out." They were the first programs to feature British traditional singers and songs. Recently I heard David Attenborough recalling how his postbag had contained a letter from a retired Brigadier in Cheltenham, saying, how jolly splendid it was to hear these gems of the folk tradition, but why couldn't they get "proper" singers to sing them?

I want to give you some idea of how I hope to counter the damage that has been done through the process I have just described. However, before

---

[1]   Richard Llewellyn, *How Green Was My Valley* (London: Michael Joseph, 1959; reprint, London: Penguin Books, 1991), 171.

[2]   Ibid.

coming to my workshops, let me tell you a little about my background and the experiences and elements I draw on that have contributed to my approach.

First, I have long had a passion for, and involvement with, the traditional music of the British isles. My singing "apprenticeship" began in the folk revival from the early 1960s. By the mid-seventies I had worked for years with leading folklorists and singers such as Ewan MacColl, Peggy Seeger, and A. L. Lloyd, and had made a number of solo and group recordings. Although I briefly had singing lessons from a highly reputed *bel canto* teacher in the mid-sixties, he regarded traditional women singers as "cackling hens," so the development of my vocal quality was very much trial and error. I spent time listening to and emulating such singers (live and on record), which both centered my voice more fully in my body and reduced the roundness of tone, leading to a full sound but with a sinewy edge (the quality so poetically described in the Richard Llewellyn quote about the miner's choir). For a while I over-used my laryngeal muscles to produce this sound but, with experimentation, found I could produce it more effectively with a relaxed open throat.

This open-throated approach was reinforced when I attended a number of Ethel Raim's Balkan singing classes in the States during singing tours there between 1973 and 1975. Raim is a folklorist and singer, and founder of the Penny Whistlers, the influential Balkan singing group of that time. She had developed a method to encourage people out of their "choir" voices to find the quality appropriate for singing Balkan songs. Much of this was based on simple call and response and on constant encouragement, rather than judgement, as we sat in a circle, amazed at the speed with which she could have us sound akin to a Bulgarian village choir. By this time, I had trained and worked as a social worker for some ten years, and the social worker in me recognized at Raim's workshops what a potent tool this way of working with the voice was for building individual confidence and for creating group support and cohesion.

A major factor in the importance to me of voice was that, from the age of sixteen, my sight had been failing due to conditions that had gone undiagnosed as a child, and by 1975 my sight was so limited that I was registered blind. Both as a social worker and throughout the development of my voice work, I relied increasingly on the subtlest nuances of breath and voice for my perceptions of people. Back in London, I passed on Raim's approach, initially running sessions for friends and friends of friends. These sessions grew into a weekly class and when we were no longer able to meet in the pub room where MacColl's and Seeger's folk club had been held, we moved to a dance studio with a wonderful acoustic, but no chairs. Neither standing nor sitting on the floor were ideal for any length of time and hence a quantum leap in the workshops occurred — necessity being the mother of invention. It was much less tiring to move as we called, chanted, and sang, so simulated work movements and simple "dances" became a hallmark for my work. This organic relationship between voice, movement, and rhythm continues to fascinate me; through involvement in theatre workshops and co-running courses with movement teachers and other voice teachers, I have adapted many exercise, games, and improvisations and added them to my repertoire.

Concurrent with the start of running these weekly workshops, I also began teaching Assertiveness Training and, as part of becoming an Action Research worker, developed evaluation, team development, and group training skills. Not surprisingly, all these different skills folded into and influenced each other. Much of my learning about voice has also come from participants, from their feedback and observations. My synthesis of this is helped by knowing how to ask useful questions, to evaluate responses, and to adapt my approach to increase its effectiveness—which comes from this Action Research and Social Work background.

As a result of the enthusiasm of my original participants, I have been invited to work with teenagers, psychiatric patients, at women's centers, folk and arts festivals, social work and therapy training courses, and theatre courses, amongst others. I still work with groups that span professional voice teachers and youth drama groups in rural villages. In all these contexts, my commitment is to empower people with confidence in their right to their own melodic voice and with a belief in their innate musicality as a birthright. The workshops also give people an all too rare sense of being part of a communal celebration. (I no longer work as a social worker, though I continue to use these skills, especially when training others to be facilitators).

A crucial aspect, which I inherited from Ethel Raim and have since considerably elaborated, is to give people the experience of speech, heightened speech, chant, and song as a continuum with no mystifying disjunctures. Having the group echo phrases made up of hollas, calls, gossip, chants, yodels, and "song" (and often sliding from one to another in the same phrase) takes us into what children do naturally, the seamless switch from the spoken to the sung.

While exploring this and listening to the numbers of participants who have said, "You snuck it up on me; I found myself singing before I knew I was doing it," it struck me that this approach often allowed people previously deemed tone deaf to sing perfectly in pitch right from the beginning of a workshop. I realized how I could help undo the negative, restricting labels put on so many people as children.

As I said earlier in this article, many music teachers and choir masters/

mistresses seem imbued with the idea that some of the children in their charge can sing and some cannot, and that part of their job is to weed out the latter. They therefore "test" this by playing a note or series of notes on an instrument, usually a piano, or singing in their genteel voices for the children to match pitch.

The difficulties that children face here are twofold. First, it can be an anxiety-provoking situation—some will pass and some will fail. There seems to me nothing like anxiety or panic to cloud the ability to listen calmly and hear clearly. The second difficulty is what I term a "translation" issue. Let me describe a sequence I often do in workshops, which I nickname "Same note—Different sounds." After talking briefly on what an incredibly flexible instrument the human voice is and how varied are the sounds one voice can produce, I tell the group I will make many different qualities of sound using one note. Calling on my body and imagination, I "color" it in many different ways, moving from deep rounded timbres via clear open sounds to more edgy or nasal ones (the "yeh, yeh, ye-yeh yeh" of the school playground) and from the softer nasality of many folk cultures to lighter "angelic" head sounds.

This is not, in itself, at all difficult, once the possibility is opened up, yet most people have never been encouraged to play and discover in this way; hence many find it hard to believe I have been singing the same note throughout. We can then discuss how the fundamental note does not change in this exercise, but how the human voice can color the sound so variously that it does indeed sound higher or lower and hence, for some people, it is difficult to hear that it is the same pitch. It is then that I suggest that many people deemed to be "tone deaf" were probably "tested" (most often between the age of five and eight) on an instrument or with a voice whose timbre was not familiar or congruent with their own voice, hence hesitation and inaccuracy in responding. So the problem is one of "translation," how to correlate the sound being given you with the sound heard inside one's own head.

As I have said, many people recognize this scenario, and say that this understanding helps release them from the label (of "non-musical", "tone deaf," or "can't hold a tune") they have carried for most of their lives, and they begin to believe in the possibility of learning or relearning the skill of pitching. I am convinced that the success I have had in helping those so labeled lies in starting the melodic aspect of my workshops with spoken tones and "calls" for the group to respond to. Not only has this pattern been used since time immemorial, but the timbre of the calling voice is remarkably similar in men, women, and children—i.e., there is little "translation" problem. I believe that, if teachers introduced singing with small children by finding a suitable timbre in their own voice (not high and piping—listen to children singing to their skipping and counting games), then nearly all children would slot into hearing and reproducing the pitch in a relaxed, untraumatized manner. It is also axiomatic that the teacher must believe in the innate musicality of the children. I do not blame the adults who so debilitated the thousands I personally have worked with (let alone the millions more); they were simply passing on received wisdom and did not have the sense to question it.

Nowadays, there are many more music educators who have a wider vision and a passionate desire to encourage, rather than inhibit, their pupil's musicality. Together with those of us who came to singing through less formal avenues and have developed our idiosyncratic ways of encouraging anyone and everyone to reclaim their singing voices, we may slowly erode the damaging myths that have robbed so many people of their birthright — the right to continue the many thousands of years of culture, beauty and function, necessity and art, living in and through us, via this most basic form of expression.

6

SINGING ACTING

Elizabeth Nash

I cannot remember when I did not want to have a career in opera. My musical aspirations were encouraged by my mother, who had been an English musical comedy star, and by our neighbor, Frederick Jagel, a leading tenor at the Metropolitan Opera for twenty-four years. "Uncle Fred" regaled me with stories of his career as well as with fascinating anecdotes about Geraldine Farrar, Enrico Caruso, Kirsten Flagstad, Rosa Ponselle, Zinka Milanov, Giovanni Martinelli, and Leonard Warren. He was a walking encyclopedia of twentieth-century American operatic history. Little wonder I was captivated by the world of opera. In later years, Frederick Jagel served as Chairman of the Voice Department at the New England Conservatory of Music in Boston.

I began singing lessons at thirteen with Mother's American teacher. Mary Ludington never accepted students under sixteen years of age, but Mother prevailed upon her to teach me simple exercises and folk songs. "She's copying singers on the radio," Mother told her, "and could develop bad vocal habits." Thus within a few years, I had attained a firm grasp of abdominal breathing, vocal placement, and even registration.

When Father was stationed with the United States Army in Munich, Germany, I continued my voice studies. Miss Ludington had introduced us to Berta Morena who advised me to have singing lessons with Frau Doctor Henny Schoner. Madame Morena had been the Munich Opera's *prima donna assoluta* for twenty years until the advent of Adolf Hitler, whom she loathed. Since she made no attempt to hide her feelings, Madame Morena's state pension was revoked and her possessions confiscated. Her stories enthralled me.

I followed her advice to study singing with Frau Doctor Schoner who was Europe's leading pedagogue of coloratura sopranos. She was a charmingly independent spirit, who declined the Paris Conservatoire's invitation to conduct master classes on "her method." She maintained there were only two methods of teaching singing—the right way and the wrong. "I," she replied, "merely teach the right way."

In addition, I attended numerous performances at the Bavarian State Opera, sitting gratis in the center box formerly occupied by Royalty and by Führer Hitler. Fortunately, the American Commanding General disliked opera and allowed military dependents to use his loge.

During undergraduate years at Columbia University, I frequently attended the Metropolitan Opera. My operatic idol was Renata Tebaldi. She was a magnificent singer whose acting consisted of statuesque poses. Suddenly, Maria Callas arrived on the scene and burst open the doors of my theatrical imagination. Her portrayals of Gaetano Donizetti's Lucia and Giacomo Puccini's Tosca are seared in my memory. I still remember Callas' gliding descent of the stairs as the crazed Lucia and her horror at having to touch the dead hand of Baron Scarpia. I became painfully aware of my own inadequacies as an actress.

My opera training classes were devoid of acting instruction, and I relied upon my singing to carry a scene or aria. I recalled the fine acting I had seen in German opera performances and applied for a Fulbright Scholarship, which led to studies in Stuttgart, Germany. Also, I returned to lessons with Frau Doctor Schoner in Munich. During the next two years, my voice developed from a lyric soprano to a dramatic coloratura. On one occasion, Frau Doctor asked her dear friend and former student, the renowned singer and teacher Maria Ivogun, to evaluate my singing. Frau Ivogun listened attentively to my labored rendition of the closing phrase in the "Martern aller Arten" aria from Wolfgang Amadeus Mozart's *The Abduction from the Seraglio*. With a kind smile, she told me to attack the passage confidently rather than approaching it tentatively. I soared through the cadenza. "That's the breakthrough we needed," rejoiced Frau Doctor. From then on, the vocal pyrotechnics of my coloratura repertoire were flights of delight rather than onerous challenges.

As a student at a State Conservatory, I was allowed to observe Wieland Wagner's and Gunther Rennert's fascinating rehearsals and to attend all performances at the Wurttemberg State Opera. Wagner's and Rennert's stage directions were very specific to soloists and chorus alike. I learned much about period and stylized movement from watching them.

Following the completion of my scholarship, I remained in Germany for ten years performing in numerous European opera houses. With the assistance of excellent stage directors, talented colleagues, and a superb teacher of operatic acting, I gradually became a successful singing actress.

The most instrumental director was Fritz Dittgen, a Baroque specialist. He turned a production of Domenico Cimarosa's tedious comic opera, *Il Matrimonio Segreto*, into an histrionic success. Herr Dittgen honed every element of the work from choreographed walks to finger poses. He spent twelve hours rehearsing one of my solo scenes and instructed the ballet personnel to teach me eighteenth-century deportment. Six weeks under his direction were invaluable lessons in acting for the lyric stage. I was able to apply many of his techniques to other stylized roles such as Mozart's Susanna in *The Marriage of Figaro*, Konstanze in *The Abduction from the Seraglio*, and the Queen of the Night in *The Magic Flute*, as well as Giacchino Rossini's Rosina (*The Barber of Seville*) and Richard Strauss' Zerbinetta (*Ariadne auf Naxos*).

Another learning experience was the portrayal of Johann Strauss, Jr.'s Adele in *Die Fledermaus* which I memorized in six days with the aid of a versatile colleague. The operetta contains extensive dialogue, and Jutta Weinkauf perfected my diction as well as made suggestions on interpretation and stage business. Since I was speaking a foreign language, it was necessary to learn my colleagues' lines in addition to my own. We changed the pert Viennese maid into a Broadway dumb blonde. The public and press were charmed by the characterization, which would never have come to fruition without Jutta's generous assistance. One evening a guest Rosalinda completely forgot her lines, and I was obliged to combine them with mine. Jutta's hours of cueing me on text saved the performance.

Jutta Weinkauf was a remarkable young woman who had spent four years in Siberia's Gulag Archipelago as a political prisoner of the Russians. The deprivations and brutalities inflicted upon her did not embitter Jutta, who was the kindest and most selfless person I ever met in opera. She once told me that life is very precious when one has suffered every human indignity. I shall always remember this extraordinary colleague.

Frau Doctor suggested I study acting for opera with Professor Marie-Theres Gernot in Munich. Frau Gernot had been a noted singer before beginning her career as a teacher. She gave me a secure acting technique and method of role creation.

Like the great singing actresses Pauline Viardot and Geraldine Farrar, Frau Gernot stressed the importance of visiting art galleries, museums, cathedrals, palaces, and other noteworthy edifices in order to acquire an eclectic knowledge of history's accoutrements. Once, when needing a particular pose for the musical interlude to Konstanze's "Martern" aria, I discovered the ideal model in a statue of the *mater dolorosa* near the high altar of Munich's St. Johann Nepomuk church. I took a photograph of the statue and kept it on my dressing room table during the production's run.

Frau Gernot's method of teaching consisted of blocking an aria or scene for me and then developing the characterization in three stages. First, I would mime the action, next add spoken text, and finally, sing the lines. Movement, text, and music were fully integrated. When I eventually taught acting to opera students at Indiana University's School of Music, I always used this method of instruction. After they had obtained knowledge of and security in stage deportment, it was easy to add the element of singing in which they felt fully competent.

Also, I served as an assistant stage director for several opera productions. The most challenging was Richard Wagner's *Parsifal* involving numerous soloists and a chorus of over fifty men and women. The stage director was bereft of ideas, and I was asked to coach the leading tenor, mezzo-soprano, and baritone.

All three singers were students of my teacher, Eileen Farrell, and I was determined to have them do her credit. The mezzo-soprano was an excellent actress and was soon writhing voluptuously to Kundry's sensuous music. The tenor and baritone, however, were not histrionically endowed. During a frustrating session on stage with the baritone, who objected to nearly all of my directions, Miss Farrell's voice came from the murky auditorium ordering him to follow my instructions. All protestations ceased. In my first rehearsal with the tenor, I led him to the back of the raked stage and told him to struggle against my pinioning of his arms. As he was voicing his fear of hurting me, I gave him a shove which sent him stumbling down towards the footlights. When he turned to glare at me, I called out: "That was great!" Jumping up, he grinned and replied, "What's next?" For the following two weeks, we staged and polished his actions.

But the major crisis occurred at the dress rehearsal during the entrance of the fifty Flower Maidens who ran on stage crashing into each other and falling down. "It's a mess, Liz," said the director, "You take over!" Turning on his heel, he left the auditorium, and I marched on stage. Recalling Wieland Wagner's militarized movements of the chorus in his production of Ludwig van Beethoven's *Fidelio*, I divided the singers into six lines with three of them on each side of the stage. At their musical cue, they moved towards the center of the stage with the six lines meeting and intermingling until they had formed a compact phalanx. Swaying rhythmically, they slowly moved apart into designated areas where they undulated seductively. I had instructed them to face the auditorium and focus their eyes just above the conductor's head in order to see his beat. "Keep your eyes on the conductor!" became the leitmotif.

On opening night, I joined Miss Farrell and her family in the auditorium where we sat glowing over her students' fine singing and acting. And the Flower Maidens were a smashing success!

Aside from teaching the opera workshop and assisting the production program, I taught singing and supervised the School of Music's thirty voice associate instructors along with their three hundred students. In addition to my own voice studies with Miss Farrell, she allowed me to observe her teaching of other singers. Opera had been my sole interest until Eileen Farrell introduced me to American popular music by pronouncing one morning in a singing lesson, "You are an opera snob and need to expand your knowledge of vocal music." She was herself a unique mistress of musical styles from Johann Sebastian Bach, Richard Wagner, Giacomo Puccini, Giuseppe Verdi, Alban Berg, and Francis Poulenc, to jazz, blues, and popular songs. Miss Farrell's best selling recording had been "I Gotta Right to Sing the Blues," and recently she has issued a series of compact discs featuring the songs of Harold Arlen, Johnny Mercer, and Rogers and Hart. She explained to me that "jazz is today's expression of eighteenth and nineteenth centuries florid bel canto singing. Listen to Ella Fitzgerald's improvisations." Then she stated that Barbra Streisand's vocal technique resembled her own but on a smaller scale and in a different style. Soon I began listening to popular singers and learned to appreciate Ethel Merman's pistol shot consonants and Frank Sinatra's smooth vocal line. Eileen Farrell opened to me a new world of musical expression, enabling me to teach both classical and popular styles of singing.

Upon completion of my Ph.D. degree in theatre history and literature, I obtained a position at the University of Minnesota to develop and teach a voice and speech program in the Department of Theatre Arts. When the students learned of my musical background, however, they requested the addition of singing instruction to the curriculum.

I soon discovered that teaching singing to actors involves quite different requirements from those of opera students. Actors thrive on dramatic interpretation but shy away from singing. I have found it necessary to assign musical selections well within their vocal ranges in order for them to attain confidence by concentrating on textual interpretation and actions. As their sense of assurance increases, I can fine-tune their breath support, tonal placement, and quality. Then they are ready to attempt more vocally challenging material.

In 1989 and 1992, I was invited to teach singing at the Theaterhochschule Hans Otto in Leipzig, Germany. I was greeted at the border by a hostile guard who grudgingly granted me admittance into the German Democratic Republic. And then the Leipzig Police confiscated my passport for several days. But the students and my charming hostess colleague, Frau Ursula Haibel, welcomed me royally since I was the first Visiting Professor at their institution in ten years. The young actors serenaded me with the performance of a German folk song and a jazz rendition of "Deep River." At the conclusion, the students stood stiffly awaiting my comments until I started showing them that jazz requires supple movement and snapping fingers. Breaking into gales of laughter, they swept around the classroom singing and dancing. This began two weeks of breathing, singing, and articulation exercises. They especially enjoyed drills involving the American central-palatal "r" glide which they referred to as "the tiger growl." We also worked on Shakespearean interpretation in German and English. One evening I attended a marvelous outdoor performance of *The Taming of the Shrew* and was very touched when the student actors welcomed me in English from the stage before the play started.

My German colleagues were fascinated with the use of singing exercises in voice production training for actors. "We hadn't realized its potential for development of vocal range and vowel placement," they commented. Singing lessons are for opera singers in Germany! They took copious notes and asked many questions, even requesting analyses of their own vocal ranges along with those of the students.

Wonderful visits accompanied by gracious colleagues to neighboring cities were part of my scheduled activities. "You are sharing Shakespeare with us, and we wish to share Goethe with you" was my introduction to Weimar. And several days later, I was escorted to a performance of Christoph Willibald Gluck's *Orfeo Ed Euridice* at the magnificent reconstructed Semper Opera in Dresden.

Upon my return to Leipzig in 1992, the border guards were gone, and no one even asked to see my passport. The students and I concentrated on the performance of selections from George Gershwin's *Porgy and Bess* in English. Next time, we hope to stage a musical.

Twenty years ago, when I began teaching actors to sing in a spectrum of vocal styles from folk songs to operatic arias, little did I think what an exhilarating adventure was ahead of me. I wonder what the future holds?

7

ON TRAINING AND PLURALISM

KATE BURKE

A few years ago *ARTSEARCH* announced a voice and speech position at a West Coast university, an appealing post in a lush setting. Having at that time a vested interest in new challenges, I felt my interest quicken. Then my heart sank as I read on to find a particular kind of training specified in the announcement. Could I apply? Should I apply? Would my application even be considered? Thinking myself a capable, experienced, and professional teacher, yet not exclusively espousing the method indicated, I forged ahead. It goes against the grain to take oneself out of the running, to forego the hazard of the race.

I wrote the requested philosophy of teaching. Writing clarified my thinking about systems, master teachers, and trends:

> My teachers and my students teach me something valid about the human voice that transcends method or system. I shy away from rubber-stamping my work with someone else's name. My teaching derives from past training and experience, and my gratitude to my teachers is great, but my methods and my interpretation are my own. I must take responsibility for my own work and cannot fob it off on Ms. Berry, Mr. Lessac, or Ms. Linklater. Our master teachers/book authors are not circumlocutors. They reach a limited number of students firsthand. In making a present reality in a room with a particular student or group of students each voice and speech teacher weaves an integral piece of a larger tapestry.

I never received a reply to my application for the West Coast job, but a year later I heard that I had made the short list when, suddenly, funding for the position was withdrawn. It was gratifying to know that I was under consideration, but had I taken that restrictive job description at its word, I would not have been in the running at all. As I read the words I wrote years ago and ponder current method-specific job announcements, I am disturbed. This method-specifying calls to mind the sick-making "No Irish need apply" chapter of our national history, fundamentalist zealotry, and provincial fear of the unknown. It smacks of shrill "Who's Hot, Who's Not?" tabloids. Where is Voltaire's spirit of tolerance embodied in his retort to an adversary, I may disapprove of what you say, but I will defend to the death your right to say it? (In the end I may even come around and agree with you.)

All sincere teaching approaches should be considered and applied when they touch on the universal, but they are merely the clothes that cover the integrity of the teacher/human being within. Think of Lillian Hellman's eloquent proclamation to The House Un-American Activities Committee, "I cannot and will not cut my conscience to fit this year's fashions."[1]

Several years ago I embarked on teaching acting students in a California M.F.A. program. The head of the training program observed my class, responded enthusiastically, and asked, "What do you call what you do?" I replied, "You've just seen it. What would you call it?" I know the sanctity of a name, and naming things smooths communication, but facile labels do not mirror reality. I want neither myself nor my work labeled with someone else's name. Certification is a worthy goal among voice trainers, but certification in only one area is suspect. Labels are seductively spare and one-dimensional.

Do administrators and theatre trainers call for Berry, Lessac, or Linklater training without a working knowledge of these approaches? One might posit that familiarity with a single teacher might prejudice an employer positively or negatively toward that teacher's method or toward other teacher's methods. A "good" Lessac teacher or a "bad" Linklater teacher will enhance or damage the reputation of these master teachers. By rights, these "good" and "bad" teachers should take responsibility for their own methods. One might also posit that theatre training programs adopt one voice and/or speech approach in emulation of other programs, such as Yale or Julliard, without looking at a range of options.

Our reach has got to exceed our grasp, or what is a heaven for? One might place a personal ad trawling for a gangly, bookish Celt, only to go gaga for a bunchy, mud-wrestling Latin. Cannot we agree that some aspects of the human voice are universal, that we are liable to stumble over vocal truth in many guises, and that diverse and improbable teachers will lead us to that truth? As a trainer and performer I am indebted to Virginia Hahne

---

[1] Eric Bentley, "Are You Now or Have You Ever Been?" in *Rallying Cries: Three Plays*, The Republic Book Co., 1977.

and Greg Bostwick, my teachers at Ohio University. Having had two Lessac summer Intensive Workshops, I am indebted to Arthur Lessac, Sue Ann Park, Lisbeth Roman, and Richard Cuyler. I must also credit Jane Ridley, Richard Nichols, Sarah Barker, Yrek Bogayeich, George Sherman, Bill Burnett, Sarah-Jane Kerr, Katherine Verdolini, Mary Corrigan, and Dorothy Mennen for their perceptions of voice and language. I am recently beholden to Ivan Midderigh, Frankie Armstrong, Cicely Berry, Andrew Wade, and Patsy Rodenburg. I would be remiss not to credit my four-year-old great niece, Sammy Jo, for her exuberant, unadulterated, instructive displays of vocal virtuosity. Were I to fashion a label for my work which paid tribute to all those listed above, I would use it. All of these teachers have informed me, yet I do not teach a survey, surface amalgam of their work. I pride myself that my own teaching is derived and yet distinctive. No method clone, I teach in my own way under my own name, bring my own passion to bear, and provide continuity. Continuity in training makes a vocal sea change, but the journey is a maze replete with wondrous twists and turns.

In an age of affirmative action, of fair practice in the workplace, of women and minorities finding toeholds in the work force, why this short-sightedness? In an era of openness, with the Berlin wall down and the Soviet door open (at least for now), why this myopic narrow vision? Let theatre and voice trainers rise to the challenge of the millennium of diversity with similar spirit. *Webster's Collegiate Dictionary* defines pluralism as:

> A state of society in which members of diverse ethnic, racial, religious, or social groups maintain an autonomous participation in and devel-opment of their traditional culture or special interest within the con-fines of a common civilization.[2]

Adding the word "gender" to the above, let us proceed. We are, after all, plural and not singular. We are the people. We are all in it together. If we are patient with each other and respectful of our collective diversity, perhaps academic administrators, heads of training programs, and artistic directors might more fully appreciate and more creatively deploy our wide-ranging gifts.

As a corollary and seeming contradiction, I would like to have a word about voice and speech training as a discipline closely related to movement, but necessary and viable in its own right. I have just spoken from the heart about teachers and students, coaches and actors drawing from many wells. Let me admit to this concern: today's job bulletins featuring more and more dual specialty positions. One sees calls for applicants versed in acting and

---

[2]   *Webster's Collegiate Dictionary*, Editor-in-Chief Frederick Mish, Merriam-Webster, Inc., Springfield, MA, 1993, p. 896.

directing, movement and combat, or acting and voice. These pairings make sense. Consider for a moment, though, the voice and movement pairing. No one denies that these two are Siamese twins, operating in synchronous or disastrous union. I wonder, though, if this pairing might not, over time, devalue the voice specialist's function, casting out baby and bath? Voice and movement are close bedfellows in the warm-up process, but they are sometimes platonic friends in the teaching process. Let me explain.

My teaching experience leads me to believe that a voice is born largely against a background of energized stillness, in an economical, kinesthetic "listening" with the body. It seems to be a matter of refining down to what Peter Brook calls a "panic-free emptiness" within. I might amend that to a chaos-free emptiness within and without; the focus and attention, the awareness and preparedness of the woodland doe; or what my University of Virginia colleague Colleen Kelly calls "the universal point of departure." When a voice is a-borning, as sounds release from deep within for the first time, extraneous movement, habitual movement, punitive "work-out" movement may confuse and obscure the very feedback that roots and frees the voice. Having said that I fear I may be branded anti-movement. Not at all! Having taught with several superlative movement specialists, I respect and have come to depend on the parallel and correlative aspects of their work in conjunction with mine. Just as I am no advocate of awkwardness or vague stasis, I am no advocate of movement for movement's sake. It is probably semantics and stereotyping that make me prefer "voice/stillness" or "voice/silence" or "voice/ease" specialist to "voice/movement" specialist.

Are there movement specialists sensitive and true who would agree with this line of thinking? There are those, I know, in the training disciplines who are of the "get them up and moving/make them suffer" school, inadvertently promoting vocal strain, who might lump movement and voice together in an arranged, shotgun marriage. To those who argue that we can no longer afford specialists in theatre training, just as in the health care the demand for specialists is declining as the need for practitioners of general medicine is increasing: my concern is that voice will somehow get lost in the shuffle. In a "what you see is what you get" world, movement is a visual art: voice is not. Those who do not have the ears to hear the vocal world perhaps cannot perceive vocal contributions to theatre art. Gesture, blocking, character physicality/movement, and dance are identifiable, visual phenomena. Breathing, pitch, placement, projection, intonation, inflection, and dialect are not so clearly discernible.

I champion our right and our responsibility to focus on sound, on voice, on listening, on acoustics, on resonance, not in splendid isolation, but as a priority, and with all the attendant awarenesses and energies of the body, its physicality, and its movement in play.

Finally, I offer a public paean to the unsung heroes and heroines of the voice and speech world, the teachers in the trenches who quietly suppress their egos and do not cultivate a national reputation in order to more fully focus on students' progress. These are the teachers who have not authored texts, no master teachers engaged in self-marketing, teachers who work with all manner and level of student. Success is predictable when one works with the crop's culled cream and faces few obstacles. This is the equivalent of driving a power-steered vehicle with one finger. The teachers I am talking about are the chauffeurs of manual transmission, gear-grinding bumper cars, whose wild rides and breakdowns and sheer endurance guide students to a vocal finish line. These teachers are our bedrock barometers. They bring to new texts, new methods, new points of view a lack of bias which helps them see what is universal in the new. These teachers are perhaps the true pluralists of our discipline, those who maintain autonomous participation in development of the voice within the confines of a common civilization.

The true teacher sees through semantics and vocabulary to the essence within. The true teacher combines disparate elements. The true teacher is inclusive and non-competitive. The true teacher knows that any vocal method or system codifies a quest for the basic, universal tenets of voice function coupled with artistry, or it is not worth its salt. The true teacher also knows that a system or method may excel in certain areas more than others.

Although the performance training arena has not been as open and inclusive of voice methods as it might be, it is my observation that some voice and speech trainers in that arena have embraced affiliation, cooperation, and dialogue. The formation and growth of the Voice and Speech Trainers Association attests to this good faith. For my part, I must own that through membership and participation in this organization I have become more a citizen of the world and a person of the theatre. My professional paranoia has decreased, as well as its academic counterpart, what University of Virginia Dean of Arts and Sciences Ray Nelson whimsically calls, "the heebie-jeebies." The generous spirit of VASTA, a gathering of sages and explorers, is contagious and promotes respect, collegiality, and cross-germination in our discipline.

Recently the National Endowment for the Humanities put out an endowment-wide call for proposals pertaining to American pluralism and identity. Sheldon Hackney, Chairman of the NEH, could be talking about our voice and speech microcosm when he said this:

> All of our people — left, right, and center — have a responsibility to examine and discuss what unites us as a country, what we share as common American values in a nation comprised of many divergent

groups and beliefs. For too long, we have let what divides us capture the headlines and sound bites, polarizing us rather than bringing us together. I am proposing a national conversation open to all Americans, a conversation in which all voices are heard and in which we grapple seriously with the meaning of American pluralism.[3]

Voice and speech trainers might expand American pluralism to an international perspective. The recent Theatre Voice Conference in Stratford-upon-Avon catches the spirit of Mr. Hackney's words and transcends localized patriotism. Let us indeed focus on the international, but let us begin among ourselves to view our diversity as richness rather than as fragmentation.

3   Sheldon Hackney, *A National Conversation on American Pluralism and Identity — Endowment-Wide Call for Proposals*, National Endowment for the Humanities: US Government Printing Office, 1994, 301-265/00016.

II

THEORIES OF VOICE

8

PRINCIPLES OF SKILL ACQUISITION APPLIED TO VOICE TRAINING

Katherine Verdolini

As a young vocalist and voice trainer, I kept thinking that if I could only identify the "right technique," if I could only figure out with certainty which body part should go where during voice production, then I could sing well and I could also be a good voice trainer. Even beyond the rather frightful omission of emotions and art in this thinking, there was a serious fallacy: knowing that you should hike up your larynx to your eyeballs when you sing (if that were the conclusion) is not equivalent to knowing how to do it or how to teach it. In fact, even as my knowledge of voice physiology increased, my ability to "do it" and to "teach it" was not necessarily improved proportionately. A gulf remained between my explicit, analytical knowledge about voice, and voice production itself. At first, the gap annoyed and perturbed me. Then it became interesting. What was the nature of "learning how"? How was it different from "learning that," or "book learning"? These and other questions prompted me to pursue studies in skill acquisition in a department of psychology.

As luck would have it, during the same historical period in which I initiated those studies, a theoretical approach to learning and memory was developed that focused on the very distinction that intrigued me: the distinction between "knowing that" and "knowing how." Based on observations of amnesic subjects as well as normal learners, it was proposed that there are different memory systems or information processing modes with distinct neuroanatomical and cognitive substrates: one system or mode that governs "knowing that" and one that governs "knowing how."

Few subjects could have been more interesting to me. This essay is an attempt to summarize in a simple way what I consider to be among the most important findings on this topic and on skill acquisition in general, as they may apply to voice and voice training.

Throughout this essay, I repeatedly refer to "memory system" and "processing mode" side by side. The reason is that a debate has been going on for a few decades now about whether to consider memory structurally, as a "system," or whether to consider memory dynamically, in terms of its processing characteristics. My use of the terms "memory system" and "memory processing mode" in the same document reflects my decision to acknowledge both theoretical views equally, essentially because I think both have merit, and I think that the distinction is an artificial one.

Some leaps will be necessary. Most of the experiments have been done using verbal or hand-eye coordination tasks. None have been carried out using voice tasks. Also, most of the experiments investigating the cognitive characteristics of the memory type we are interested in have been carried out not looking at skill acquisition per se, but rather at a parallel phenomenon called "priming," which will be discussed in some detail shortly. Despite these limitations, I think that it is reasonable to make some generalizations from these studies to skill acquisition in voice training, awaiting the proper studies.

THEORETICAL BACKGROUND

Among the earliest contemporary observations leading to a distinction between "knowing that" and "knowing how" were those reported by Dr. Brenda Milner, a Canadian neurologist. A patient of hers, a now-famous "H.M.," had undergone a bilateral resection of his temporal lobes (parts of the brain surface) as treatment for a debilitating seizure disorder. After his surgery, H.M. could not acquire new, conscious memories of post-surgical events. He did not remember from one moment to the next that he had eaten or that he had met someone. Somewhat surprisingly, he could remember how to do new things. For example, he improved with practice on a task that required tracking a rotating target with a wand.[1] So, he was indeed able to form new memories: those governing improved perceptual-motor performance with practice. He just did not know that he had acquired the memories. (In fact, a "memory" is any record of the past, regardless of whether the memory is "remembered," or experienced in consciousness, or not.)

The theoretically important implication that eventually developed from

---

[1]   Antecedent observations were made as early as Plato (see for example, Stumpf, 1975) and Descartes (see Haldane & Ross, 1967), and were later made by psychiatrists (Freud & Breuer, 1966; Janet, 1893, 1904), psychologists (Ebbinghaus, 1885; Hull, 1933; Thorndike & Rock, 1934), neurologists (Clarapede, 1911/1951; Korskoff, 1899), and others (see Schacter, 1987 for a review). However, Milner's reports more directly led to the current formulations discussed.

this report and similar ones was that there must be a neuroanatomical system or processing mode that governs practice effects without conscious remembering, and that is spared in amnesia, as well as a system that governs memories that we experience and can talk about. The brain parts resected in H.M.'s surgery, and specifically the hippocampus and the amygdala in the temporal cortex, were clearly important for the latter but not the former type of learning and memory.

What are the characteristics of the memory system (or processing mode), preserved in amnesia, that appear to govern perceptual-motor skill acquisition? Information about this system and how it works might elucidate some useful principles for voice training. A look at some recent findings will shed some light on this question.

Characteristics of the Memory System and Operations Preserved in Amnesia, Which Appear to Govern Perceptual-Motor Skill Acquisition, i.e., "Implicit Memory"

The memory system (or processing mode) preserved in amnesia governs not only skill acquisition for perceptual-motor tasks, but also other functions, including "priming."[3] Priming is facilitated performance on previously encountered stimuli, as compared with performance on new stimuli of the same class. For example, if a subject first studies a series of words and then is shown studied and non-studied words extremely rapidly (say 35 ms. [milliseconds] each), priming is shown by better identification of the studied versus the non-studied words, regardless of whether the subject remembers the studied words or not.

So, to reiterate, both skill acquisition and priming remain intact in amnesia; as such, they can be considered together as part of a set of memory functions called "implicit memory," or to use Squire's term, "procedural memory." Specifically, implicit memory is reflected by any performance benefit from prior practice or exposure to stimuli, without learners explicitly remembering those stimuli (Graf & Schacter, 1985; see also Schacter, 1987, and Roediger, 1990, for excellent reviews). Not only amnesic learners but also neurologically intact subjects show implicit memory, as described next. In the discussion that follows, we will assume that the characteristics of implicit memory — most of which are known from studies on verbal priming — are consistent across all types of implicit memory, including perceptual-motor performance without awareness. This assumption may ultimately be shown to be incorrect, but I am willing to make it in the meantime.

Implicit Memory is Memory Without Awareness

Implicit memory, as it has been defined in theoretical research, is memory without awareness. That is, implicit memory involves a memory type without conscious remembering of events leading to memory development or conscious remembering of what has been learned. At best, conscious awareness is irrelevant for implicit memory. At worst, it may interfere with it (Verdolini-Marston, 1991).

Given this characteristic of implicit memory, it would seem that this memory type could be shown only in amnesic subjects, who do not remember much of anything. On the contrary, implicit memory can also be shown in normal learners. Graf and his colleagues (Graf, Handler, & Haden, 1982) reported a classic study in this regard. In that study, the investigators essentially simulated amnesia — and showed implicit memory — in neurologically intact learners.

Healthy adults were first asked to study a list of words (for example, they might have been asked to study "defend, repair, engage" etc.). Subjects were later asked to complete word stems (for example, "def...") with the first word that came to mind. Each stem could be completed with several different words ("defend, define, default..."). However, subjects tended to complete the stems with previously studied words, *which they did not necessarily remember*, at a greater than chance level (priming). Thus, the effect of prior exposure was seen on current performance, without the apparent assistance of conscious remembering. This finding constituted evidence of implicit memory or memory without awareness in normal learners.

Implicit Memory Appears Fundamentally Governed by Perceptual Processes

This point is the most important one to focus on regarding implicit memory, to my thinking. Implicit memory, at least as reflected by priming, fundamentally involves the mental processing of perceptual — or sensory — information: sight, sound, smell, taste, and touch. As important, implicit memory generally does not appear to involve "associative processing," or the relating of perceptual information to other mental contents and operations that make it "meaningful" or symbolic.

The study cited above by Graf and colleagues is an example of the many, many experiments that have pointed to this conclusion (Graf et al., 1982). Recall that in the initial phase of that investigation, subjects studied a list of words. In fact, during the study phase of the experiment, subjects studied the words under different conditions. In one group, subjects studied the words by processing their meanings (subjects rated how much they "liked" each word, related to its *meaning*). In another group, subjects studied the words by processing their perceptual or *surface* characteristics (subjects indicated whether each word had any letters in common with the preceding word).

During the subsequent test phase of the experiment, it turned out that the likelihood of remembering or recalling the studied words was increased if the subject had processed the words' meanings during study. However, the likelihood of spontaneously completing a word stem with a previously studied word (or implicit memory) was unaffected by the earlier study task: words that had been examined for their meaning and words that had been examined for their surface or perceptual characteristics were equally likely to be produced as word stem completions, even when subjects did not recall which words they had studied. The conclusion was that implicit memory (reflected by word stem completion in this case) can develop any time one is exposed to a stimulus and processes its perceptual characteristics. The processing of stimuli's meanings, or associative processing, appears irrelevant for the development of this memory type. Numerous other studies have pointed to similar conclusions, although qualifiers do need to be added. One qualifier is the topic of the next subsection.

Implicit Memory Requires Attentional Processing

Some studies have pointed to the likelihood that when *new* stimuli are encountered, for effective perceptual processing underlying implicit memory to occur, full attention must be directed to the stimulus. This principle was perhaps most clearly demonstrated in a series of studies by myself, for my dissertation (Verdolini-Marston and Balota, 1994).

My studies involved a perceptual-motor task, "pursuit rotor." In this task, the object is to track a rotating stimulus with a wand. When there is contact, a counter is driven. If the subjects involved were amnesic subjects who did not remember that they had ever done the task before, improvements with practice would constitute evidence of implicit memory, i.e. memory without awareness. However, we used neurologically normal subjects in our studies, who did remember that they had done the task before from session to session. Thus, to investigate implicit memory, we had to come up with some measure of perceptual-motor learning *without awareness* in these normal learners. We essentially used a priming paradigm. Subjects first practiced on several different stimuli. Later, they returned for a test on the old stimuli, as well as on new stimuli of the same difficulty. Implicit memory would be shown by a performance benefit for the old as compared with the new stimuli, assuming that subjects did not remember which stimuli were old and which were new. In our first of several experiments, we demonstrated such priming for the pursuit rotor task.

The main objective of theoretical interest in our studies was then to investigate the type of mental processes that regulated priming for this perceptual-motor task. We thought that priming might be governed by perceptual processes, as had been found for verbal priming. Our experimental strategy was to give subjects in different groups different instructions about what to do mentally during the initial practice phase. In some groups, subjects were instructed to use images to assist their performance, such as stirring in a bowl or imagining a locomotive wheel as it turned. (According to earlier pilot work, subjects thought that these were good images to help performance.) In other groups, subjects were instructed to pay attention to the task, and to concentrate on it. Finally, in other groups, subjects were not given any instructions about what to do mentally during practice.

During the later test phase, it turned out that subjects showed priming (a performance benefit for old stimuli, without remembering which stimuli were old, or implicit memory) only if they had not been given any instructions about what to do mentally during practice. Subjects who had received instructions, whether they were imagery or concentration instructions, failed to develop priming or implicit memory.

We were a bit perplexed by the findings, but our explanation was ultimately as follows: perceptual processes underlie implicit memory in the perceptual-motor as in the verbal domain. However, for tasks that are novel to subjects — such as the pursuit rotor task — in order for perceptual processing to occur, subjects must devote their full attention to the task. (Perceptual processing might occur more automatically for familiar stimuli, such as words.) When instructions of any type were imposed, subjects paid attention to the instructions, and not to the perceptual array associated with the task. Thus, priming (implicit memory) failed to develop.

What we have said here may seem to be a paradox: implicit memory involves learning without awareness, yet attention is required. How can we be unaware of various aspects of a task, and yet attend to it? Thinking carefully, awareness and attention are actually different phenomena. Awareness involves knowing that one has done something specific (performed on a given stimulus, or perhaps moved the arm this way or that way). Attention refers to alertness, or the reception of information without any necessary conscious organizing of it in time or space. In a word, attention refers to "being in the moment," "being here, now," without judgment or comment or conclusions (awareness).

Another important finding in our studies, which may be of greater interest for this readership, was that not only implicit memory (priming, in this case) but also learning for the pursuit rotor task in general was poorest when subjects were given mental strategies to use during practice. Relatively poorer overall performance was seen for both imagery and concentration groups, as compared with the no-instruction group. Equally as interesting, subjects who used imagery and concentration strategies thought

that those strategies were very helpful for learning and performing the pursuit rotor task. The implication is that imagery instructions or even concentration instructions may not be as useful as we sometimes think they are, regardless of students' informal impressions about their benefits.

Implicit Memory Depends on Repetition

One of the strongest factors affecting implicit memory is repetition. The size of performance benefits for previously encountered or practiced stimuli increases as the number of exposures or repetitions increases. This principle seems obvious enough, so I will not drag you through the evidence (the interested reader is referred to Jacoby and Dallas, 1981). However, as noted in the preceding sections, for repetitions to be effective in producing implicit memory, apparently they must involve the processing of perceptual, or sensory information. The repetitions must also occur in the same modality as will be required for later tests of implicit memory. This issue is discussed next.

Implicit Memory is Modality and Context-Specific

Implicit memory appears to be a quite literal and inflexible memory type in that it is modality-and context-specific. If you change the performance modality between study (training) and test (for example from the auditory to the visual modality), or even if you change the environment in which study (or training) and test occur, (from a swimming pool gallery to a games arcade), implicit memory fails to develop normally.

An example of the modality-dependence of implicit memory was reported by Jacoby and Dallas (1981). In one of their experiments, words were presented to subjects either visually or auditorily during an initial study phase. In a later test phase, subjects were required to identify words that were presented visually, extremely rapidly (for 35 ms). Some of the test words were from the earlier study list and some were not. A better ability to identify studied as compared with non-studied words would constitute evidence of priming or implicit memory. In some cases the modality was consistent between study and test modality (visual-visual), and in some cases modality was inconsistent between study and test (auditory-visual). On average, subjects showed better identification of studied as compared with non-studied words (implicit memory), *provided* that the study and test modalities were consistent (visual-visual). When study and test modalities were inconsistent (auditory-visual), implicit memory was not shown. The implication is that implicit memory depends on modality consistency between training and later performance.

Implicit memory also fails to develop fully when the context (or environment) changes from study to test. An example of this principle was reported by Graf (1988). In his study, subjects studied the usual word list during an initial experimental phase, either in a swimming pool area or in a games arcade. Later, subjects performed on implicit memory tests (word stem completion and another conceptually similar test, a "category production" test), either in the same setting in which they had studied or in the other setting. Priming, or implicit memory performance, was greater when the study and test environments were consistent. Thus, implicit memory depended on environmental consistency.

OTHER PRINCIPLES OF SKILL ACQUISITION

There are numerous other important principles of skill acquisition that have been investigated within other frameworks besides implicit memory. Schmidt (1987) provides a comprehensive review of this literature and pertinent issues. For our purposes, three of what I consider the most important principles are discussed next.

Skill Acquisition Requires Information About Performance During Training (Knowledge of Results)

For skills to improve with practice, learners must have information ("knowledge of results," or KR) about how well they have done relative to the target performance. An example of this quite intuitive principle was illustrated in a study by Bilodeau and colleagues (Bilodeau, Bilodeau, & Schumsky, 1959). In their study, subjects practiced what is called a "linear positioning task," which requires subjects to learn to displace an object to a criterion position. Some subjects received KR after each of twenty practice trials, some subjects received no KR for twenty trials, and other subjects received an intermediate amount of KR. The result was that no learning was observed in subjects who had not received information about their performance, or KR. Therefore, KR was apparently required for learning.

The interesting thing is that, from this and other studies, although KR appears required for learning, more is not necessarily better. In another study by Johnson, Wicks, and Ben-Sira (1981), using a similar linear positioning task as in the study by Bilodeau and colleagues (Bilodeau et al., 1959), some subjects received KR after each of ten trials. Some subjects received KR on 25 percent of forty trials, and some subjects received KR on 10 percent of one hundred trials. Thus, in each subject group, subjects received KR on ten trials. However, there were differences in the number of intervening trials between KR provision. During the training phase of the experiment, subjects who received relatively infrequent KR appeared to do somewhat worse than other subjects. However, when subjects were tested later, during a delayed test, subjects who had received the infrequent KR actually did the best.

The implication is that although frequent KR may be useful for *immediate performance during training*, less frequent KR may enhance actual learning shown by better performance at a later time. It may be that when learners are not pounded with KR during training, they can process information relevant for learning and "make it their own," with performance benefits at later follow-up.

To be able to perform acquired skills along with other tasks, consistent responding is required during training. One of the goals of training in many domains, including voice, is to skillfully produce the target behavior while at the same time performing other critical tasks, for example talking, moving, or dancing. Some work suggests that the ability to run a new, acquired behavior off skillfully along with other behaviors requires that during training, the behavior be consistently produced in the target fashion. This principle was evident from a series of studies by Schneider and Fisk (1982). In their studies, subjects were first shown a series of cards with letters on them, in rapid succession, and were required to indicate in which position on a card a target letter had appeared. In some cases, a given letter (for example, "M") was always a "target" when it appeared. This was called a "consistent mapping" condition. In other cases, a given letter ("M") might be a target to watch for on one trial, but not a target on the second trial (i.e., "X" might have been the target, and "M" a distraction). This training condition was called "variable mapping." Later, the task was made more complicated by asking subjects to look for new letters as well as previous target letters. The result was that when this additional task was added, subjects were able to retain their previous skill level in position identification for the original target letters only if previous training had involved consistent identification of those letters, or "consistent mapping." If previous training was inconsistent, or variable (requiring the identification of different letters on different trials), earlier skill levels were not retained in the face of the new task. An excellent way to summarize the conclusions from this study is found in a much earlier quote by a renowned American psychologist, William James:

> *Never suffer an exception to occur till the new habit is securely rooted in your life.* Each lapse is like the letting fall of a ball of string which one is carefully winding up; a single slip undoes more than a great many turns will wind again. *Continuity* of training is the great means of making the nervous system act infallibly right. (James, 1890).

Generalization to untrained variants of tasks is enhanced by practice under variable conditions. Practice under variable conditions appears to enhance the generalization of specific trained behaviors to other behaviors in the same class. An example demonstrates this principle. McCracken and Stelmach (1977) had subjects practice knocking over barriers with their hands within a given time-period on numerous trials. Some subjects received practice with a constant hand-to-barrier distance, and other subjects received practice with different hand-to-barrier distances on different trials. During the training phase, subjects with the constant distance did better. However, when all subjects were tested later with a distance that was new for all of them, those who had previously received variable practice did better.

The point from this and other studies is that to maximize the generalization of a trained behavior to new, untrained situations, practice should involve varied practice conditions, perhaps with varied materials.

APPLICATIONS TO VOICE AND VOICE TRAINING

Having gone through some of the details, what do we do with this information in voice and voice training? In this next section, we take a second look at each of the principles discussed above, one by one, and try to make some links to voice and voice training. Then in the final section, we attempt to tie all the principles together into a cohesive whole.

You may discover that you already employ several of the suggested strategies. In this sense, the following section might provide support and encouragement for what you are already doing.

Specifics

Implicit memory is memory without awareness. Based on studies with amnesic subjects, implicit memory is a memory system or processing mode that appears to govern skill acquisition and does not involve conscious awareness of what has been learned. In fact, awareness may be indifferent for implicit memory. Explicit knowledge about learning contents may actually interfere with the development of implicit memory, in some cases (see for example, Verdolini-Marston, 1991).

The implications might be quite surprising to some trainers: although knowledge about voice science may be extremely helpful to you as trainers, that knowledge is not *necessarily* helpful to your voice students. In particular, *a mechanistic awareness about voice production in training, such as "expand your ribs here and drop your jaw there" may be fruitless or even counterproductive.* I realize that this is a strong statement, and may not extend to all situations. However, I encourage you to explore it.

Implicit memory appears fundamentally governed by perceptual processes. From this principle, we understand that one of our main tasks as trainers is to promote our students' processing of perceptual — or sensory — information during training. We should show students what good alignment for voice production looks like. We should let them feel a deep breath. We should let them hear the sound of a focused voice.

The emphasis on sensory information is not new to theatre. The Alexander Technique is profoundly based in this principle (see for example, Jones, 1976). Lessac also focuses on sensory information, going so far as to include "tasting" and "smelling" various aspects of voice production (Lessac, 1967). There are many, many other examples of theatre trainers for whom sensory information is a critical part of the training program.

A discomforting corollary is that metaphoric images ("imagine rowing a boat as you breathe"), which are commonly used in voice training and which involve meaningful or associational processes (as opposed to perceptual processes), may work against voice development in some cases.

Implicit memory requires attentional process, where novel stimuli are concerned. The implication from this principle is that any operations that divert away attention from perceptual or sensory information related to voice may interfere with memory development. Attention can be diverted by too many instructions about mental strategies, so that the learner attends to the strategies and not to sensory information. Attention from perceptual information can also be diverted by emotional responses. ("That was so *terrible!!!* — foot stamping optional). Attention may be affected by low motivational levels. Most of you are empirically familiar with these and other apparent perils to attention.

As already mentioned, I think that the best way to describe what attention to perceptual information "looks like" is "being in the moment," "being here, now." Theatre trainers are all assuredly very familiar with this concept.

Implicit memory depends on repetition. This principle is quite straightforward. PRACTICE! Or, as Lessac (1967) suggests, "Don't practice, do it!" (repeatedly).

Implicit memory is modality- and context-specific. Here we have an interesting point. There has been much talk about different "modality" strengths across learners in theatre training. According to this view, some people would be "visual" learners. Others would be "auditory" learners. Still others would be "digital" or verbal learners. The suggestion is to modify your teaching input to match the student's modality strength. The finding that implicit memory is modality-specific suggests a different tack. Within this framework, the best modality for training is the modality required for task execution. For voice production as for any motor task, ultimately, perceptual (not verbal) information guides central nervous system output commands. Therefore, training should occur in the perceptual realm, including auditory, kinesthetic, and visual modalities, depending on the specific task. If we train a student in the "digital" or verbal mode, at best a translation of that information to a perceptual code will be required before voice can be produced; the transformation takes time and precious information may be lost or distorted in the process. The verbal mode is right if you want the student to learn to talk about voice production. But the verbal instructional mode is wrong for voice training, if you want the student to actually learn to produce voice better, *regardless of the student's relative "modality strengths.*

Also, training benefits may be greatest when training occurs in the same or similar environments as will be encountered for performance. We all think about conducting classes on a stage, but I for one do not do it nearly enough.

Skill acquisition requires information about performance (knowledge of results). Students need information about how they are doing relative to what you want them to do. However, intensive feedback is not necessarily good. Withholding information about performance for several trials may enhance the student's own processing of information and later performance, or learning. This conclusion may be especially valid later (as opposed to earlier) in learning. So, not giving any feedback for several trials may help the student generalize from what you have worked on for one vowel to another vowel, from one monologue to another, and so forth. The translation of this principle to simpler language is, "Give your student space!"

To be able to perform acquired skills along with other tasks, consistent responding is required during training. I have heard theatre trainers talk about this principle: if the student is to use a certain voice production mode on stage while acting, dancing, emoting, etc., that same mode or a similar mode must be consistently used, even offstage. What it boils down to is that we cannot summon a physiological operation in voice on stage, adding other task requirements, if we do not consistently use that mode in all or most situations when it is appropriate.

Generalization to untrained variants of tasks is enhanced by variable practice. The use of varied training materials will probably enhance the student's ability to generalize a target voicing mode from trained to untrained materials. For example, if you are working on a focused voice, you should train it on many different vowels, phrases, monologues, etc. In that way, when the student encounters new materials, generalization of focused voice should transfer to those materials. Similarly, you should include different performance materials in training: different monologues, dialogues, comic and tragic material, etc.

TYING IT INTO A COHESIVE WHOLE

For a few years, I found myself incorporating many of the principles described here in a helter-skelter fashion in voice training. My mind leapt from one to another to another of the principles, like the proverbial monkey in a tree. I was run ragged by the job, and my students and patients were probably stunned. What was the classic "banana" that would quiet the mental monkey? If we accept the principles discussed here, how can we tie them all together into a cohesive whole? Let me share what I have come up with so far.

The kingpin of what I call my "skill acquisition package" is the notion that skill acquisition fundamentally involves *attention to perceptual information*, in numerous repetitions, with varied tasks. If the student effectively processes perceptual information, several of the principles that we discussed will be satisfied as a by-product. We avoid a mechanistic "awareness" of voice production. We stay in the relevant modality, which is perceptual, not verbal. Numerous repetitions occur, with consistent performance required across different tasks. An additional notion is that I attempt to supply "some" but not "too much" feedback (knowledge of results).

What does all this look like? I have a hierarchy of five steps that I think represent a start. Let us take breathing as an example. Say that we want the student to expand the abdomen on inspiration, and press it in during expiration (and voicing). How can we get the behavior trained, following the principles outlined? The steps that I use are:

Step 1. *Direct the student's attention to the body in general*, and ask him to notice any sensations. ("Scan your body with your mind's eye. Do you notice any sensations?") Do not ask the student to describe the sensations verbally, just to attend to them. Often, the desired physiological behavior will appear with this simple step, without further work. If not, proceed to Step 2.

Step 2. *Direct the student's attention to the specific body part of interest*, in this case, the abdomen. ("Focus on your abdomen as you breathe.") Again, the desired behavior may appear with this step. If not, proceed to either Step 3 or Step 4 (they are interchangeable in order).

Step 3. *Model* the behavior for the student. For example, without saying anything, place the student's hand on your abdomen as you breathe in and out.

Step 4. *Manipulate* the student's body so that the target behavior is likely to occur. In this case, you might stabilize the shoulders and chest so that only the abdomen is available for movement during breathing.

If the student still does not produce the behavior, as an absolute last resort, proceed to Step 5, which violates the principle of perceptual training:

Step 5. *Tell* the student what to do.

This sequence, which I think I came up with on my own, has a similar flavor to what Timothy Gallwey describes in his book on tennis learning, *Inner Game of Tennis* (1974). In that book, he also emphasizes the processing of perceptual, or sensory information. The sequence that I outlined can be used with just about any behavior that you want to train. If a student is "squeezing" in the throat while talking, direct the student's attention to the body in general, and ask her to notice any tension. If the tension does not dispel, direct her attention to her throat. If that does not work, model tight versus free voice, and have her mimic you in both. Or, manipulate the neck or other body parts in a way that is likely to free the throat. Finally, if you must, tell her to let go of her throat, for heaven's sake.

Once the student has produced the behavior for simple tasks, you proceed (of course) with many, many repetitions, in different and increasingly complex contexts (for example, simple vowels, words, phrases, short discourse, conversation, monologues). Gradually fade models so that the student depends less and less on your input.

With this type of sequence as a part of your training technique, you will discover that you are talking and explaining less and less, and "doing" more and more. Bonnie Raphael referred to this principle at a recent VASTA workshop (1993), "Every year I promise myself, 'Half as many words.'" I agree with her, and consider minimized yammering an indication of principled and, I think, effective training.

SUMMARY

In this essay, we have discussed several principles of skill acquisition, mostly derived from a theoretical construct called "implicit memory." This type of memory, to which skill acquisition appears tightly linked, is a memory without awareness, it involves attention to perceptual or sensory information; and, it develops with numerous and consistent modality- and context-specific repetitions of target behaviors. It is optimal training for voice performance since it likely maximizes attention to sensory information, minimizes verbal analytic explanations, and includes training with a variety of materials and in physical environments that will be relevant for performance. The approach described here is, in sum, "something to experience."

WORKS CITED

Bilodeau, E. A.; Bilodeau, I. M.; & Schumsky, D. A. "Some Effects of Introducing and Withdrawing Knowledge of Results Early and Later in Practice." *Journal of Experimental Psychology* 58 (1959): 142–144.

Clarapede, E. "Recognition and 'me'ness." In D. Rapaport, ed. *Organization and Pathology of Thought* (pp. 58–75). New York: Columbia University Press, 1951. (Reprinted from *Archives de Psychologie* 11 (1911): 79–90).

Cohen, N. J., & Squire, L. R. "Preserved Learning and Retention of Pattern-Analyzing Skill in Amnesia: Dissociation of 'Knowing How' and 'Knowing That.'" *Science* 210 (1980): 207–210.

Ebbinghaus, H. *Uber das Gedachtnis* [Memory]. Leipzig: 1885. Duncker and Humblot. Evarts.

Freud, S., & Breuer, J. *Studies on Hysteria.* (J. Strachey, Trans.) New York: Avon Books, 1966.

Gallwey, W. T. *The Inner Game of Tennis.* New York: Bantam Books, 1974.

Graf, P. "Implicit and Explicit Memory in Same and Different Environments." Paper presented at Psychonomics, Chicago, 1988.

Graf, P.; Mandler, G.; & Haden, D. E. "Simulating Amnesic Symptoms in Normal Subjects." *Science* 218 (1982): 1243–1244.

Graf, P., & Schacter, D. L. "Implicit and Explicit Memory for New Associations in Normal and Amnesic Subjects." *Journal of Experimental Psychology: Learning, Memory, and Cognition* 11 (1985): 501–518.

Haldane, E. S., & Ross, G. R. T., Eds. *The Philosophical Works of Descartes.* Cambridge: Cambridge University Press, 1967.

Hull, C. L. *Hypnosis and Suggestibility.* New York: Appleton Century, 1933.

Jacoby, L. L., & Dallas, M. "On the Relationship Between Autobiographical Memory and Perceptual Learning." *Journal of Experimental Psychology: General* 110 (1981): 306–340.

James, W. *Principles of Psychology* (Vol. 1. p. 123). New York: Holt, 1890.

Janet, P. "L'amnesie continue [Continuous amnesia]." *Revue Generale Des Sciences* 4 (1893): 167–179.

Janet, P. "L'amnesie et la dissociation des souvenirs par Demotion [Amnesia and the dissociation of memories by emotion." *Journal de Psychologie Normale et Pathologique* 1 (1904): 417–453.

Johnson, R. W.; Wicks, G. G.; & Ben-Sira, D. "Practice in the Absence of Knowledge of Results: Acquisition and Transfer." Unpublished manuscript, University of Minnesota, 1980.

Jones, F. J. "Escape from the Monkey Trap: An Introduction to the Alexander Technique." In F. J. Jones, *The Alexander Technique: Body Awareness in Action.* New York: Schocken Books, 1976.

Korsakoff, S. S. "Etude medico-psychologique sur une forme des maladies de la memoire [Medical-psychological study of a form of diseases of memory]." *Revue Philosophique,* 28 (1899): 501–530.

Lessac, Arthur. *The Use and Training of the Human Voice: A Practical Approach to Speech and Voice Dynamics.* Mountain View, CA: Hayfield Publishers, 1967.

McCracken, H. D., & Stelmach, G. E. "A Test of the Schema Theory of Discrete Motor Learning." *Journal of Motor Behavior* 9 (1977): 193–201.

Milner, B. "Les troubles de la memoire accompagnant des lesions hippocampi ques bilaterals [Disorders of memory accompanying bilateral hippocampal lesions]." In *Physiologie de l'Hippocampe.* Paris: Centre National de la Recherche Scientifique, 1962.

Roediger, H. L. "Implicit Memory." *American Psychologist* 45 (1990): 1043–1056.

Schacter, D. L. "Implicit Memory: History and Current Status." *Journal of Experimental Psychology: Learning, Memory, and Cognition* 13 (1987): 501–518.

Schmidt, R. A. *Motor Control and Learning: A Behavioral Emphasis* 2nd ed. Champaign, Illinois: Human Kinetic Publishers, 1987.

Schneider, W., & Fisk, A. D. "Degree of Consistent Training: Improvements in Search Performance and Automatic Process Development." *Perception and Psychophysics* 31 (1982): 160–168.

Squire, L. R. "Mechanisms of Memory." *Science* 232, (1986): 1612–1619.

Stumpf, S. E. *Socrates to Sartre: A History of Philosophy* (2nd ed.) New York: McGraw-Hill, 1975.

Thorndike, E. L., & Rock, R. T., Jr. "Learning Without Awareness of What is Being Learned or Intent to Learn It." *Journal of Experimental Psychology* 17 (1934): 1–19.

Verdolini-Marston, K. "Processing Characteristics of Perceptual Motor Memories with and without Awareness." Ph.D. diss., Washington University, St. Louis, 1991.

Verdolini-Marston, K., & Balota, D. A. "The Role of Elaborative and Perceptual Integrative Processes in Perceptual-Motor Performance." *Journal of Experimental Psychology: Learning, Memory and Cognition.*

9

VOICE IN A VISUAL WORLD
A NEURO-LINGUISTIC PROGRAMMING
PERSPECTIVE ON VOCAL TRAINING

ROBERT BARTON

For your own sakes, (the writer) bade me say:
Would you were come to hear, not see, a play.
The playmaker would therefore have you wise
Much rather by your ears than by your eyes.

Ben Jonson

Learners respond in visual, auditory or kinesthetic modes. They are seeing, hearing, or feeling information. The science of Neuro-Linguistic Programming (NLP) has demonstrated that each of us tends to prefer one of the three at any given moment.[1] If teachers can adjust information to the modes in which students are responding or students can change response modes, progress soars. For vocal coaches and teachers, mode adjustment can be the key to freeing actors from vocal prisons and letting them fly.

---

[1] Neuro-Linguistic Programming was founded in 1976 by Richard Bandler and Jon Grinder, who studied three brilliant therapists (Virginia Satir, Milton Erikson, and Fritz Perls) with the research question, "What do brilliant communicators do that can be taught to others?" The resulting system (Neuro-brain and nervous system, Linguistic-language and non-verbal communication, Programming-shortcuts and codes) includes a series of exercises for studying and changing learning and behavior patterns. It is now taught at over one hundred institutes in the U.S. and a similar number throughout the rest of the world. NLP has impacted significantly on the fields of therapy, business, law, and is making some inroads in early childhood and elementary education. It is new to theatre arts, but offers numerous useful and applicable processes for the training of actors.

For obvious reasons, a voice specialist is likely to function frequently in the auditory learning and teaching mode. A typical rehearsal situation may involve a director with an intensely visual orientation, an auditory vocal coach, and an actor responding kinesthetically. Each may be trying valiantly to communicate while limited by learning frameworks. It requires considerable sensory acuity to recognize when you have gotten caught in a mode. It is possible to mistakenly judge others as dense or difficult or yourself as inept. When an entire class or cast is involved, the challenge increases. A voice specialist with learning mode flexibility could be the crucial mediator in the threesome above and in all contexts the one who helps others learn to hear, a capacity increasingly at risk in our society.

ADJUSTING

Two conditions present in acting classes and rehearsals are:

1. At the introductory levels, the vast majority (often up to 80 percent) are visual learners. Information must be presented in a way that can be accepted by this group without alienating others. Since our educational system strongly favors visual learners, it is also important to identify students of exceptional potential who have not yet "bloomed" in part because of the system itself.

2. At the advanced levels, a more pronounced portion of acting students will be kinesthetic and auditory learners because this discipline often encourages those who respond in these modes, even if society in general does not. Auditories often excel at the full range of voice and speech work, simply because they hear sound distinctions others miss. Kinesthetics dominate in sports and dance, since a member of this group has the uncanny ability to watch an act and "feel" what it is like to recreate it successfully. The physical challenges of acting are therefore likely to come easily to this group. Kinesthetics are also highly responsive to both tactile and emotional feelings.[2] Such access is rewarded behavior in acting. What NLP calls "second position" is the capacity to put one's self totally in the "shoes" of another. This core component for characterization might challenge a Kinesthetic less than it would other learners.

---

[2] I suspect Kinesthetic actors do particularly well in film, where "one great take" as well as the capacity to give something fresh but real each time the camera rolls is prized, but may do less well in live theatre where a strong technical need for consistency dominates. This may also offer a partial explanation why an actor can do superb work in one film and fail utterly in another. I suspect that actors who succeed over the long haul strongly develop all three modalities. Since no research exists at present, these conjectures are worth testing.

FUTURE CHALLENGES

I believe that visual domination will continue to increase, while auditory learners decline, making us a culture of pictures with less and less use of sound as a communication tool. While national S.A.T. score averages have risen in other basic testing areas, *verbal* scores have dropped a full five points since 1990 and remain over thirty points lower than in the early seventies. NLP founder Richard Bandler's research has shown that Americans repress the auditory component to such a degree that mental patients often are haunted by voices, which supports the contention that what one resists persists. Modern music often favors volume and rhythm over more subtle variations. Contemporary students habitually experience music at levels designated as risks and as a result may be hearing impaired.

Are we as a culture speaking less than in the past? While a fascinatingly untested research topic, anecdotal evidence suggests that fondness for the art of conversation, appreciation of subtlety and nuance in verbal interaction are losing ground. If there are more people who communicate exclusively in sound bites or the barest minimum verbal signal, if we as a culture are hearing and speaking less, vocal expression is jeopardized. The art of acting, particularly in the classics where sound and language capture experience, is at risk. Shakespeare and his contemporaries wrote plays to be heard. How can these language-based masterpieces merely be seen? Each year my new students seem slightly less aware of their own volume, pitch, breath, articulation, pronunciation, quality, tempo, rhythm, word choice, and use of non-verbal sound. They often drop a few more medial and terminal consonants almost as a matter of course. They struggle a bit more to capture their experience in words. They choose fewer words (anything at this moment may be "awesome," "cool," or "suck" as basic ratings). Many no longer make distinctions between partner verbs such as can/may, could/would or even want/need. Many get caught in the now omnipresent "up-speak" where each statement ends on an upward inflection and this same pitch pattern recurs over and over. So each statement sounds like a question. They are still teachable, but more astonished by the all too new world of voice. From games (arcade to hand-held) to music videos, they experience an almost exclusively sight-centered pop culture.

In class, these students seem to experience greater difficulty simply listening. They appear less likely to "hear" an assignment if it is not given to them in writing or on the board. Many favor what I would call a "non-voice", one not so much flagrantly dissonant or distracting, but almost free of character. Their expressiveness is at first narrower, less adventurous and freewheeling than their predecessors.

These challenges can compound when working with directors. A professional director does not necessarily train to listen to a play. Many in this profession have succeeded through their sense of picturization, not their capacity to sound a text. I am consistently astonished at the number of directing programs with no voice and speech component and the number of aspiring directors who do not themselves consider it important to their training. Many directors are so insecure in the world of sound that their relationships with production vocal coaches are wary, guarded, even suspicious. Other adequately trained directors get discouraged about pitching a play for a largely visual audience. I have certainly been guilty of assuming the audience would not "get" the words and therefore working out visual solutions before exploring ways to help my listeners hear.

So how do we face the future? I believe we need to start with simple pattern recognition. The first step toward mode mastery is recognizing the signals for each. While many subtle blends exist, the archetypal patterns will be presented here.[3] These learning patterns have been observed through thousands of NLP studies and are remarkably consistent. They are far easier to learn if presented first in their purest form. After mastering these, the teacher/coach can move on to recognizing overlaps and combinations of patterns. But there will be some students who are the archetypes. As these patterns are reviewed, you are likely to recognize people you have known.

VISUALS

Someone in a strong Visual learning mode is characterized by a *stiff spine* which rarely touches the back of the chair when sitting; *tension in the shoulders* (which are often raised); *high, shallow breathing*, rarely allowing air deep in the torso; *high, unvarying pitch*; a tendency toward *breathiness*; an extremely *rapid tempo* (because their thoughts are coming faster than they can express them); and *chin pulled down* into the throat to intensify eye contact. Such learners use very little movement and like to work alone, with no interruptions. They like charts, lists, graphs, films, outlines, subheads, and summaries. They have difficulty remembering verbal instructions and their minds wander with too much verbal input. They are frequently not highly aware of themselves from the neck down. Additionally, they favor visual verbs, saying, "I don't see what you mean," or, "It's not clear." These verb choices are literal representations of their experiences. Visual learners are

---

[3]   Most of us blend modalities and favor different learning modes for different circumstances. It is also possible to employ one mode for taking in information, another for searching, another for affirming that what one retrieved was what was intended, and yet another for sharing the response in consciousness. The pure "types" are presented here simply to clarify the major distinctions. It is far less valuable for actors to decide what type of learner they are than to begin to notice the mode they are in at any given time.

often organized, good spellers, neat, orderly, and of course, observant. This learning mode dominates in our culture, with the remaining 20 percent almost equally divided between the other two modes. Unfortunately, the highlighted characteristics in the paragraph above form a virtual checklist of "problem areas" addressed by voice teachers. It is rare, when in full visual mode, to produce a voice that could be described as full, rich, rooted, or free. The teacher may experience frustration because the student, when guided out of shallow breathing or narrow pitch, may also be guided out of the learning mode in which he feels most receptive and productive.

AUDITORIES

Auditory students tend to nod their heads encouragingly as you speak to them. They often tap something — a pencil, foot, or fingers in rhythm — and may sing or hum during activity. Auditories may touch their own faces with some regularity and cover their mouths when embarrassed. They sometimes actually take the phone position (head resting on one hand) while listening. They often repeat what you have just told them almost word for word and may move their lips when reading or computing information. They may use prolonged exhalation when thinking. They speak easily and often talk to themselves. They are distracted by background noise, learn by listening, discussing, reading out loud, tape recording, and playing back. They will literally say that they "hear you" or can "tell" what you mean. Sometimes when you want them to share a single detail with you, they will feel compelled to share the entire story of their experience leading up to that detail. If you interrupt them, they sometimes go back to the beginning and start all over.

Auditories can be subdivided into four categories. An "Auditory Digital" is someone for whom precise word choice is important but who has little sensitivity to nuance in sound. Such a person frequently corrects others on vocabulary, but may speak in a relative monotone and evidence some other almost robotic characteristics of the visual learner. An "Auditory Tonal" is likely to have the most modulated sound and to be extremely sensitive to tone of voice, but less concerned with wording. These two may overlap with a tendency towards either "Auditory Internal," a constant inner voice which the student is hearing, or "Auditory External" where the student talks out loud to herself regularly, in fact seems to need to talk in order to think.

KINESTHETICS

The first signal of a Kinesthetic learner will be the need to take up a great deal of space and to gesture broadly. Kinesthetics often sit with their buttocks far from the back of a chair, while leaning back, with shoulders sloped. They change rhythms easily, and may squirm for a while, then lapse into what appears to be comatose stillness. They breathe low in the torso and often have low pitched, soft-spoken voices. They touch and rub their torsos and appendages, sometimes quite literally as in placing a hand over their heart when discussing a feeling. They may take large pauses and let statements trail away. They may point, especially when reading. They may say they are struggling to "grasp" a point or that they think they "can handle it." They learn by doing and respond to physical reward: touching, hugging, standing close. They need to walk through or act out, demonstrate, change positions, pick up and feel samples, and take frequent breaks to load information.

While simple mode recognition can lead to compassion and progress, there are some other possible solutions.

PACING AND LEADING

Meet Visuals on their own territory and then lead them into others. Match their predicates, support their needs and gradually move them over. Realize that they must take notes and often need handouts. Encourage them to score their manuscripts — highlighting some words, marking stresses, underlining in different colors for various effects. Remember that when they look at this rainbow script it greatly stimulates them. Consider videotaping them or showing them model videos of experts at work. Even if you are predominantly working with their voices, they often feel a need to see what they look like doing it appropriately (and inappropriately) or to see it done exceptionally by others for it to compute. Encourage them to keep the script handy and to look at the words regularly for stimulation. It is especially useful to put them in front of a mirror and show them what they look like forming the sound the right, then the wrong, way.

An intensely Auditory actor may wish to record rehearsal, and certainly will benefit from recording herself in presentation and then tape your comments in order to listen to them again and again. A Kinesthetic actor will bloom once props, rehearsal costumes, and physical contact enter. Consider adding these elements even when you work one to one. It may not seem important to coach an actor vocally with that person wearing the right shoes, but perhaps that actor is so intensely kinesthetic that the shoes provide the key to responsiveness.

With each mode, when communicating, simply try meeting, then leading. "Tell me what you see when you enter. Now tell me what you hear," or, "Let's dig down past these images and imagine a soundtrack swelling behind you. What does that sound do to support you?" or, "How does that vivid picture make you feel? What sensations does it produce?"

All children start as Kinesthetics and evolve into their modes of choice. Sometimes a warm-up releasing childlike whimsy instantly transports the entire group back into this mode. All habitual modes are intensified when one is under stress, so sometimes relaxation exercises can free responsiveness to other patterns. Pacing and leading works equally well with actors of all ages. Even though the techniques may seem to favor children, a remarkable number of actors reach maturity without recognizing their own most responsive modes, much less moving gracefully into others. And actors are never too mature to respond to encouragement in their mode of choice.

APPROPRIATE REWARD

Each modality responds to a different form of praise or reinforcement. Visuals need to see (in your eyes) that you mean your praise and they love encouraging written notes and drawings. Auditories can hear the subtlest encouragement in your voice, and are particularly delighted if everyone in the group is asked to tell them how wonderful they are. Consider a message on their answering machine which may be played over and over, several times if they choose. Kinesthetics simply crave touch. You can lavish them with praise but if there is no pat or hug, it may not quite take. Sometimes the slightest adjustment in your habitual way of giving encouragement can matter enormously.

A Visual learner may be distressed by negative internal pictures, so substituting other pictures can be powerful. A Kinesthetic may associate overwhelming pressure, weight, and temperature with poor work or experience a sensation like "gut-wrenching pain" when fearing a performance, so suggesting other more pleasant, substitute sensations can offer relief. An Auditory may be virtually haunted by an inner critical voice, but, as Bandler found, any learner may experience this phenomenon. Many athletes hum an empowering tune or repeat a positive affirmation specifically to still such a voice. It is worthwhile to explore with the individual performer the impressions he or she gets when feeling unempowered.

ADJUSTING SUBMODALITIES

Sometimes you can achieve change, not by changing modes, but by helping the actor adjust the dials for the mode he has already favored. For Visuals, making the image flatter/deeper, clearer/less focused, nearer/farther, more vivid/more muted, lighter/darker, more active/more static can offer tremendous variation. For Auditories, having the sound continuous/interrupted, soft/loud, fast/slow, harmonious/dissonant, external/internal, near/far, stereo/monaural can be revealing. For Kinesthetics, adjustment in perceived temperature, pressure, texture, weight, movement, and tactile sensations can lead to vocal changes.

WARMING UP AND CONNECTING TO ALL THE MODES

Attend to all three processes during warm-ups. After analyzing the group or individual, tailor the warm-up so that whatever mode is least accessed by this group is employed. A huge number of warm-ups actually favor the two minority modes, possibly because teachers long ago recognized, albeit unconsciously, that actors were not producing in these areas.

A classic acting class exercise is to play a tape with cuts of music from various cultures and styles, asking students to respond by moving the way the music moves them. While opening many other levels of freedom (and often more associated with movement than voice training), this exercise is a basic reawakening for both auditory and kinesthetic modes. For the time being there is no visual input (although a student may see internal images); instead the student is asked to hear and to allow the sounds to enter the body, which then is asked to respond, manifesting the sound. The auditory component may be punched up by asking actors to produce sound complementary but not identical to the music, their own auditory response. Many of us already have exercises like this one in our working repertoire that can expand modes of response. We simply need to reconsider what we already know.

Here is another popular activity for the scanning of verse. Ten actors go up in front of the class with two others waiting in the wings. Observers suggest very famous lines from Shakespeare. When the group onstage receives the line, it tries to physicalize. Each person becomes a stressed or unstressed syllable by standing or kneeling. So "If music be the food of love play on" might have the odd-numbered actors kneeling and the even-numbered standing with no need for the back-up team because there are only ten syllables, not eleven or twelve. The group goes back over the line and discuss how the stresses might vary. A syllable with low stress might slump down near the ground, one with very low stress might crawl all the way into a fetal position. A strong stress might jump in the air. An extremely strong stress with an explanation point might leap in the air with arms thrust high above him. If elision is needed, the actor might scrunch in as if he had been hit in the stomach. The line is first done with each person speaking and physicalizing his syllable, first for a straight scanning, just recognizing stressed and unstressed syllables. Then it is repeated for a more refined line reading, acknowledging other factors. This gives the body, the voice, and the eye the experience of a line of verse.

Many of us have found these kinds of exercises useful without actually recognizing the reason. Before I studied NLP I failed to recognize the vocal component in the first exercise. In the second, I knew it worked but did not realize that fully loading all three learning systems was why it never seemed to miss. If an exercise fails to connect, we should always ask if one of the modalities has inadvertently been neglected. As we are tweaking or modifying exercises, we should always stop to ask if all modes have been honored.

SYNESTHESIA

A powerful way to communicate with actors and directors is through synesthesia or connecting modes. Here are ten fairly typical examples:

1. "Caress the sounds."
2   "See your breath change color."
3. "Give each sound a shade, then a texture."
4. "Let your vowels breathe. Give them freedom and room."
5. "Use your consonant as a weapon. Shoot it like a dart."
6. "See the space between sounds. Then fill it."
7. "See the floating ribs welcome the breath. Hear their greeting."
8. "Feel the string pull the sound effortlessly across the room."
9. "Stop the gentle, waterfall vowel with a firm, iron dam of a consonant."
10. "The unstressed syllables in this line are played by a cool flute, then stressed by a hot kettle drum."

Most of us employ such phrases, recognizing that they are somehow evocative and loaded with imagery, without necessarily noticing (in consciousness) that they cross, combine, or blend modes. If you can connect with two or more modes in a single sentence, you reach more people and take each of them farther above and beyond their old habits. The title of this book, *The Vocal Vision*, is synesthetic. It is intriguing not just because its powerful alliteration makes it pleasant to speak, but because it suggests a provocative blend of distinct modes, with the human voice somehow reverberating on the horizon so that it can be seen as it sounds. It suggests voice reaching far into the future. It implies sound as illumination.

POWERFUL BACK-UP STIMULI

In early NLP research the Olfactory and Gustatory modes were isolated, but have subsequently been clustered largely with other Kinesthetic impulses. While all actors have preferred modes, these two prove powerfully stimulating in a pinch. Give a word or an image a scent or a taste. It tends to stimulate all learners. And even Visuals and Auditories respond well to intensely physical activities because such activities tend to load information past their immediate responses to deep within the body.

It would be a mistake to lump all voice specialists in the auditory club.[4] Long ago voice teachers found that the lessons learned sitting calmly at a desk tended to dissipate once the actor had a rapier in hand leaping off a platform. It is certain that voice classes have become more active. It is useful to ask periodically if enough activity has occurred recently and if it is the kind that will awaken the body to the sounds and words at hand.

CULTURAL BRIDGES, INFLUENCE, AND UNDERSTANDING

Consider identifying (or asking students to identify themselves as) various learning modes in the class and having those in one mode teach another to enter theirs. A great deal of respect (and relief) is created because this often provides an explanation for perceived tension between individuals who had thought themselves hopelessly mismatched and beyond connection. It is great fun to spend some time in each mode and then switch. The best exercise I have found is to work in groups of four and to begin telling a familiar story such as a fairy tale. At the given signal the next person continues the story but in a different mode. The story remains the same but with fascinating temporary variations. After a time, students become sufficiently adept at ad-libbing conversations in any mode, then deliberately matching and mismatching each other. Having students who favor similar modes work together as partners is effective at the beginning of the term. Later deliberately mismatching partner modes gives students an interesting and rewarding challenge. Shifting modes helps actors drop judgment and reach the state of unconditional positive regard for others that is so conducive to genuine collaboration. Obviously, it would serve any actor to ultimately master any mode and we might well consider this part of our basic training.

While the trends in our culture are alarming, the voice specialist has the tremendous potential to save and heal within this chaos. The capacity for recognizing learning patterns, the use of pacing and leading, offering appropriate reward, warming up and connecting to all modes, adjusting submodalities, employing synesthesia, offering powerful stimuli, and building

---

[4]   Obviously not all voice teachers are purely auditory and there can be tremendous variety even within a single modality. Kristin Linklater has a powerful kinesthetic and visual component to her work (some would claim the auditory element is least focused); Edith Skinner's work is intensely auditory yet involves visual use of phonetics. Those most comfortable with the IPA are probably also visual learners. (Phonetic pillows represent a move to connect the kinesthetic — fabric, texture, the simple act of throwing and receiving the pillow — with an intensified visual component of color and pattern for each pillow). Arthur Lessac's work is intensely kinesthetic in a form quite unlike Linklater's. The three predominant dialect systems appeal to diverse learners. Blunt requires you to see the symbols, Machlin to hear and reproduce sound, Stern to "feel the resonance" as you separate one dialect from another.

cultural bridges are all ways in which responsiveness to sound can be achieved. Such efforts are unquestionably challenging, yet the gratitude of students, once reached, is thrilling. Since many of them have had little genuine auditory action in their lives, it is like opening a whole new galaxy of experience to them. Once the words of Shakespeare reverberate in their ears and in their bones, deep in their pelvises and their hearts, they are never the same. To suddenly be given the gift of hearing, feeling and speaking after a largely visual life is extraordinary. For the Auditory and Kinesthetic learners to at last be honored after a school system of disregard, is fully, genuinely liberating. While some directors are too set in their ways to change, many may be reached through mode adjustment and the spirit of giving implied therein.

Certainly all theatre artists could benefit from an understanding of NLP, but in the hands of voice teachers, these learning patterns are a particularly powerful and vital tool. Voice specialists are often mistakenly regarded as first aid kit staff, with bandages and ointment to fix little hurts. Given the shifts in our society, we must now regard them as Warrior Healers, the stewards of vocal life, and ultimately, those charged with its very survival.

WORKS CITED

Andreas, Connirae and Steve Andreas. *Change Your Mind — and Keep the Change.* Moab, Utah: Real People Press, 1987.

———. *Heart of the Mind.* Moab, Utah: Real People Press, 1989.

———. *Successful Parenting.* Boulder, Colorado: NLP Comprehensive.

———. *Introducing NLP.* Boulder, Colorado: NLP Comprehensive.

———. "Briefer than Brief," *Networker* (March/April 1990): 37–41.

Bandler, Richard. *Using Your Brain for a Change.* Moab, Utah: Real People Press, 1985.

Bandler, Richard and John Grinder. *Frogs into Princes.* Moab, Utah: Real People Press, 1979.

Bell, Nanci. *Visualizing and Verbalizing.* Paso Robles, California: Academy of Reading Publications, 1986.

Barton, Robert and Rocco Dal Vera. *Voice: Onstage and Off.* Forth Worth: Harcourt Brace, 1995.

Campbell, Lindagail. *NLP Institute Of Oregon Training Manual.* Medford, Oregon: Lindagail and Associates, 1994.

Cameron-Bandler, Leslie, and Michael Lebeau. *NLP Home Study Guide: Demonstration of Patterns.* Boulder: NLP Comprehensive, 1984.

———. *The Emotional Hostage — Rescuing Your Emotional Life.* San Raphael, California: Future Pace, 1985.

Dilts, Robert, Suzi Smith, and Tim Hallbom. *Beliefs: Pathways to Health and Well Being.* Rapid City, South Dakota: Golden Egg Publishing, 1987.

Dilts, Robert and Todd Epstein. *Tools for Dreamers.* Garde City: Meta Publications, 1991.

"Gap Closing on SAT Scores." Washington: Associated Press. August 25, 1984.

Grinder, Michael. *Righting the Educational Conveyer Belt.* Portland, Oregon: Metamorphosis Press, 1991.

Faulkner, Charles, Kelly Gerling, Gerrmy Schmidt, Tim Hallbom, Suzi Smith, Robert McDonald. *NLP: The New Technology of Achievement.* Niles, Illinois: Nightingale-Conant Corporation, 1992.

Masters, Robert and Jean Huston. *Listening to the Body.* New York: Delacourte, 1978.

O'Connor, Joseph and John Seymour, *Introducing Neuro-Linguistic Programming.* San Francisco: Aquarian Press, 1990.

10

PSYCHO-PHYSICAL TECHNIQUES AND THEIR RELEVANCE TO VOICE AND ACTOR TRAINING

MARY CORRIGAN

A common goal in the training of an actor is to produce an actor who has achieved well-coordinated functioning and an integration of voice, body, and emotion. This fusion of energies has the potential to enable the individual actor to freely and effortlessly express acting texts of any style or period. Many voice teachers currently employ psycho-physical techniques when teaching voice production because these techniques are methods which engage some aspect of a person's physical, mental, or emotional functioning.

What is the relevance of these techniques to the teaching of voice and speech? Are there benefits to be gained from them? Or are there problems associated with the use of these techniques in voice classes?

Webster's Dictionary defined "psycho-physical" as the following:

> **psycho-physical** ... when we conceive physical and psychical stimulation to exist together; a sharing of mental and physical qualities.

"psych-" or "psycho" is defined as:

> Gk fm. *psyche* breath, principle of life, soul; akin to *psychein* to breathe, blow, cool.[1]

Yoga, T'ai Chi, Chi Kung, Aikido and Suzuki training are examples of

---

[1] *Webster's New Collegiate Dictionary* 3rd. ed. (Springfield, Mass.: G & C Merriam Co., 1975): 930–31.

psycho-physical techniques derived from Eastern or Asian cultures. Some European contributions to these techniques are Moshe Feldenkrais's Neuro-Muscular exercises, Alexander Lowen's Bio-Energetics, Ida Rolf's Structural Re-integration (Rolfing), and Mathias Alexander's focus on body alignment and the head/neck relationship.

These are but a few of the many current methods in the burgeoning compendium of psycho-physical techniques presently being adapted as useful adjuncts in voice and actor training programs. The following are some commonly held principles of psycho-physical techniques:

1. All of the approaches encompass the totality of the participant's psychological and neurological organization.

2. They all involve, to a greater or lesser degree, some reorganization of the individual's consciousness.

3. When these techniques are properly executed, it is possible to promote deep and profound changes in the individual. The application of many of these methods can be both potent and subtle.

4. Psycho-physical techniques seem to provide immediate access to deeper blocked areas in the individual that may previously have appeared to be relatively inaccessible.

5. Neurologists have stated that most individuals use only 5 to 10 percent of their full mental potential. These techniques usually enable the individual to experience a greater percentage of that potential.

6. These techniques help to free the participant by establishing a more effective mind/body unity.

7. Most of these approaches have an impact upon the individual's awareness of his/her inner self. The individual frequently experiences a greater degree of self-awareness and personal autonomy, i.e., a sense of feeling "centered."

8. None of these methods strive for relaxation per se, because relaxation tends to be viewed as total collapse. These methods attempt to induce a heightened kinesthetic awareness in the individual.

9. Most of these techniques enable the individual to become more freely functioning, as a result of greater muscular and psychological autonomy.

10. Almost all of the psycho-physical methods stress an altered relationship of the body in space.

11. All the techniques stress that neuro-muscular habits can be permanently changed and the body's flexibility can be enormously increased.

12. Most of these approaches encourage modification of the participant's mental attitude.

WHAT ARE EXAMPLES AND APPLICATIONS OF THESE TECHNIQUES?

The **Alexander Method** attempts to alter the postural behavior of individuals, both when performing activities and also when the body is not in motion. In "The Alexander Technique," P. J. MacDonald states:

> Alexander is a technique for altering the reaction of the individual to the stimuli of the environment and can be applied to the whole range of human activities: whether these be regarded as just thought processes or processes involving predominately muscular activity.[2]

Rolfing is defined as a technique of deep body massage designed to bring the body's major segments — head, shoulders, thorax, pelvis, and legs — toward a vertical alignment. Rolfing generally lengthens the body and reinforces a body in which the weight remains close to a vertical central axis. Rolf's work contributes to the correction of the individual's bodily imbalance. Previous injuries and poor posture contribute to the body's imbalance. Over the years these imbalances deepen and the body moves progressively further from its central axis. Rolf's work can help to realign the body.

T'ai Chi and **Chi Gung** are disciplines that focus on the energy flow of the body, in addition to the relationship of body parts to total body functioning. **Aikido** is also a mind/body discipline that stresses body flow in response to external resistance.

Following are some common assumptions in the application of these techniques:

1. *Trying too hard gets in the way of the learning process.* Too much self-absorption, or trying too hard, produces excessive self-consciousness and self-monitoring, both of which constrict and tighten muscles, thereby interfering with the freeing process.

2. Most of these methods stress the *importance of "learning to let go,"* to avoid what Alexander termed *"end-gaining."* If a person pushes too hard in the beginning, he can only practice in the old way, repeating his old pattern.

3. Sufficient time is essential when working with all of these techniques. Practitioners stress the importance of *repetition of the exercises over time.* It is crucial to have time for that intermediate step — time to do nothing — time to establish new neurological pathways.

4. It is also important, *when experiencing change, not to get caught up in the*

---

[2] Patrick J. MacDonald, *The Alexander Technique — Psycho-Physical Integrity*, article printed by W. E. Baxter, no. 2, Cattlegate, Swanborough, Lewes, Sussex.

analysis of it. Psycho-physical changes are not always immediately accessible to the conscious mind.

5. *Do not force change, or make it happen; "let it happen."* This is a recurring theme in voice and acting classes, because an anxious student will interfere with the process by over-analyzing the mechanics of the exercise or will limit development by prematurely attaching labels to the outcome of the exercise.

    Note: An example of the above is reflected in the process involved in voice production. Because the muscles of phonation are not subject to direct voluntary control, the most effective voice and speech improvement occurs when the teacher creates a comfortable, stress-free psychological climate, and when the student is encouraged to experiment without force. Vocal tone becomes harsh and pinched when the actor/ singer constricts the throat or "pushes" the tone. In Eugene Herrigel's famous essay, *Zen in the Art of Archery*, the student archer is instructed by the master archer who says:

    > The right art is aimless; purposeless! The more obstinately you try to learn how to shoot the arrow for the sake of hitting the goal, the less you will succeed in the one and the other will recede. What stands in your way is a much too willful will. You think that what you do not do yourself does not happen. You must learn to wait properly; achieve a purposeless tension.[3]

    Practitioners of the Alexander method and teachers of voice production talk of avoiding "end-gaining" and letting go of "trying." Students begin to realize that if they have practiced their exercises and done their homework, they do not have to try. It begins to come by itself without forcing. Denise McLuggage states:

    > Try to lift your right arm. Did you do it? If so, you didn't try. You simply did it. It had nothing to do with trying. One either does it or one does not. Try again. This time did you not lift your right arm?[4]

6. Most practitioners of psycho-physical techniques stress *not doing and not end-gaining.* They suggest that it is best not to have a strong desire for change, in order to allow time for the process to work. Students who spend too much time "trying" frequently miss the point of a given exercise. Patrick MacDonald, in a lecture to the Society of Alexander Teachers in London, stated:

    > . . . learn to become consciously disinterested in what is going to hap-

---

[3]   Eugene Herrigel, *Zen in the Art of Archery* (New York: Vintage Books, 1977): 34.

[4]   Denise McLuggage, *The Centered Skier* (Vermont Crossroads Press, 1977): 78.

pen and to behave not as if being taught something but rather as if watching someone else being taught.[5]

It is essential to become "disinterested" because recent studies suggest that tension and stress resulting from trying too hard can actually impede learning. (The problem inherent in this is that, as a consequence of the preceding statement, beginners may assume that a disinterested philosophy implies that practice is unnecessary.)

7. *Belief systems help to structure the reality of the event.* In other words, "If we believe that we can do it, we can!" Psycho-physical practices rest on a belief system that is imbedded in a question of not what we can do, but what we *think* we can do. As in the children's story *The Little Engine That Could*, "I think I can" becomes translated into "I can."

The James-Lange Theory states that the experience of emotion is the experience of bodily changes. For example, their theory rests on the principle that labeling the event helps to fashion the event.

Dr. Moshe Feldenkrais writes:

> A human being is like a computer that is capable of thousands of things but we put in a card that lets us do only one thing. Until we change the card, that is all the computer will do — that one thing over and over... The difference between human beings and machines is that we make the cards. If one card doesn't work, take it out and put in a new card.[6]

8. If belief systems (i.e., language) structure reality, it is also correct to say that emotions such as anger, joy, or anxiety are mental labels that describe bodily reactions to a given event. Words such as "anxious" or "nervous" can be essentially interchangeable with excitement because it is *the label we employ which determines our individual reaction to a given event.* If we learn to modify our language to an event, we will perceive and experience the event differently and the event can be restructured more positively in our consciousness.

9. *Selected exercises can change neurological patterns, and if changed, conceptual patterns will also change.* As individuals, we can perceive ourselves differently. As we perceive ourselves, so others will perceive us, and that is what we will become.

10. Many theorists maintain that the way many people hold their bodies is

---

[5]   Patrick J. MacDonald, "On Giving Directions: Doing and Non-Doing," Lecture to the Society of Teachers of the Alexander at the Medical Society of London on November 12, 1963, 4.

[6]   Ryan Thomas, "The Feldenkrais," *New Realities* vol. II, 23.

a result of what they have in mind about some belief or position in life. They believe that *our musculature is a reflection of our mental states*, and, reciprocally, that *our mental states affect and shape our musculature*. Jan Sultan, a Rolfer, says:

> A person's body and set (alignment) reflect his emotional past as well as physical trauma that may have happened to him...If a person maintains a particular attitude long enough, it will show outwardly as posture. This posture will eventually modify the structure that it is imposed upon and if it is continued, it will become habitual. Once the body has accommodated the attitude, it will then determine the attitude.[7]

Studies have demonstrated that activities such as Transcendental Meditation, Yoga, Rolfing, Silva Mind Control, Feldenkrais, and T'ai Chi cause significant alterations in neural activity and brain functioning. The physiologist Edmund Jacobsen (*Progressive Relaxation*), conducted studies as early as the 1920s, in which the subjects *imagined* themselves doing certain actions, such as walking, jumping, and running. He found the muscles employed in those tasks registered definite small but measurable contractions. Appropriate neurological pathways were being activated *as if* the person was actually doing the action. It is now clear that mentally practicing a motor skill can be as valuable as the physical practice itself.

Edward de Bono wrote in *Lateral Thinking* that the mind is a pattern-making system. He was one of the first to state that the information system of the mind creates patterns and recognizes them. The implication of that belief is that it is possible for a performer to *think* his way through voiceless and physical limberings and to receive vocal and physical *benefit* from doing so. These mental exercises can be helpful to a performer before going on stage if s/he is in a situation that does not permit vocal or gestural warm-ups at that moment.[8]

However, it is essential to recognize that mental practicing cannot be drawn from a vacuum. The mental practice effect is possible only if a strong muscle memory has been previously established. It is necessary to establish the requisite neuro-muscular habit patterns. The participant must initially establish a strong synaptic pattern. In addition, mental practicing requires profound concentration and highly specific visualization.

11. *Most psycho-physical techniques have an implicit recognition of the differences between right and left brain functioning.* Split brain studies have profound

---

[7]   Gene Vier, "Rolfing: How It Works," reprint *Let's Live Magazine*.

[8]   Edward de Bono, *Lateral Thinking* (New York: Penguin Books, 1977).

implications for persons in the arts. Both hemispheres of the human brain are involved in higher cognitive functions, yet each hemisphere employs distinctly different modes of processing information.

The left hemisphere is largely analytical, digital, linear, and verbal. Right brain activity (spatial awareness, intuitiveness, imagery, metaphor) is essential for persons in the arts. Exercises are generally most effective when imagistic language (right brain) is employed in teaching specific voice exercises. Note: there will always be a few students in each class who will respond more readily to linear, logical, sequential, left brain language. Those students will prefer highly specific non-imagistic exercises. The most effective teachers will employ both approaches in a voice class.

It is also important for teachers to remember to create a comfortable psychological climate in the classroom. The muscles of phonation are not under direct voluntary control, and it is much easier for singers, actors, and public speakers to obtain better coordination of breath and tone when they feel comfortable enough to experiment with new ways of making sound.

Speech therapists frequently suggest specific technical exercises which are often very effective in the improvement of certain speech problems. Speech pathologists and other clinicians might be most successful if they engage both hemispheres of the student's brain by combining highly technical instruction along with the language of imagery and metaphor. Creative persons generally have easy access to the right brain hemisphere. Betty Edwards writes:

> One of the marvelous capabilities of the right brain is imaging: seeing an imaginary picture with your mind's eye. The brain is able to conjure an image and then look at it, seeing it as if it were "really there"... We see things in this mode that may only exist in space and see how parts go together to make up a whole. When something is too complex to describe, we gesture, thereby employing our right hemispheres. Try to describe a spiral staircase without making a gesture.[9]

It is just as difficult to describe a beard without use of gesture. Perhaps because the visual image is so strong, most persons will use their hands to illustrate a beard rather than describing it as a growth of hair on the chin, thereby relying on the right hemisphere.

These right brain functions are very valuable to the performer. The right hemisphere can aid in the "Ah-Ha!," that moment of synthesis

---

[9] Betty Edwards, *Drawing on the Right Side of the Brain* (Los Angeles: J. P. Tarcher, Inc., 1977).

when all the disparate elements fall into place. That moment of synthesis is the act of alchemy for the actor. That is the moment when memorized words are "lifted off the page," fused with intention by the actor's expressive voice and filled with meaning. That is the moment when the actor is transformed into the character. Such moments of fusion between actor and text are examples of right and left brain co-functioning.

The teaching of voice and allied acting skills can be rendered more effective and teaching can be amplified by images — word and sound pictures — in addition to providing sequential series of lip, tongue and mouth positions.

> Split brain studies of Robert Ornstein and others have demonstrated that imagery and muscles are inseparable. It comes to this: any movement needs an accompanying image, however unconscious we are of the image. In short, no image, no movement. Teachers need to remember that images are what instruct the body. Talk to yourself in words if you want to, but be sure the words are translated into sight images, sound images, feeling images! That totality of sensation is what gets the [message] into the body.[10]

Alexander Lowen stated the following:

> Bio-Energetics principle and practice rests upon the concept of a functional identity between mind and body. This means that a change in personality is conditioned upon a change in functions of the body. The two functions that are most important in this regard are breathing and movement. Breathing and movement determine feeling. The depth of respiration affects the intensity of feeling. By holding the breath, feeling can be reduced or deadened; just as strong emotions stimulate breathing, the activation of respiration evokes suppressed feelings.[11]

12. Psycho-physical techniques stress the value of a non-judgmental frame of reference: *a no judgment/no blame ordering of internal reality.*

The participant is urged to surrender his/her relentless inner eye, the overly severe judgmental self, and is encouraged to quiet the compulsive chatter of the super-parent in the brain. This approach represents a total departure from competitive striving. These methods stress release and freedom from the tyranny of being either right or wrong and provide permission not to be "right" all the time. This attitude enables the performer to become a better risk taker and to take chances. It gives permission to be less stereotyped and may even encourages the

---

[10]   McLuggage, 78.

[11]   Alexander Lowen, "Breathing, Movement and Feeling," Lectures given at the Hotel Biltmore, New York City, Fall 1965.

performer to take a chance with a dangerous (and, perhaps, more interesting) line reading. Practitioners of these methods attempt to create a psychological climate in which students are freed from the need to impress, the fear of criticism is reduced and objective problem solving becomes the norm.

13. *Excessive expectations are burdening and limiting.* They heighten contrast between desire and actuality and limit potential growth because the individual's self-perception is limited or negative.

14. *All these methods stress some form of detachment and encourage a "che serà serà" attitude.*

Charlotte Selver, one of the pioneers in the Sensory Awareness movement, states:

> At some point, the insight comes that all these sensations are simply personal reactions which can be accepted without evaluation and labeling and can be explored for new and fuller understanding, and that "right" or "wrong" are inappropriate here. The receiving and accepting of messages from inside and outside without feeling pangs of bad conscience or a sense of failure when they are not as expected, contribute greatly to one's sense of independence, and of course, lead to further and clearer sensing and to surer discoveries.
>
> Little by little the tendency to expect diminishes and vanishes, so that sensations can arrive just as they are and gradually the general tendency to notice only in terms of what feels pleasant and unpleasant diminishes too . . . Is it possible to give up watching, a kind of looking into what happens when the eyes are closed? Is it possible to give up associative, compulsive "thinking," the internal gossip, the talking to oneself? It simply happens this way — I don't have to try; it comes by itself.[12]

15. *Legitimacy of the immediate "now," rather than what will be.* The "now" is surely at the core of the voice/speech/actor/performer process.

A SUMMARY OF SOME ADVANTAGES OF PSYCHO-PHYSICAL TECHNIQUES:

1. Most of these methods have a common goal of attempting to free rigid computer-like brains, frozen emotions, and wooden bodies.

2. They afford the participants with capacity for greater range of physical and emotional experiencing.

3. Exercises are designed to encourage flexibility, responsiveness, and a more expansive response repertoire.

---

[12] Charlotte Selver, "Report on Work in Sensory Awareness and Total Functioning," in *Exploration in Human Potentialities*, Herbert A. Otto, ed. (Springfield, Illinois): 487.

4. Visualization exercises can jog participants' evocative senses, which enables them to more deeply invest in their acting texts.

5. These techniques, if used sparingly and creatively, can stimulate a singer/actor/performer to more fully engage all his/her senses.

6. Visualization and "self-talk" techniques, if used imaginatively, can reduce or eliminate a performer's stage fright.

7. Visualization techniques and judicious use of imagistic language can free and release the human voice.

8. Performers who have participated in these techniques are reputed to have a clearer understanding of their feelings and have less restrictive self concepts. If it is possible to discard self-limiting strictures of right and wrong, it is then possible to view one's work with some degree of detachment.

9. Many of these techniques can create a studio climate that will encourage students to take chances and to perceive constructive comments as suggestions in a joint problem-solving venture rather than as personal attacks. Comments, suggestions, even criticism, simply become events in a continuum, thereby providing additional opportunity for individual growth. When face-saving is allowed, risks are reduced, and students become more capable of objectively assessing their own work.

10. Creative selection of these techniques can enable participants to achieve a heightened sense of spatial and body awareness. Voicing and making sound becomes more fluid because the manner of regarding it is changed; it becomes not a style of speaking or singing, but fluid coordination of tone and articulation. Students learn to restructure judgments regarding sound and space. They become multi-dimensional.

11. Selected psycho-physical techniques can also re-invest language and metaphor. Language is an actor's major vehicle of self-expression; ironically, it can also be an actor's major stumbling block. It is imperative that an actor vividly and specifically experience a given text.

12. These techniques provide a performer with a clearer, stronger sense of his/her uniqueness; no one else can do that for the individual. It is that major factor that distinguishes one actor from another.

13. Vivid imagery can improve one's capacity to memorize and retain the text.

14. Right brain imagery can engender increased creativity and insight by effecting a synthesis between the intuitive and rational sides of the brain (the "Ah-Ha!" phenomenon).

In spite of the many potential advantages of these methods, there may be problems associated with their use in the classroom. The following represent some potential pitfalls associated with injudicious use or over-application of psycho-physical techniques in actor training programs:

1. Sufficient TIME is a major issue in all training. These exercises can seriously interfere with or impede the skills acquisition that is required for an actor's voice training because too much classroom time can be expended "freeing" the individual actor. Such freeing work must be placed in the context of the overall training program, without sacrificing the quality of the specific voice, movement and acting training. Unfortunately, this is not always done.

2. Genuine perils are attached to some of these more potent methods if they are casually or indiscriminately applied. Some of these exercises can rapidly access deeper emotional centers in the unprepared student. For example, Moshe Feldenkrais conducted a workshop that I attended many years ago. Several of the participants were so stimulated by the exercises that they reported sleeplessness and disturbing dreams, in addition to experiencing upsetting emotions and feelings that they had long forgotten. Some of those same participants later expressed enthusiasm for Feldenkrais exercises; nonetheless, they vented dissatisfaction because of the sleeplessness, the dreams, and the fact of disrupting emotions they had experienced. They reported that it took them some time to re-establish a sense of internal order. (Dr. Feldenkrais's exercises are said to re-structure the neurological response systems and are reputed to effect a new balance in the organism. Homeostasis may be the stated goal; but occasionally, like Humpty Dumpty, all the pieces cannot immediately be put back together again.)

3. If these techniques are to be employed, it is essential that the teacher who introduces the technique has experienced *sufficient training* and has *thorough grounding in that discipline*. An inexperienced teacher may not be aware of the possible problems associated with inadequate presentation of certain exercises. Additionally, an inexperienced teacher will not be as likely to detect problems associated with a given exercise or method.

4. Frequently, these methods are presented without any rationale as to why they are being done, too often falling into the category of busywork or "filler." Sometimes there is no clearly stated goal on the part of the instructor nor any statement as to the possible outcome or application, thereby undermining valuable class learning.

5. Another pitfall is the potentially synergistic effect of these combined

techniques that may be haphazardly gleaned from weekend conventions and brief workshops. The combinations of all these bits and pieces of different methods may physically work against each other in combination; or at the very least, the smorgasbord of methods may be confusing or counterproductive. Student evaluations at the University of California have demonstrated that students prefer exposure to fewer guest teachers rather than a continuous passing parade. They preferred to experience a given method in greater depth.

6. Another problem with imprecise exposure to a given technique is that students often express a sense of erroneous sophistication because they may believe that they have totally experienced that method, whereas they may have merely grazed the surface. Conversely, other students may have disliked a method only because of the inexpertness or insufficiency of the training. Students are then deprived of experiencing the genuine benefits of that method, which might be taught by a qualified instructor at a later point in time, when that student might have received a more expert and thorough exposure over an extended period of time.

7. Any method is diminished if it is not presented in the context of its theoretical framework. The inexperienced or uninformed teacher may neglect to present the conceptual or historical framework of the technique. This is particularly true of disciplines that are steeped in tradition and history like T'ai Chi and Yoga.

The dictates of time and room space in teaching voice and acting generally require a trade-off; one method or approach must be sacrificed for another. Students enroll in a course for voice or actor training, not necessarily for better mental health or interpersonal functioning. If the latter should occur as a by-product, all to the good, but it is not the basis of voice or actor training.

It is also important to suggest that we who use these techniques avoid the temptation of playing psychotherapist with a student; i.e., "Joan, you really need to clean up your relationship with your mother (boyfriend, father, brother, etc.) before you will be free to really fulfill the work."

We must also create a psychological climate that permits students to comfortably reject a given psycho-physical method if it is uncomfortable for them.

Occasionally a student will experience strong emotions that s/he will want or need to talk through. If that need arises, it will be helpful to the student if we as teachers are *informed referral agents*. We should provide the student with the names of thoroughly qualified therapists in the area. It is essential that we do not confuse the nature of our task by taking on interpersonal responsibilities that we as voice teachers are not trained to undertake. It is essential that students receive professional help when necessary and that our role as voice professionals not be compromised.

In conclusion, many psycho-physical techniques can be effectively incorporated into actor training programs. However they must be responsibly employed. A voice or acting teacher who employs these techniques would be wise to continually raise the following questions. Why am I using these techniques? Am I qualified to responsibly teach them?

Concepts and exercises from sensory awareness, guided fantasy work, T'ai Chi, Yoga, and Feldenkrais all present potential exercises, if employed with discretion and knowledge. We always need to know the how, why, and wherefore of a given exercise. The techniques should be used always with the awareness that they are supplanting other theatre techniques and skills that might be more valuable.

As to my own teaching, I have had the greatest exposure to the Alexander Method and Yoga. I have also had the greatest personal enrichment from them. It probably naturally follows that I have found the judicious use of Alexander and Yoga exercises to be most helpful in my work as a voice teacher. Certain techniques appeal more to one student than another. However, I have also participated in and have been enriched by work with Feldenkrais, Rolf, and Lowen.

However, these methods present no easy answers. Teachers usually experiment in order to determine what is best for their teaching. These techniques are merely tools to free the body and to stimulate the imagination, in order to facilitate teaching voice and acting.

The techniques should not be used to replace specific training, only to supplement it. Unfortunately, there is barely enough time to teach the requisite skills, techniques, and tools that modern actors must have to survive in the market place as part of a larger vision of what theatre can be.

Let us always ask ourselves: Why am I using this exercise? How does it relate to enhancing the skill and proficiency of this class of students? Do I have sufficient expertise to responsibly teach these techniques? Will it help them as actors?

11

VOICE AS A SOURCE OF CREATIVITY
For Acting Training, Rehearsal, and Performance

Sue Ann Park

The titles of Arthur Lessac's books, *The Use and Training of the Human Voice* and *Body Wisdom: The Use and Training of the Human Body*, give no hint of the exciting processes they offer for acting training, rehearsal, performance, and directing procedures.

The creative possibilities available to actors through the use of this training are almost mysteriously and magically practical. It is an incredibly fast way for an actor to break out of established habit patterns of voice and body, out of linear, left-brain thinking, and activate the inner harmonic sensing systems, evoking new physical and emotional behavior. It is remarkable to watch facial expression and body posture change and tears come simply as the result of feeling the gentlest staccato tap of a "T" following the humming vibration of an "N" in a word like "fond." However, we have all experienced music as a natural relaxer/energizer and probably everyone has experienced being transported to the past when hearing a particular melody. Lessac treats the whole body as a musical instrument—a Stradivarius—and the sensory experience of the music of its voice acts not just on our ears, but also resonates in our bones and travels our nerves, accessing our deepest feelings, significant experiences, and memories.

The comprehensive development for voice, body, and acting offered by this synergistic, sensory-based work is unique in that it does not depend on ear training, imitation, outside images, inspiration, or rote. It is based on responding to sensory awareness in parts of the body over which we have voluntary control because we can *feel* their function. All of these body actions are natural body relaxer/energizers, familiar events that can be used as a basis for training. It is an incredibly labor-saving process because each of the voice and body energy states, beyond its many individual benefits, contributes synergistically to the optimal function of the others. This training aims at skillful use of the voice and body energy states rather than at developing new vocal habits. It works qualitatively rather than quantitatively; works for carefree, not careful vocal use; develops the voice simultaneously for speech and singing; and is a self-teaching journey of discovery. It is effortless from the beginning except for the concentration of attention.

My introduction to the work came in the Spring of 1961 when the Director of The Goodman School of Drama of the Art Institute of Chicago handed me a copy of Lessac's voice text, saying a friend had written it. He suggested that I evaluate it in the light of our own program.

I was initially intrigued by Lessac's unique *sensory* approach that relies on vibratory, muscular, or tactile awarenesses for voluntary control of the voice rather than on ear training. I found that in each of the Vocal Energies — Consonant, Tonal, and Structural — I had already experienced some aspects of the process without ever perceiving what caused them to work or what the wider implications were for complete vocal development. For example, I had somehow often used full mouth space on [uː] for richer tone as easily as on [aː], never realizing that if I could do full space easily on both the smallest and largest rounded lip openings, the same could be done for all of the IPA back vowels from [uː] to [aː], except for [ʊ], by gently yawning the cheek muscles forward as Lessac described, thus avoiding the tension-producing use of the jaw muscles or the facial flaccidity of simply dropping the jaw to get optimal reverberation space in the mouth.

Lessac's metaphor of the Consonant Symphony Orchestra struck an immediate chord with me! I had always used the advice of Constance Welch, the legendary acting teacher at the Yale School of Drama, who maintained that the sustainable consonants [n, m, and ŋ] "are the golden chain of resonance on which the other sounds are strung." But it had never occurred to me that if these three vibrating consonants can be sustained, why not [v, z, ð, l, and ʒ] also, giving us the melody, rhythm, and tonal colors of *eight* sustainable consonant "instruments," (strings and woodwinds, as Lessac treats them in the Consonant Energy Orchestra), instead of only three? Starting with such recognitions as these, I used what I could understand of the work with private students during that summer. The Tonal training especially produced such satisfying results that I asked to introduce the work to the Goodman's first-year classes. It had been my observation that our speech training was fairly successful, but our students' voices and vocal skills did not improve much during our three-year program and in many instances became worse—strained under the heavy performance schedule they carried along with classes. I was convinced that the Lessac work would improve our training.

It did, although the first year was a rocky one. I had only one six-hour session with Lessac in New York before the Fall semester began, but he was generous in responding to letters and emergency phone calls. The following Spring, he came to the Goodman and for three days I was able to watch him teach all my classes. For the next ten years I went to New York every summer for continued training.

The most exciting discovery of the first year's teaching was the realization that the same work that was improving the voice and speech of our students so effectively was simultaneously turning out to be an experience in *acting* training, rather than just *actor* training.

As we worked and played through the developmental exercises, I discovered that even on single words and sentences I was feeling other things happening beyond the improvements in traditional voice and speech skills such as articulation, good voice quality, diction, projection, etc.

1. I felt changes in emotion that occurred without any thought of investing an emotion in the speech. This eventually eliminated my need to do "emotional recall."

2. I felt internally evoked images of intention, action, and relationships.

3. When playing with Consonant melodies and pitch range, I experienced feelings of laughing and crying that developed into a dependable way to release and control these emotions on cue and with qualities appropriate to the character. (I was unaware that Lessac had already developed this process; my discovery of it was simply evidence that working well with the Vocal Energies teaches us new things we didn't expect.)

4. I realized how the Vocal Energies made it easy to learn and teach dialects.

5. I discovered that feeling one Vocal Energy as dominant, with the other two supporting, can perfectly define the physical or emotional distance between characters on stage without losing either audibility or intelligibility for the audience.

6. I realized that the Lessac Tono-Sensory Phonetic System provides a spoken identification and a production instruction for each sound without the necessity of my speaking the sound itself. This allows me to ask actors for a sound change without asking them to imitate me. Imitation is a deadly anesthetic to creativity. Creative people usually resist imitation and many actors are simply unable to imi-

tate. Ear training is of necessity imitative; Lessac sensory training eliminates this barrier to learning.

7. In exploring familiar and well-loved Shakespearean passages, I simultaneously discovered fresh meanings and more music in the poetry, especially through the new use of the consonants.

The two Lessac texts, published eighteen years apart, deal with the use of three Vocal Energy States (Consonant, Tonal, and Structural) and four Body Energy States (Buoyancy, Potency, Radiancy, and Inter-Involvement). Although each acting process described here has been done in conjunction with the Body Energy States since 1978, which infinitely increases the variety of experience, I will concentrate here only on the uses of the Vocal Energy States that I discovered or experienced in my first ten years of teaching the work.

The major characteristics of the three Vocal Energies described briefly are:

Consonant Energy: The music of the singing voice is carried on the vowels; the music of the speaking voice is carried on the consonants. Each of the twenty-six consonants is recognized as having the musical qualities of an instrument in a symphony orchestra and each is identified by a feeling of vibratory or tactile sensation. The Consonant instruments are responsible for intelligibility; for melody, rhythms, and sustained tonal colors; and for variety and contrast in speech.

Tonal Energy: Consists of using the awareness of vocal sound waves vibrating through the hard palate and head bones to control voice production, tonal resonance, voice quality, vocal expressiveness, and to affect the emotional experiencing system. It protects the voice, heals the voice, guides the voice, attacks and cures bad voice quality; defends against stress and destructive emotions; and trains both the speaking and singing voice. Identifies and perfectly produces two vowels: The Ybuzz, [i] and the +Ybuzz, [ei].

Structural Energy: The yawn-like forward stretch of the cheek muscles creates the most optimal, adjustable size and shape for the human vocal sound box (the mouth cavity, not the larynx) and a relaxed and energized forward facial posture while relieving tension in the jaw, neck, and throat. Consistently *optimal* use of this easily adjustable sound box space regulates color, body, resonance, strength, and esthetic quality of vocal tone in any voice and speech situation. (*Optimal* means using as much of any Vocal Energy as possible without effort or conscious use of breath, and without distracting from communication.) Eleven vowels and diphthongs are perfectly produced and identified by the full use of Structural Energy, and its optimal use improves the quality of all other vowels.

The first step in the training sequence for each Vocal Energy is to do the body action that creates the energy, concentrating on your awareness of the physical sensation that accompanies it, and recognizing your response to it. The recognized sensation is then used to produce the action again so that you can explore all its dynamic possibilities. The bio-dynamics of each Vocal Energy can be felt and explored in all degrees: high and low, long and short, fast and slow, concentrated and diluted, voiced and voiceless. Each of the Vocal Energies perfectly produces and identifies two or more English sounds. Each Vocal Energy is developed first by improvising melodies on the sounds it produces to fully develop the esthetic qualities.

The next training step is to explore the use of each Vocal Energy in single words, then successively in sentences, paragraphs, and dramatic texts. At each of these stages, the exploration is first done by sustaining a fully concentrated experience of the Energy much longer than you habitually would, until you feel a response that is different from what you expected. Even though deliberately long sustentions are used, explorations never seem slow because you are filling time with energy which, when responded to, produces recognizable communicating behavior even though it may be an extremely unusual, emphatic, unique, or peak experience. All plays contain such behavior in the subtext of the character's action if not in the context.

The printed scoring of the three Vocal Energies below suggests the possibilities. The markings are simply aids to developing skills with the Vocal Energies until the actor learns what might be called "sensory sight-reading." (Explorations of prepositions, articles, and auxiliary verbs are optional and therefore are not marked in some instances.) Sustainable consonants are underlined twice. Percussive drumbeats are underlined once; and consonants that are only "prepared" but not "played" are slashed. Each word is linked to the next up to a pause for breath or interpretation.

Cons. Energy:	Oh, that this too, too solid flesh would melt
Str. Energy:	Oh, that this too, too solid flesh would melt
Tonal Energy:	Oh, that this too, too solid flesh would melt

— Shakespeare, *Hamlet*, Act I, Sc. 2

GENERAL EXPLORATIONS

When one Vocal Energy dominates in connected speech it is called the "leading" Energy, and it produces an experience called a General Exploration. Even before we had completed work on the three Vocal Energies during the first year at the Goodman School of Drama, it was obvious that doing a General Exploration of a text successively with each Vocal Energy would produce very different acting experiences.

I am loathe to even suggest what physical, emotional, mental, and spiritual experiences might be evoked because, since each of us has stored within a different life journey, one never knows what part of the past experience will be tapped by the exploratory energy. However, in a general way it can be said that when Consonant Energy leads in exploration or communication, it produces behavior using quiet speech of varying rhythms and tempos depending on the incidence of sustainable or percussive consonants. I have experienced it as quietly conversational, intense, intimate, secretive, casual, sinister, fearful, grief-stricken, passionate, etc.

When Tone is the leading Energy in exploration or communication, the most concentrated "Mother" tone is used. This pure, fully resonating tone produces heightened behavior that I have experienced as commands, exhortations, and intense, often ecstatic experiences of grief, rage, hysteria, laughter, etc. In the lower pitch ranges, skilled exploration using this concentrated tone evokes unusual emphasis, and quiet, unexpected intense emotion, completely projected without increase in volume.

When Structural Energy leads, it is characterized by rich but generally dilute tonal quality which I have experienced on various texts as expansively conversational, comfortably sociable, quietly authoritative, pompous, pedagogical, casually indifferent, flippant, even as stunned horror or quiet amusement, etc.

While Structural Energy in its creation of a relaxed and energized facial posture improves everyone's looks (I've had two actresses bring me before-and-after snapshots revealing a previously invisible upper lip) it has a much more significant value for all actors. Its focus on the optimally forward stretch of the cheek muscles, with softly rounded lips easily capable of changing size and shape, breaks up the habitual, protective arrangements of facial muscles humans use to function socially without showing inner feelings, whether it's done with a constant smile, a blank mask, clamped teeth, or compressed lips. Structural Energy makes the face malleable, vulnerable, and immediately responsive to both inner turbulence and outer confrontation.

I experienced this in a rehearsal exploration of the Countess Aurelia's scene with the King of the Sewer Men in *The Madwoman of Chaillot*. The director noted that Structural Energy unexpectedly produced a very effective flirtatious quality in my quizzing of the Sewer Man. It is my belief, or conceit, that I do not know how to flirt, and I would have had a hard time using flirting as an action if I had been so directed. However, by using Structural Energy as a "leading" vocal action in the scene, I could retain the flirtatious facial animation in performance without feeling self-conscious about it.

In my private pre-rehearsal explorations for *'night Mother*, the dominance of Structural Energy in Thelma's lines to her suicidal daughter created a moment of utter horror that transposed directly into performance and broke me out in goose-flesh and tears every night:

Who am I talking to? You're gone already, aren't you? I'm looking right through you! I can't stop you because you've already gone.

I was able to use Structural Energy to recreate that horror in every performance without having to imitate or remember how it first happened.

After first exploring with sustained and concentrated experiences of the three Vocal Energies, the successive stages of General Explorations shorten the sustentions until the speech is at a tempo as conversational as it can be without losing the dominant feel of the exploratory energy.

All of these explorations are done more than once but should never be repetitions; they are truly living-in-the moment experiences. The remarkable thing is that while doing these explorations slowly so that you have time to improve the esthetic quality of every sound before you leave it (skill development that is retained as the sustentions are subsequently shortened), it is concentration on feeling the finest sensation of the specific sounds being explored that agitates the inner harmonic sensing systems and triggers new physical reactions, new emotions, new meanings, new communicating behavior. *Vocal skill development and the creation of new behavior go hand-in-hand.*

As soon as just two or all three of the Vocal Energies have been experienced in connected speech, whether it is sequentially as given in the text, or concurrently, as we teach whenever possible, an even wider range of creative experience is available by combining Vocal and Body Energy States in both General Explorations and Specific Explorations.

SPECIFIC EXPLORATIONS

In the General Explorations, no matter how productive or how diligently done, we often quite unconsciously still cling to our own interpretation of the script — especially our "line readings." The next level of exploration calls for a more specific use of the Vocal Energies to break out of personal habit-patterns, to break out of preconceived ideas about the character or the meaning of the text, and most important, to experience the subtext in many ways.

No analogy exactly parallels what a Specific Exploration feels like. I see it as similar to successfully negotiating white water in a kayak — the paddle gives you enough control to keep the craft upright, but you are caught up and carried along by irresistible currents that determine what the journey will be. It feels dangerous but is endlessly exhilarating and exciting.

The Specific Vocal Exploration proceeds by deliberately giving dominance and therefore sentence stress *only* to the words that contain the exploratory Energy, a process that shifts you ever more deeply into a right-brain mode; it takes you off the beaten path to "wander in wilderness" *without ever losing your connection to the text.* If you can accept a momentary imbalance or disorientation as you depart from your literal, left-brain understanding of the text and allow your body to experience fully the sensory esthetic of the Vocal Energy in the new configurations, the sensation makes a connection with your unconscious, with your reservoirs of physical and emotional experience, creating new behavior, new recognizable realities, believable and complete. And because these responses have been created internally and experienced physically, they continue to exist as part of the role whether in the context or subtext, foreground or background, as the character develops.

It is my perception, for example, having explored Hermione's trial scene in *The Winter's Tale* (Act III, Sc. 11), that she is dismissing Leontes' threat of death, is defending her honor, and is not breaking down in grief over the loss of her children, which happened offstage. However, Vocal Energy explorations can give an actor a physical and emotional experience of that grief which surely is subtext in this scene. The following lines, for example, I have always found most evocative; there is something about Shakespeare's repetition of consonant combinations here, particularly in the third line, that never fails to bring tears. Note the three playable T drumbeats before the three initial M's:

> My third comfort,
> Starr'd most unluckily, is from my breast
> They innocent milk in it most innocent mouth
> Hal'd out to murder:

This level of exploration is first done self-to-self and is most productive when shadowed by one of the Body Energy States.

Obviously, on a new script the exploration is done with eyes open (memorization happily happening simultaneously) as you do all the variations. On lines already memorized, it is most exciting and evocative to actually work blindfolded so that the experiences are completely internal and "self-to-self." In our summer workshops, the initial explorations are done with the actors blindfolded and spaced out on the Body Work mats as they progress through Body Energy, General, and finally Specific Vocal Explorations on the same memorized two- to three-line selections. Actors are randomly chosen to explore by a number on the blindfold, and although this work happens about halfway through a summer workshop, even these initial explorations change the vocal, physical, and emotional experiences of the text so much that actors are often unable to recognize their fellows.

After doing self-to-self Specific Explorations for each of the three Vocal Energies *where the Vocal Energy determines the behavior*, the actor does a "self-to-other" exploration, in which he pursues whatever that moment's perceived intention of the material is, letting *her behavior determine the interaction of the three Vocal Energies.*

As I mentioned before, a "self-to-*self*" exploration evokes among its many experiences, a relationship to another person; but in a "self-to–*other*" exploration the "other" may be newly evoked as the intention is played, or may actually be envisioned as the character addressed in the script, depending on where we are in rehearsal.

CHARACTERIZATION AND ROLE DEVELOPMENT

It is important to understand that the Specific Explorations are pre-rehearsal preparations for a role. There is no set way to use explorations; my own practice is to do Specific Explorations daily on each "beat" and scene. First I do them "self-to-*self*" and "self-to-other" *as myself*, not as the *character*, in order to break out of my own patterns and for memorization. I make no choices or decisions until I gradually feel the character developing through growing knowledge of the script, interaction with the other actors, and the director's concepts. Naturally, I cannot do Specific Explorations in rehearsal with other actors or directors who are not Lessac-trained, but my pre-rehearsal experiences of the text prepare me to respond both to the actors and the director. And I continue to use everything I learned about acting in my forty years before Lessac, or have learned from others since then, if it is compatible with Lessac principles.

Sometime after we have been through the whole play on our feet at least once, I begin doing Specific Explorations again and again *as the character* exploring more deeply the actor's task: what am I doing, why I am doing it, and how I am doing it?

Here is Clytemnestra's speech to the chorus after murdering Agamemnon, marked for all the Vocal Energies, Structural with an arc (⌢), Tonal with a dot (·), and Consonants with underlining. Exploring produces different answers to the three questions that define the actor's task.

> I spoke so many empty words,
> Words of love, and my heart a cinder of hate
> Now I throw them all to the ground
> And think no shame on it.
> > Aeschylus, *The House of Atreus*

When I first began doing explorations, the Goodman approach to script analysis included describing a character's action as an infinitive: "My action is to threaten," something that *is going* to happen. For me the immediate difference in Explorations is experiencing and recognizing, in the moment, what I *am doing*. When I explore Clytemnestra's speech with Tone, I feel *I am triumphing*; with Structural Energy, *I am rejecting* blame; and with Consonant Energy, *I am warning* the Chorus not to interfere. In cast rehearsal these are actions I can experiment with supported by the exploratory experience. Explorations with all the combinations of Vocal and Body Energies would produce many other possibilities for either context or subtext.

The explorations feed the daily rehearsals and the rehearsals feed the explorations so that neither grow stale or static.

CREATING THE CHARACTER'S VOCAL LIFE

For a new characterization it is essential to break out of one's own mind set in order to experience what the playwright has written.

In some instances, of course, the character is described in the stage directions or in comments of other characters in the script, but the actor's understanding of this will necessarily be a left-brain judgment that is colored or guided by his own dominant traits or acquired mannerisms. Olivier, in his autobiography, described doing outrageous, wild antics during early rehearsals in order to leave recent characterizations behind. However, while antics and improvisations may break habit patterns and produce new experiences, they do not simultaneously move an actor productively into the new script.

I have been a character woman since the age of ten when I played Jim Hawkins' mother in a children's theatre production of *Treasure Island*. Over time I have been pleased to be told that my characterizations are very different from each other and are also not like me. If this is true, I believe it comes from doing these sensory explorations of each playwright's unique vocabulary, sentence structure, and punctuation. For me the best clues to the character are in these physical experiences, whether the playwright has given a written description or not.

A simple vocabulary of mostly monosyllabic words, which usually means far fewer sustainable consonants, greatly changes the rhythms and may give generally quicker tempos to the character's vocal and physical life — much different from a script using polysyllabic words where the greater incidence of sustainable consonants creates more complex rhythms and tempo changes. But it is the matrix of the writer's words that is so endlessly challenging and exciting. With the Vocal Energies I can deliberately ring a hundred changes on a single word, but what is more fascinating is the playwright's juxtaposition of words — and what happens when I feel the sensory experience at the end of one word move into the wave of unknown physical and emotional sensation that will wash through me on the next word. When these differences are experienced kinesensically through the voice and body energies, one is already breaking out of one's own voice, rhythms, tempos, pitch range and power, and wandering through wilderness to discover directly the new person in the script now inhabited.

I never try to think up a vocal characterization; it evolves through exploring to discover what are the dominant Vocal Energies in a character's lines. I believe I can always find, through explorations, a vocal characterization that is right for the character, even the most unpleasant character, without hurting my voice or inflicting unintelligibility or an excruciating voice quality on the ears of the audience. Even if the playwright seems to have given a character a dominant vocal energy throughout the play, it still need never be limited and boring, since each Vocal Energy has a total range of dynamics and is always supported by the other two Energies to give variety and contrast within the characterization.

FINDING THE CHARACTER'S PHYSICAL LIFE

Long before we had the Body Energies to play with, I discovered body actions and gesture, quality of gestures, and ways of walking that happened as the result of vocal explorations. How Prince Hal, in *Henry IV*, Part 2, handles the crown on "Lo! here it sits..." occurs quite differently with each of the Vocal Energies and with different actors doing the Vocal Explorations. The original kinds and qualities of movement arise from inner agitation by the voice. When I directed *Under Milk Wood* with twelve undergraduate actors, they developed the many characters that each played during cast explorations with Voice and Body Energies.

FINDING THE EMOTIONAL LIFE OF THE CHARACTER

Actors delve into their own pasts to find experiences and degrees of, anger, grief and fear that will bring emotional truth to the creation of a role. For me, explorations have eliminated the need to deliberately use "emotional recall," a process that can be painful, exhausting, and even destructive, as one consciously relives either resolved or unresolved emotional experiences. I suspect that having to resort to "emotional recall" may well contribute to some actors' use of drugs and alcohol to deal with the resulting emotional wear-and-tear.

In doing Specific Explorations directly on the text, the vocal sensations plug directly into the unconscious where the connection to the actor's stored experience creates not a recollection of the actor's life but an instantaneous physical and emotional experience in the character's life which will eventually appear as foreground or background in that life in actual performance. It is important to recognize that one does not make a "cafeteria"-type choice from the exploratory experiences. In Specific, subtext explorations, the occurrence and experience of the exploratory Vocal Energy *determine the behavior*; in follow-up, "context" explorations, the character's perceived intention, determine the interactions of the three Vocal Energies. The experiences of these explorations continue to evolve during the entire rehearsal period.

The actor does not need to try to recreate or imitate something that happened previously in a general or specific exploration. Actually, imitation, especially of oneself, is an anesthetic to creativity, killing the illusion of the first time. But with performance based on Vocal Explorations, one can always be "in the moment," trusting that as needed in the next moment, a vocal energy can evoke from the text the desired emotion and physicality as spontaneously as when the text was first explored.

I had been surprised through the years by the dependability with which tears would appear on single lines I used frequently for demonstration, but strangely enough I had never done a role that required sustained tears on cue during the run of a show. At the conclusion of the first read-through of *Grace and Glory*, Tom Ziegler's two-women play about Grace, an illiterate, ninety-year-old mountain woman dying of cancer, and Glorie, an unwelcome hospice volunteer, we were both sobbing almost uncontrollably. The director commented that it would undoubtedly be the last time we would get that kind of reality until after tech rehearsal. But it was not so.

During my pre-rehearsal explorations of that final scene in which the hospice worker arranges for Grace to video-tape a letter of love, faith and farewell to her great niece, I found that Structural Energy would both release and control tears every time we worked the scene and in every performance.

I imagine most actors have looked at some part of a script with dismay, thinking, "How can I ever do this believably?" Again, in *Grace and Glory*, Grace, nearing death, has an attack of pain so excruciating that she finally accepts the morphine she has resisted for months. The morphine takes effect during the ensuing monologue. I have neither experienced this level of pain nor seen it in real life, and the consultant from the Hospice Program insisted that pain is so subjective in patients that she could not prescribe what its physical manifestation might be in Grace.

The monologue begins at an hallucinatory pitch with three repetitions of the words "Sweet Jesus" and runs an emotional gamut that ends in sobbing whimpers. I found it very difficult.

Finally, in regular cast rehearsals, the director allowed me to shift into successive Vocal and Body Energy explorations without interruption as I came to the monologue. Gradually, without discussion or suggestions from the director, a multi-layered experience evolved through the explorations into a roller-coaster ride of physical and emotional pain.

Eventually, the three repeats of "Sweet Jesus" started low and rose through two-and-a-half octaves on long, drawn-out syllables into trembling fear of death; anguished tears for two dead babies; thrashing and howling in despair over an humiliating, loveless marriage; intense raging at Glorie for judging my life wasted; and finally collapsing in whimpering defeat.

Throughout, the Vocal Energies also provided the control to stay intelligible and to be ready to handle the explosive humorous release that Ziegler provides so deftly to rescue the actors and the audience from each traumatic emotional peak.

I got no "notes" on this scene from the director, but the audience cried and laughed nightly and the Hospice Consultant said that "roller-coaster" accurately described the experience hospice workers have with dying patients.

Although I suspect that over the years I have been regarded as a fanatic about Arthur Lessac's work, I have never been a blind follower. I was a very linear, right-brain, habit-oriented person when I began his work. It's a marvel I was open-minded enough to even try it. However, as I struggled to teach it in the very early days, the Voice work taught me how to use myself freely as an actor. It has been a long and joyful journey of discovery, problem-solving and satisfaction. The role in *Grace and Glory* was a lovely bonus I received in 1995, eight years after retiring from university teaching.

WORKS CITED

Aeschylus. *The House of Atreus.* Translated by Robert Bly. Minneapolis Publishing.

Giraudoux, Jean. *The Madwoman of Chaillot.* NYC: The Dramatists Play Service. 1947; English version by Maurice Valency.

Lessac, Arthur. *Body Wisdom: The Use and Training of the Human Body.*

———. *The Use and Training of the Human Body.*

Norman, Marsha. *'night Mother.* New York: Dramatists Play Service. 1983.

Olivier, Laurence. *Confessions of an Actor.* NYC: Simon and Schuster. 1982.

Shakespeare, William. *Hamlet, Prince of Denmark.* Act I Sc. 2

———. *Henry IV, Part 2.* Act II Sc. 5

———. *The Winter's Tale.* Act III Sc. 2.

III

THE VOICE IN HISTORICAL CONTEXT

12

VOICE TRAINING:
WHERE HAVE WE COME FROM?

DOROTHY RUNK MENNEN

"A voice is a voice is a voice."
Tyrone Guthrie

W HY STUDY VOICE?

What lures us to study voice? Why are we voice teachers so impassioned about our work? What is it that makes us become so intense that we feel we must know everything about the voice — all its capabilities and the reasons why people use their voice in certain ways? How can we help the interpreter of language and text to a better understanding of the skills that free the voice to bring us into the realm of imagination and expression?

Perhaps somewhere in our early lives we sensed or felt the power of human voices to affect our feelings and decisions. Many of us as children were moved by the voice of a teacher, an actor, a singer. What was there about a voice that could change a mood or a conviction, carry us to heights of imagination, or convince us through the power of vocal persuasion? The next step was discovering the fascination with our own ability to change our voice, to reflect or to evoke a mood or a feeling in others when we spoke, read aloud, or sang.

At an early age it seemed natural for me to think of singing and speaking as expression that moved freely back and forth. Later I realized that there was a great degree of variance in an individual's speaking and singing. As my interest in theatre grew I was curious about actors' voices. With that same curiosity I observed the speech of all kinds of persons, ineffective and effective. What made these differences? In my undergraduate days I pursued the vocal work available through classes in oral interpretation and singing lessons. Speech of all kinds, debate, public address, oratory offered great opportunities to develop my skills further. I discovered all this experience gave me an advantage over the other actors in college plays. I did not, at that time, consider voice teaching as a recognized profession.

Instead of finding myself on Broadway, necessity sent me to public school teaching. With the philosophy that every step in life is another adventure I realized that I liked teaching and was a good teacher. It was then that I became convinced: "If you can speak you can sing!" To help the so-called "non-singer" sing and students to speak well became my goal. The seed was planted and began to develop as I guided the vocal development of singing and speech students in both public and private teaching and in pursuing acting.

WHEREFORE VOICE AND SPEECH TRAINERS ASSOCIATION?

In 1968 the first concerted effort was made to address the neglect of vocal training in actor training programs in the United States. The American Educational Theatre Association (AETA), representing theatre in higher education, devoted most of its national conference programming to history, literature, architecture, and, occasionally, directing and acting. Too little attention was paid to what happened on stage. More attention was given to the literature than to how the literature was spoken. The academic theatre, as well as the commercial theatre, was still under the influence of the "method." There was a need to be "American" and to disavow the "classical" approach which "they" said was artificial and not believable. How the actor felt was the focus, not the voice or the speech. As I became a part of academia, the complete neglect of voice/speech, particularly at the national conferences, alarmed me. This voice teacher's determination led to a passionate discussion with Lewin Goff, an officer in AETA, at a national conference. Fortunately he was sympathetic and responded by urging me to begin the crusade! So be it!

For the annual conference of the American Education Theatre Association in Los Angeles, August 1968, I chose the topic "Actor Training the United States." Kristin Linklater, Sue Ann Park for Arthur Lessac, and Robert Parks for Edith Skinner spoke urgently to the topic. I had chosen these three for I felt they represented strong, vital training with methodologies which could affect the standards of vocal training in the theatre, both academically and professionally.

At the conclusion of the forum, there was avid discussion among those attending; we met immediately to organize Theatre Voice and Speech. We became a recognized project in AETA in 1968. (An interesting note is that the board of the organization titled the project Theatre Speech, but at my request and with my arguments the name was changed to Theatre Voice and Speech Project.)

In the lively discussion on that memorable day we revealed our own feelings and attitudes about the neglect of this crucial work in voice and speech. We recognized that there was voice and speech training around the country, but it was occasional and at random. Across this country there have always been individuals who believed strongly in training the voice. These individuals were making a personal struggle and having some excellent results among their students. The problem was that each of these teachers was fighting a personal battle, and often they persisted because their own personalities were so convincing that they were "allowed" to work. Most of us are very aware of the debt we owe to Tyrone Guthrie in drawing attention to the state of actor training in the United States. Coming from the English tradition, where the voice is the strongest aspect of the actor's craft, he decried the training in the United States: "...we require a much higher standard of vocal competence from quite minor singers than we demand from even the greatest actors." The Guthrie Theatre has had a vocal coach from the outset.

The "we" in this discussion refers to those teachers in the academic programs who were a part of acting training programs. When the American Educational Theatre Association changed to the American Theatre Association, one of its objectives was to encompass the world of theatre, wherever it might be. Theatre Voice and Speech, from its beginning in 1968, encouraged the participation of freelance and conservatory teachers. Many of us taught private students, and a few were adjunct faculty at conservatory programs. VASTA continues that integration.

WHY THE STRUGGLE?

Much of the frustration and lack of interest in our goals was a result of our own history. Voice training was not new. We were not inventing a new idea; we were only asking for voice and speech training to have its rightful place in performance training. This included all professional voice use, but at that moment we were concentrating on theatre training, and particularly in the programs that were growing in higher education. Speech, rhetoric, and voice have been cultivated and studied from the beginning of written history. Attention to quality, style, charisma, and persuasion by the voice has been written about orators, politicians, and of course, actors (more actors of the past than the present). Whether one refers to Cicero, Edmund Burke, David Garrick, Sarah Bernhardt, James Earl Jones, Abraham Lincoln, Franklin D. Roosevelt, Martin Luther King, John F. Kennedy, or Bill Clinton, their vocal characteristics are paramount in our reflections. Historians refer to the elocutionists, the schools of oratory, and the acting schools from the 1890s to their decline in the 1920s, in terms of the demise of the interest in voice/speech study.

More than that was the wave of naturalism that swept this country with influences such as the Group Theatre and, even more so, Strasberg's "method," which some incorrectly thought was Stanislavsky's. In *Building a Character* we learned how wrong that was. Stanislavsky had an established regimen of acting training that strongly emphasized voice-speech and singing. The wave of renunciation of the voice and speech of an actor in order to be realistic, natural, meant the study of speech and voice was discarded in American acting at the same time that higher education was incorporating theatre study into its curriculum. With the increase in theatre departments at universities, history, technology, scene design, theatre management, directing, and acting were filling the courses of study. If the department was to put on a play it needed a set to be designed and built, a director, and actors. The first two were the responsibility of faculty members (in smaller programs it might be the same person); the actors could be students, faculty, or townspeople. As the programs grew, the generalists remained, but specialists were added. The acting area began to consider dance and then movement. The acting teachers might have some speech/voice background, but unless they came from a training program that considered voice/speech a major requirement for an actor, they were unprepared. Even the more qualified found more prestige in adding more acting classes than working on the fundamentals of voice production. This was the history that confronted those of us who met in 1968.

Through the years schools or groups or individuals offered specialized training in acting, and particularly well-known actors set up studios. The attention given to voice training was dependent not only on the skills of the individuals teaching, but also on their philosophy of acting. If it were "method," or if the instructor felt inadequate, little fundamental training was given. Often vocal instruction was limited to "sound grouchy," or "just feel it," or "use a sexy voice."

The few conservatory programs we have in this country have always given voice and speech a place in their curricula. Often today they depend upon adjunct faculty. However, reading a school or studio's advertisement does not reveal what kind of training is offered. They may offer a limited number of special classes, groups of classes, or semesters ending in an associate degree. The degree programs vary from two to three years.

The American Academy of Dramatic Arts, founded in New York in 1884, identifies itself as the first school to provide professional education for actors and is still offering courses. Other conservatory programs developed, among them the better known Neighborhood Playhouse. It is important to point out that despite the rise and fall in the popularity of vocal training for actors, we must give credit to those singing teachers through many generations who saw the affinity of singing and speaking. Some found their work with actors more interesting than with singers. It was a retired singer who guided the famous voice of John Barrymore. Singing teachers believe the Italian admonition: *"Canta bene parla bene."* ("If you sing well, you speak well.")

Theatre Voice and Speech Project (TVSP), true to our mission to promote voice training, steadily pursued that goal through the years from 1968 to the early 1980s. We sought to integrate our work with the movement, acting, and directing programs of American Educational Theatre Association (AETA) and, later with AETA's successor, the American Theatre Association (ATA). The TVSP organization began to influence other programs and offered workshops in Washington, Minneapolis, San Francisco, Los Angeles, and New York. We are proud to say that, though some of the other programs in the national organization fluctuated in interest and membership, we never did. As professional training programs began to be added to higher education we saw our mission as more imperative. Some of our members moved back and forth from conservatory programs to university programs, a logical compatibility.

Bill Ball, in founding the American Conservatory Theatre (ACT) in 1965, established both a conservatory program and a theatre. His work with Edith Skinner at Carnegie Mellon convinced him that actors need to develop vocal and movement skills. Ball was the first to embrace the importance of the Alexander work. ACT offers an MFA in Acting, as well as summer courses.

The Julliard School, founded in 1968 by John Houseman, followed the guidelines of the famous teacher-director Michel Saint-Denis. Thus voice and speech would be essentially a part of fundamental acting training. Elizabeth Smith, from Central School of Speech, London, led the voice program and expanded the department. Edith Skinner came to the program and later brought in her protégé, Timothy Monich, who has taken Skinner's speech work into the film industry. Robert Neff Williams has been an essential part of their program. Julliard offers a BFA and four-year diploma program in acting.

California Institute of the Arts (Cal Arts) in Valencia, California, was established in 1965 with a bequest from Walt Disney. Cal Arts encompasses all of the arts but has a strong actor training program and offers an MFA in Acting.

For a comprehensive view of the history of voice training one should read the excellent book by Nan Withers-Wilson, an active VASTA member,

Vocal Direction for the Theatre. The chapter on "The History of Voice and Speech Training for the Actor" gives a good overview of VASTA's history.

However, I hasten to say that we must give credit to two strong influences on voice/speech training not included in Dr. Withers-Wilson's excellent book. Dr. Evangeline Machlin gave us a legacy we cannot ignore. For many years she was Director of Speech Studies at the Neighborhood Playhouse School of the Theatre and a Lecturer in Speech at Columbia University. She trained many actors in New York, then went to Boston University to set her mark on the voice and speech training in their Theatre Training Program. Her book *Speech for the Stage* has been widely used since the early seventies. Van Machlin contributed immeasurably to the growing influence of the Theatre Voice and Speech Project in AETA and ATA. She was a founding member of the Board of Directors of VASTA and its first Honorary Member.

The other influence which has given us a great legacy and must be given credit is the area of oral interpretation. The names of Charlotte I. Lee, Robert Breen, Lila Heston, and Alvina Krause are among the many oral interpretation teachers who made their contribution to actors. Northwestern University owes much to the great reputation of its oral interpretation faculty and graduates. Aspiring actors went there to study with influential persons. Oral interpretation was the only resource for students in many colleges and universities. As a senior member of the profession, I have already attested to my early training in oral interpretation and singing as invaluable.

In the sixties I began to develop the first voice curriculum for a professional actor training program at Purdue University. I had no idea what direction to take. Where should I go to learn a method of teaching voice? Should I study with Gwynneth Thurburn at the Central School of Speech? Clifford Truner at the Royal Academy of Dramatic Art? Iris Warren at the London Academy of Music and Dramatic Art? London seemed to be the logical place to study since it was the center of many schools whose influence shaped the study of voice in England and in a number of conservatory programs in this country.

What choices did I have for texts? For methodologies? For a blueprint for vocal development of the artistic voice? I wanted to look to the American scene. There were some old standby voice and diction texts which are still used in beginning courses. Acting texts often have only one inadequate chapter on voice and speech. Oral interpretation books still have essentially very good material. However, these texts do not attempt to pursue developmental vocal study with the continuing demands of professional voice use, nor do they pay particular attention to the artistic use of the voice. Those administrators or directors who have had little experience with oral interpretation at its best discourage actors from taking these courses. (At times I longed for the student actor to have taken such a course, if for no other reason than to have a semblance of knowledge about oral literature.)

Arthur Lessac's book *The Use and Training of the Human Voice* came out in 1960. It was the first major work in the United States to train the voice for the actor or professional voice user. Published first by himself, and then in 1966 by Drama Books, it is now available through Mayfield Publishers. Lessac's treatment of voice/speech, personally developed through years of work and teaching, is based on a sensory-awareness approach that considers voice/speech as a single discipline that he believes "will lead to a superior American speech standard, elegant and beautiful and effective enough for the highest artistic use — and at the same time practical and natural enough for the most utilitarian application." Though it seemed a little awesome for the novice who wanted a book for a basic course, or for the teacher who had studied another method and was not willing to deter from a beaten path, it offered thoroughly researched, fundamentally sound, imaginative techniques that developed the voice progressively. As a singer and musician, Lessac also understood through research, experience, and disciplined practice the potential of the body and voice. His book was an exciting discovery for me, a singer and voice teacher.

Evangeline Machlin's book followed. *Speech for the Stage*, published in 1966, was a little more reassuring to the novice, but demanded a certain discipline. She carried her skill and artistry into dialect study for her actors. Her text *Dialects for the Stage*, with accompanying tapes, was published in 1975. Her work was influenced by her years in England, Canada, and the United States.

When Kristin Linklater's *Freeing the Natural Voice* was published in 1976 it was enthusiastically received. Born in Scotland, trained at the London Academy of Music and Dramatic Art under Iris Warren, she credits Warren for the basis of her work. Since coming to the United States in 1963, Linklater's own work has expanded, gone beyond what she gained from Iris Warren, and evolved into her own unique approach to voice and text work.

In her later years Edith Skinner submitted to the pressure of students and advocates and published her book, which heretofore had only been available to her students. Revised with new material by Timothy Monich and Lilene Mansell in 1990, *Speak with Distinction* was greeted with acclaim. Her students often refer to the work of Prendergast McClean and William Tilly as the forbears of the Skinner method. This is undoubtedly because Edith Skinner was very careful to credit her sources. She was a modest woman, a giving mentor to her students, with a generosity of spirit that endeared her to them.

Arthur Lessac's work integrates voice and speech. Kristin Linklater emphasizes freeing the natural voice. Van Machlin treats voice and speech comprehensively, and Edith Skinner's sound principles of good speech are very specific. All voice teachers owe a debt to these innovators. Each is distinctive in his or her own way. We must recognize there are many dynamic teachers who through the years have quietly pursued their own teaching and their legacy may be less spectacular, but no less impressive, to those whose lives they have marked. Many VASTA members pride themselves on having studied many disciplines and methodologies and find through their own work their individual uniqueness. As an organization we have been inclusive in our attention to voice training.

VASTA'S CONTRIBUTION

VASTA's major contribution was establishing the organization itself. We are the only professional organization for training the artistic voice.

> VASTA Members serve as Vocal Coaches for
> Broadway shows, Repertory theatres, and
> Shakespeare companies; work with leading theatre,
> film, and television producers and directors
>
>
>
> provide voice and speech training for professional
> actor training programs, theatre and music
> conservatories, major corporations and leading media
>
>
>
> are faculty members at leading colleges and universities
>
>
>
> are recognized specialists in private practice.
>
> — from the VASTA brochure

As Theatre Voice and Speech grew, we actually moved ahead of the national organization. In 1986 when the American Theatre Association disbanded we knew it was time to establish ourselves independently as the only professional organization for voice trainers. We organized August 1986 at New York University after many long hours and days of discussion. We incorporated in 1987. As we grew and made an impact on theatre training, we would from time to time reiterate our original dual role in 1968 in the TVS Program: 1) to improve the standards of voice training in the United States and 2) to integrate the importance of voice to acting and movement training. We have enlarged our scope of networking by participating in The Voice Foundation and the Annual Symposium for the Care of the Professional Voice, founded in 1971 by Dr. Wilbur Gould. We have a growing number of speech pathologists and singing teachers as members. This often results from VASTA members bringing other specialists into their work.

OUR FUTURE

The year 1996 was the tenth anniversary for VASTA. We hope to continue our growth and our influence. Though our original goal was voice training in acting programs, to improve the voice and speech of actors and performers, it is moving beyond that. The broad talent and capacity of my colleagues are extending every day, working in and with related disciplines. We serve on teams working with speech pathologists and otolaryngologists; we have brought our expertise to the classroom teacher, the university professor, the media, and public figures.

Our greatest challenge, as we move to the twenty-first century, may be to raise the ideal of a healthy dynamic voice as a powerful means for establishing better human communication. I am reminded of a student of mine who decided to change her major. She came to me apologizing for dropping out of theatre. Her concluding words were, "I'm sorry." My assurance was, "Don't be sorry. Believe in what you have learned. Use it every day."

Why study voice? My first question. For me it is a lifelong pursuit. The pleasure it gives to me in all its manifestations, whether it be speech or song, is surpassed only by the wonderment I feel when I hear a voice, once bound, now free and fluent.

WORKS CITED

Guthrie, Tyrone. *Tyrone Guthrie on Acting*. New York: Viking Press, 1971.

Lessac, Arthur. *The Use and Training of the Human Voice*. New York: Drama Book Specialists, 1967.

———. *Body Wisdom, The Use and Training of the Human Body*. New York: Drama Book Specialists, 1980.

Machlin, Evangeline. *Speech for the Stage*. New York: Theatre Arts Books, rev. ed. 1980.

Linklater, Kristin. *Freeing the Natural Voice*. New York: Drama Book Specialists, 1976.

McTeague, James H. *Before Stanislavsky, American Professional Acting Schools and Acting Theory 1875–1925*. New Jersey, London: The Scarecrow Press, Inc., 1993.

Skinner, Edith, rev. Timothy Monich and Lilene Mansell. *Speak With Distinction*. Applause Theatre Book Publishers, 1990.

Withers-Wilson, Nan. *Vocal Direction for the Theatre*. New York: Drama Book Publishers, 1993.

13

"WHAT IS A VOICE FOR?"
TRAINING AND THE RISE
OF THE VOCAL COACH

ANDREW WADE

Working recently in Canada, I became conscious that there were very few people of a second generation in theatre. This struck me immediately, reminding me that, ironically, I am now part of a second generation of voice coaches at the Royal Shakespeare Company and part of a long line of theatrical tradition. Innovation for us is always the latest expression of a continuum.

We are reminded constantly how much the growth of our role has been tied to the development of the organization itself, the Royal Shakespeare Company. It might be worthwhile to pause a moment and consider its rather patient debut.

THE RSC CHARACTER

Although the company has operated under its present name since 1961, its history goes back beyond that date to the building of the first permanent theatre in Stratford, the Shakespeare Memorial Theatre, which opened in 1879. George Bernard Shaw described the theatre building as belonging to the late Marzipan period! Under the direction of F. R. Benson, the season consisted of two months in summer, with tours of the country in between. The granting of the Royal Charter in 1925 was a recognition of almost fifty years of work. Following the destruction by fire in 1926, a new theatre was built, which opened on Shakespeare's birthday in April 1932. It was Barry Jackson, as Artistic Director, who instigated sweeping changes, taking the Shakespeare Memorial Theatre into the postwar period. With his slogan of "productions before profits," he brought in different directors and designers for each play and nurtured young talent. Established actors, tours, invitations from abroad — all contributed to broaden the Company's outlook throughout the 1950s.

In 1960 Peter Hall became Artistic Director. This marked the beginning of the period referred to as "the crucial years," for it is since then that a vision of a theatre company imposed itself in a fuller way. The repertoire widened to take in modern work and classics other than Shakespeare. The Company's experience of classical discipline and sense of language nurtured its new contemporary awareness gleaned from modern work. The seeds of the current company were sowed in those decisive years.

The 1960s saw the development of the idea of training. Directors such as Peter Hall, Peter Brook, and Michel Saint-Denis underlined the value of experimenting, of not seeking final solutions or concrete theories in theatre. In January 1960, Hall appointed John Barton as Assistant Director of the Memorial Theatre. He was, at this time, Lay Dean of King's College, Cambridge, and an authority on Elizabethan speech and drama. John Barton led verse-speaking classes, and training was taken as a continuous process, equally aimed at confirmed and less experienced actors. Peter Hall expressed these views in no uncertain words:

> We believe that a company can only be created if each actor, in addition to his main work, is continually developed and reexamined by training in the Studio and by taking part in experiments in public. We want to increase this work.[1]

When Trevor Nunn took over as Artistic Director in 1968 all this work continued and expanded. During this time actors began to take work into schools — it was the beginning of what has become an extensive Education Department.

Expansion did not cease from then on: the Other Place opened in Stratford in 1974; in 1977 the Company made the first of its now annual visits to Newcastle-upon-Tyne; the following year established its policy of touring to small regional venues; in 1982 the RSC moved its London base to the Barbican in the City of London; and the 1986 season in Stratford saw the opening of another RSC theatre, the Swan. That same year, Terry Hands became sole Artistic Director and Chief Executive.

Adrian Noble succeeded Terry Hands in 1991. He has sought since to maintain the tradition of studio theatre in Stratford while pioneering in other areas. One of his stated aims is to make the company "the best classi-

---

[1] Peter Hall, "Avoiding a Method," in *Crucial Years* (Stratford-upon-Avon and London: Reinhardt, 1963), 19.

cal theatre in the English-speaking world."[2] Thus, part of the new policy was to expand the voice profile. I became Head of Department with one full-time colleague in London and one in Stratford. Cicely Berry remains Voice Director, and this enables her now to devote more time to specific projects.

Sitting within the organization is the current Voice Department.

THE FORMATION OF A DEPARTMENT

When one looks back at what might be called now the history of voice at the RSC, one is again reminded of the debt owed to such directors as Peter Hall, Peter Brook, and Michel Saint-Denis. These men shared a passion for form and strongly laid the emphasis on the importance of verse-speaking. Peter Brook was aware of the challenge that this entailed:

> We must get him [the actor] to see that the challenge of the verse play is that he must bring to it an even deeper search for truth, for truth of emotion, truth of ideas, and truth of character — all quite separate and yet all interwoven — and then as an artist find, with objectivity, the form that gives these meanings life.[3]

The first reference to any technical voice work was through a singing teacher called Denne Gilkes. Peter Hall was the first to employ a voice teacher, Iris Warren, who led a series of classes on Saturday mornings. It was not until 1969, however, when Cicely Berry was invited in by Trevor Nunn, that the real foundations of voice work for actors in theatre were laid. From a part-time position, it soon acquired a full-time status. Berry, thus, pioneered the role of the voice person, working as part of the production team, no longer just opening the voice out and addressing the actors' audibility in the given theatre space, but trying to find a way, with the director, for actors to connect with words.

As the company grew, particularly with the expansion of the Swan Theatre, casting needed to be changed and the workload demanded the appointment of an assistant position in Stratford. Bardy Thomas was first hired on a part-time basis. David Carey took over, and a part-time position at the Barbican was given to Patsy Rodenburg. I replaced David Carey in 1988.

A CHANGING THEATRE CLIMATE

The RSC's development naturally coincided with, adapted to, responded to the social and theatrical climate as a whole. Forms of writing and acting

[2]   Stephen Fay, "Waking from the Dream," *The Independent on Sunday* (London), 17 March 1991, p. 12.

[3]   Peter Brook, "What About Real Life," *Crucial Years*, (Stratford-upon-Avon and London: Reinhardt, 1963), 21.

styles changed. New needs emerged and, as the social, political, artistic language of the plays evolved, new challenges had to be met.

Parallel to the growth of what was to become the RSC, radical, sometimes violent changes began to shake the foundations of theatre in the 1950s and 1960s. Well before the abolition of the Lord Chamberlain's powers of stage censorship in 1968 — which could be regarded, to some extent, as the advent of these evolutions — playwrights like Brecht, Beckett, Osborne, and Pinter (to mention only a few landmarks) were the forces that transformed the theatre of Galsworthy, Maugham, and Shaw, of Eliot, Priestly, and Fry. Individuals were now portrayed in all their cosmic absurdity. Characters displayed their imperfect powers of communication, their inevitable fears and loneliness. The mood thus veered to quietism and it was no longer uncommon for actors to work in smaller, more intimate spaces. At the same time, the barrier of the fourth-wall convention increasingly disappeared. This movement also changed the artistic language of the plays. Language became less inhibited, more committed, Received Pronunciation lost its considerable hold, thereby allowing a whole variety of contemporary idioms and dialects to flourish.

The late 1960s and early 1970s pursued and developed the criticism of social values. Issues such as the destruction of the nuclear family, violence, homosexuality, and colonialism were broached upon in very outspoken ways. In the late 1970s and the 1980s, an element of fear entered progressively in drama. This led to a period of postmodern disillusionment, doubt, and loss of faith — a period which we are still largely part of. Language, however, retained some of its most outrageous, defiant, and unconventional expressions, thanks to the development, in particular, of what came to be known as Alternative Theatre, mainly in London and Edinburgh.[4]

Modern theatre has thus created its own tradition, which John Barton recently summarized in three crucial words: "situation, character, and intention."[5] This modern tradition — it is a belief commonly held by directors at the RSC — can be harmonized with older traditions, such as the Elizabethan, provided that the radical differences between them are fully acknowledged.

In the last few decades, the role of the director in theatre has reached special prominence, while — paradoxically — the age is one in which the notion of ensemble has become the ideal (one thinks of Brecht's and Helene

---

4   I am partly indebted to Harold Hobson, *Theatre in Britain: A Personal View* (Oxford: Phaidon, 1984), and Ronald Harwood, *All the World's a Stage* (London: Secker, 1984).

5   Michael Coveney, "King John, Master of the Verse," *The Observer Review*, 9 October 1994, p. 12.

Weigel's Berliner Ensemble, of Peter Brook's nomadic companies, and naturally of the Royal Shakespeare Company).

This is only an apparent paradox. Much of the pioneering work accomplished by Cicely Berry has been in response to the director's needs. But Berry became — and remains — the privileged medium of communication between director and actor, never ceasing to find means to address moral, intellectual issues practically. In this way, she has laid the ethical foundations of present voice work at the RSC, which consists first and foremost in serving the needs of both the actors and directors.

THE PRESENT: VOICE WORK AT THE RSC

The present Voice Department at the RSC has grown through the impulse of one person, Cicely Berry. Today, the structure established by her is still here, responding to the same needs but through different personalities and with broadened means. The nature of the voice work carried out currently at the RSC revolves primarily around two areas. First, we deal with the fundamentals of the actors' voices, always putting forward the intimate connections with the body. We work on relaxation, breath, resonance, muscularity of sounds and words, taking into account the different requirements of each theatre auditorium. Secondly, we are concerned with how actors relate to language within the rehearsal process and in performance.

Within the life of the RSC, these two strands are addressed in many ways. Our task consists, primarily, of being in rehearsal and of liaising with directors. We then set up calls and work with the actors away from the rehearsal room. These calls can be solos, group calls, or can take place in the auditorium. During previews and prior to Press Night, we feel it is essential to organize company calls in the auditorium.

As the season establishes its repertoire format, there is the opportunity to introduce blocks of classes. Early morning sessions, lunch-time verse work, sessions in the different theatre spaces, and taking projects out into the community are just a few examples of the possibilities. Yet, there is not and should not be a timetable or syllabus for the work. Inevitably, it has to be playing by ear and responding to the needs as they arise.

To give a more detailed account of the ongoing work, our role involves leading warm-ups before each performance, setting up solo sessions with actors, working with understudies, and monitoring performances. The same attention is devoted to the actors when on tour or when the ongoing work is transferring from one venue to the other. Voice care is not the least of our concerns either: we have E.N.T. consultants, voice therapy links, voice care talks and advice.

Whatever the area, our function as voice people at the RSC entails that we owe a total commitment to the actors and that we have a constant responsibility towards the language. The underlying concept of working with the actors is allowing them to explore without limitation, while never overlooking the demands of the production. Unremittingly, our duty is to find means to keep inviting actors to listen for and be affected by the choice of word. The issue that we are what we speak must never cease to be a central preoccupation. Making a classical structure ring true for the actors is a goal which can only be achieved by giving them choices, helping them to hear the possibilities practically and finding the meeting point of thought and feeling.

In order to discover this meeting point, it is crucial to leave aside momentarily all other concerns and concentrate on the actors' predominant means of expression: language. I believe that there is a "sound" of the language in a text which actors must hear. Some might object that we leave ideas aside. I would deny this observation by saying that my interest is precisely in the music of the thought, in the way words are chosen, and in the thought's inherent cadence. By making the actors listen to the language of the playwright, we are able to help them feel comfortable with that language without their being tempted to duck or manipulate it.

Precision of word is what fascinates me and represents the real challenge for actors. It is the journey between finding the articulatory truth of someone else's shaped thought in a carefully worded line and finding the reference point to a truth of our own. There is a definition of self when you actually achieve this. Such precision creates an elation. It is never about a descriptive, external impression, but about the absolute delight of the moment of the word. Rather than imposing our own meaning, our own tune, it is vital to hear that the shape of the writing is a tune in itself. It is thus necessary to let go of one's ego and to hear the ego of the text.

This passion and deep concern for language and text has led to the realization of many projects under the inspired impulse of Cicely Berry, in her present role as Voice Director. To mention only a handful, the Voice Department has initiated such ventures as the 1992 Theatre Voice Conference, the Edward Bond-Cicely Berry workshop, workshops with actors and writers, and the more recent Poetry Programs, directed by Cicely Berry and myself (*Journeys* in 1993 and *Words, Words, Words* in 1994). Response to both these programs has shown the current need and relevance of a return to language through poetry and storytelling.

There is a battle to fight: "the battle of the word to survive." This phrase was coined by Michael Redgrave at the beginning of the 1950s, in a period when theatre began to be deeply influenced by more physical forms of art such as mime.[6] Although the context is obviously different, the fight is the

---

6   Michael Redgrave, *The Actor's Ways and Means* (London: Heinemann, 1953), 67.

same one today. Recent changes affecting voice work in theatre schools can indeed be a little disquieting.

One must bear in mind that the RSC operates within the theatrical culture as a whole and the voice work carried out within the organization responds to and reflects the actors who work there. They themselves are a product of the theatre climate and of the training in this country. The climate is more fluid than it has been for a very long time as the traditional training establishments are being forced to restructure.

VOICE WORK IN UNITED KINGDOM THEATRE SCHOOLS

The RSC, in many ways, could be seen as an island in an ocean of generalism. I feel that training in the U.K. has slightly lost its way. As we all know, an actor today is expected to be incredibly versatile. Consequently, drama schools are torn as to what aspect or for which type of theatre they are preparing their actors. The result is that voice work is having to cater for an actor who is possibly going to work in film, television, radio, theatre, schools, restaurants, outside and inside, with classical, text-based language, contemporary writing of all qualities, in forms of art such as musicals or theatre whose reference is the visual and the physical.

Other evolutions are likewise significant: it is interesting to note that many a drama school in England was founded or run by qualified voice and speech people who also directed, as for example Elsie Fogerty, Gwynneth Thurburn, Rose Bruford, or Jean-Norman Benedetti. Only relatively recently have the majority of our training establishments been headed by directing/acting oriented people. The extension of this state of affairs seems to be that in the future more and more will be in the hands of the financial administrators.

Overall there is a climate in which fewer actors are leaving drama school with an attitude to acting beyond simply being as opposed to doing. For some time, the focus of voice work has tended to revolve predominantly around self. I refer to the emphasis on the "release" of a voice — what might be called the removal of the imposed voice, in the form of blocks, tensions, and restrictions that limit a voice. To this end a vast amount of work is done to undo tense muscles that can be seen as a barrier to a more truthful quality of voice. The psychology of the person is naturally tied up with these issues. After all, the physical is part of the mental. Unfortunately, this inward-searching can become the primary concern of our work, to the exclusion of making the private public. We must never stop asking, "What is a voice for?"

When the psychological approach is given sole prominence, there is often — in the best cases — a comfortable sound but lack of verbal presence to define it. Speech is indeed more than open sound.

It is vital in my view that we move from voice work on self to voice work that affects and can change others — from the indulgence of the self to the survival of the human, communicating being.

THE PUBLIC LIFE OF THE PRIVATE VOICE

In the last analysis, ours is a political cause. We as voice coaches have to believe that theatre is changing our lives in some way, that it is performing a valuable function in society today. In this materialistic civilization, it is of prime importance that we never cease looking at human beings as people who are able to define their lives, themselves, and their relationships to others through language. Our relation to language informs, in turn, how theatre relates to language and how appropriate that language is. Theatre must not become a museum piece: it must be a reflection and a reaction, a mirror to what is going on around it.

The more I look at my role in theatre, the more I find that, in order to defend our cause, we have to earn our role. Our rights as voice people will never be statutory, because theatre never has and never will operate in that way. Time and time again relationships based on mutual trust have to be established, renewed, sought for, with actors and directors. With unfailing fervor we must constantly earn our role anew.

Working as a voice coach at the RSC, I do realize how fortunate I am in that the earning of my role is facilitated by the organization itself. The spirit of the directors who gave such a decisive impulse in the 1960s by underlining the importance of language and form, as well as proper verse-speaking — Peter Hall, John Barton, Peter Brook, Michel Saint-Denis — is revived today by Adrian Noble, the present Artistic Director of the RSC. His passion and respect for classical language does not, by far, exclude rigor. He confirmed this in a recent television interview: "One should recognize the disciplines that Shakespeare offers which are in fact freedom."[7] His concern for language is by no means a recent one. Since his appointment as Artistic Director in 1991, Adrian Noble has sought to exorcise the ghost of that dark period when critics tended to be unkind about the Company's technical standards, especially the verse-speaking. The vision behind the present revival of the company has always been at once clear and rightfully ambitious:

> A classical ensemble is trained in the use of language, is trained not just in how to speak it, but in how you connect the living word with the human emotion and with the spirit. That's the actor's business. That's the kind of debate that we in theatre are willing to address.[8]

---

[7] The Shakespeare Laboratory, BBC2 production, 17 October 1994.

[8] Deborah Orr, "Curtains for Culture," *New Statesman and Society*, 26 October 1990, p. 25.

This profession of theatrical faith is one which could be said to guide and inspire the current Voice Department. Noble's unflinching support has also set the standards of the truthful relations which we seek to maintain with other directors.

What relations we build with the directors we have to keep building with our colleagues. The current Voice Department at the RSC tries to be a reflection of these ethics. I have sought to create a broadened environment made up of a team of people with their own individualities, their own strengths, and their own interests — all equally competent. In this context, we strive to define a voice role in a slightly wider way, staying clear from overpowering individualism.

One cannot deny that the voice world is largely one of individuals with personality and charisma. Our varied and sometimes conflicting views will, no doubt, provide us with rich debate for many years to come. However, we have to confront the fact that we can be regarded as very prescriptive sometimes, if not dogmatic in our views. It appears to me more than ever that our politics need to be clear in this matter.

Every discourse is potentially a discourse of power. As we become authors of books, articles, and so forth, we automatically become authorized voices, with views that — if we are not sufficiently cautious — may become authoritarian. Power does not only reside in a monolithic institution called the state which is largely alien to us and with which we might disagree. Power is plural; it is made up of voices using the habitual medium of power: the discourse of arrogance. Dogma feeds on such condescension and demands uncompromising acceptance. If method and theory are well-suited for the printed page, they might not be so for the stage.

Now that we voice specialists have earned a role, it is vital that we do not use the power given in trust to us for our sole purposes. This, I feel, is our responsibility as voice people, citizens, as human beings.

⌒⌒

14

"I CHARGE THEE SPEAK":
John Barrymore and His Voice Coach, Margaret Carrington

Barbara Acker

In the early days of his career, Barrymore did not need a good voice. He did not have to meet the challenge of speaking classical verse nor did he need a particularly good quality stage voice. Even when he began to tackle serious dramatic roles, such as the desperate Cockney clerk in *Justice* (1916), or his roles in *Peter Ibbetson* (1917), *Redemption* (1918), and *The Jest* (1919), critical attention focused on his physical realization of the part, not on his voice.

Theatre reviews suggest that Barrymore's voice was not his best feature. When he played Dr. Rank in *A Doll's House* (1907), his indistinct enunciation and poor projection drew criticism.[1] In the 1908 production of *A Stubborn Cinderella*, the audience again had difficulty hearing him.[2] Several reviewers faulted Barrymore for vocal monotony and a tendency to be "overemphatic."[3] It was only when Barrymore played Shakespearean roles, Richard III (1920) and Hamlet (1922/25), that the press began to pay as

---

[1]   "*A Doll's House:* Ethel Barrymore Plays An Ibsen Role," *Globe* (Boston) 1 February 1907, p. 4.

[2]   Amy Leslie, *Chicago Daily News,* 2 June 1908, p. 14.

[3]   "John Barrymore in Tolstoy Tragedy," *New York Times,* 4 October 1918, p. 11; John Corbin, "From the New Plays," *New York Times,* 6 October 1918, sec. 4, p. 2; F. H. [Francis Hackett], "After the Play," *The New Republic* 19 (May 10, 1919): 55; Alexander Woollcott, "Second Thoughts on First Nights," *New York Times,* 28 September 1919, sec. 4, p. 2.

much attention to his voice as to his physical presence. His critics then gave a collective sigh of gratitude that his voice had changed for the better.

Broadway director Arthur Hopkins put it best: "Jack had all the beauties except voice."[4] Others agreed. Barrymore's brother, Lionel, noted that although Jack's raspy voice was "good enough for comedy and an effective reed for most drama, . . . Jack did not then have a full-rounded voice and his diction was slovenly."[5] Their uncle, John Drew, a polished and accomplished actor in his own right, lamented, "Jack talks like a stable hand."[6] Constance Collier, a British actress and friend of Barrymore, saw how his voice dismayed people in British theatre circles. When he negotiated with London theatre managers to remount his production of *Hamlet*, Barrymore adopted tough-talking Bowery speech:

> [The managers] would say, "How can you expect in England, the home of Shakespeare, a man with a voice like that, to be any good in Shakespeare's plays?" You couldn't *make* Jack *not* put that voice on. He would do it deliberately to shock them.[7]

Collier herself made arrangements for the lease of the Haymarket before the manager had an opportunity to hear Barrymore's voice and to renege on the agreement.

John Barrymore's vocal problems could hardly be attributed to his upbringing. He was born into a family of actors. His sister Ethel was lauded by theatre critic Alexander Woollcott for her enchanting, lovely voice.[8] Until the age of fifteen, Barrymore spent most of his time with his grandmother, the forbiddingly correct Mrs. John Drew, who had managed the Arch Street Theatre in Philadelphia for over thirty years, and had acted ever since she was a young child.[9] Ethel Barrymore reminisced about the speech standards laid down by their grandmother:

---

[4]   Arthur Melancthon Hopkins, *Reference Point: Reflections on Creative Ways in General with Special Reference to Creative Ways in Theatre* (New York: Samuel French, 1948), 117.

[5]   Lionel Barrymore and Cameron Shipp, *We Barrymores: As Told to Cameron Shipp* (New York: Appleton-Century-Crofts, 1951), 202, 158.

[6]   Alexander Woollcott, Interviewed by Gene Fowler, Bomoseen, Vermont, 1942. Gene Fowler Collection, Special Collections, University of Colorado at Boulder Libraries, Boulder, Colorado.

[7]   Constance Collier, Unpublished Manuscript. Gene Fowler Collection, Special Collections, University of Colorado at Boulder Libraries, Boulder, Colorado, 6.

[8]   Alexander Woollcott, quoted in Ethel Barrymore, *Memories: An Autobiography* (London: Hulton Press 1956), 168; Gene Fowler, *Good Night, Sweet Prince: The Life and Times of John Barrymore* (New York: The Viking Press, 1943, 1944), 135.

[9]   Lionel Barrymore and Shipp, *We Barrymores*, 85.

I came from people who spoke well, from a family where purity of speech was a matter of course, where there was no such thing as a provincial accent. If I brought a provincialism home from school, eyebrows were raised so far that they disappeared into that thick Drew hair, and that particular provincialism would never be uttered again. In running her stock company at the Arch Street Theatre, Mummum had absolutely no patience, no tolerance whatever, for slipshod speech. At home she and everyone else spoke well. Nothing was ever said about it. It was just done.[10]

Barrymore had a flair for accents, which means he had a good ear for intonation, vocal placement, and subtle phonemic differences. He was praised for his Cockney accent in the productions of *Pantaloon* (1906) and *Justice* (1916).[11] He studied with a White Russian to perfect an accent for *Redemption* (1918).[12] Barrymore proved he could mimic speech patterns, proved he had the requisite skills to get rid of his sloppy, nasal sound. What he needed was a compelling reason to change the vocal habits of a lifetime.

Lionel Barrymore recalled that by the 1920s his brother had a group of self-appointed advisors, the "Barrymore Board of Strategy," composed of Ned Sheldon, Constance Collier, Alexander Woollcott, Robert Edmond Jones, and Margaret Carrington. Anxious as they were for Barrymore to leave the byways of comedy and establish himself as an actor in serious roles, they supported Hopkins' plans to launch a classical repertory with *Richard III*. The only stumbling block was Jack's voice.[13] Barrymore apparently agreed, for years later he told his friend Anthony Quinn that "speech was the most important thing in the world for the actor."[14] He confessed that it was the prospect of a Shakespearean role which finally forced him to deal with his nasal Bowery accent. The voice specialist Barrymore turned to was Margaret Carrington.

As a young woman, Margaret Carrington was a concert singer in Europe. When World War I began, she settled in New York and established a reputation as a vocal coach for actors. She counted among her students her younger brother Walter Huston and Lillian Gish. She was a very successful dramatic coach who could bring out the best in an actor. Huston credited her

10 Ethel Barrymore, *Memories*, 47.

11 *New York Dramatic Mirror*, 6 January 1906, p. 3; "Justice," *New York Times*, 23 April 1916, sec. 2, p. 8; "'Justice' Done Here with Superb Cast," *New York Times*, 4 April 1916, p. 11.

12 Arthur Melancthon Hopkins, *To A Lonely Boy* (New York: Book League of America, 1937), 168–169.

13 Lionel Barrymore and Shipp, *We Barrymores*, 202; Fowler, *Good Night, Sweet Prince*, 190; Hopkins, *To A Lonely Boy*, 199.

14 Anthony Quinn, *The Original Sin: A Self-Portrait* (Boston: Little, Brown, 1972), 206.

for teaching him how to act.[15] Nephew John Huston, the film actor and director, described Carrington as a "consummate actress in a drawing room."[16] John Huston's wife recalled a "riveting" performance of Carrington's when "this *thing*…came out of her when she was reading Shakespeare—one could understand how she was sought after as a coach.[17]

Carrington took only pupils who interested her and never accepted any payment for her lessons.[18] She taught how to improve voice quality, diction and breathing, and how to make the words come alive. She was not interested in "vocal gymnastics," but rather in how to link the sound and sense of words to create clear and emotionally expressive speech.[19]

When Barrymore began to study with Margaret Carrington he was already rehearsing *Richard III*. In an unfinished essay, "The John Barrymore that I Knew," Carrington said that he came to see her, shyly explained his fears of acting Shakespeare and with "devastating charm" asked for her help.[20] At first, Carrington hesitated to take him. The production was slated to open in six weeks and that was precious little time to change the vocal habits of a lifetime. She assessed his problems and observed, "His voice was tired, and in spite of its rare individual quality was of short range due to a complete lack of breath control."[21] Unable to resist the challenge, she took him as a pupil.

Carrington did not begin lessons with breathing or vowel exercises. Instead, she asked him to take a piece of fruit from a bowl on the table. As soon as he picked up an apple, she began an inquisition.

> "Mr. Barrymore, what do you have in your hand?"
>
> "I got a red apple."
>
> "You have what?"
>
> "I got a red apple."
>
> "I'm sorry, I don't understand."

---

[15] John Weld, "September Song," Unpublished Biography of Walter Huston. National Film Information Service, Academy Foundation, Center for Motion Picture Study, Beverly Hills, California. 88, 128.

[16] John Huston, *An Open Book* (New York: Alfred A. Knopf, 1980), 37.

[17] Lawrence Grobel, *The Hustons* (New York: Charles Scribner's Sons, 1989), 189.

[18] Lillian Gish and Ann Pinchot, *Lillian Gish: The Movies, Mr. Griffith and Me* (Englewood Cliffs, N.J.: Prentice-Hall, 1969), 317; Lillian Gish, Manuscript. Special Collections, Manuscript Division, Library of Congress, Washington, D.C., 27.

[19] Margaret Carrington, "The John Barrymore I Knew." Gene Fowler Collection, Special Collections, University of Colorado at Boulder Libraries, Boulder, Colorado, 3.

[20] Carrington, "The John Barrymore I Knew," 2.

[21] Ibid., 2.

"You don't understand? I got a red apple in my hand."

Then he laughed and said his speech lessons for the first two or three weeks consisted of making that apple sound like the juiciest, reddest apple in the world. She wasn't satisfied until he had created not only the imagery, but the fullness of each word. He said, "She taught me to make love to the words. Don't get carried away with the emotion, kid. Caress the word."[22]

Carrington taught Barrymore to respond to the imagery and meaning of every word. She also gave him exercises to increase his breath capacity and improve vocal quality and diction. He practiced vowel sounds as he walked along the street until he could speak a complete Shakespearean sentence on a single breath.[23] Barrymore knew that in order to play Richard III he had to change his voice. He also had to work on intonation, which indicates that Carrington was giving him lessons on stress and rhythm in the verse.[24] Director Arthur Hopkins heard improvement:

> John... whose voice was furry and not best suited to Shakespeare, had been studying diligently with Mrs. Margaret Carrington, who by some magic, entirely her own, had turned his faulty instrument into a medium of ease and beauty.[25]

The role of Richard III became a demarcation line, dividing the old Barrymore sound from the new. Critics heralded the star's new rich vocal quality, his range and control, and his clear enunciation. Francis Hackett, in the *New Republic*, was delighted the actor had eliminated his nasality and developed a voice that was "beautifully placed, deep and sonorous and free."[26] Alexander Woollcott remarked:

> Now he has acquired, out of space, a voice. His voice three years ago was dry and monotonous, his speech slovenly and sometimes common. All that is largely changed. He entered upon the Shakespearean task with a patiently acquired voice, one rich, full and flexible. This is really the advance of which he may be proudest.[27]

---

22 Quinn, *The Original Sin*, 206.

23 Carrington, "The John Barrymore I Knew," 5–6.

24 John Barrymore, *Confessions of an Actor* (Indianapolis: BobbsMerrill, 1926), np. Peters identifies Karl Schmidt as the author of Barrymore's memoirs. Margot Peters, *The House of Barrymore* (New York, London: A Touchstone Book, Simon & Schuster, 1990), 290.

25 Hopkins, *To A Lonely Boy*, 199.

26 F. H. [Francis Hackett], "After the Play," *The New Republic* 22 (March 24, 1920): 122.

27 Alexander Woollcott, "At 'Richard III'," *New York Times*, 21 March 1920, sec. 6, p. 6.

Carrington and Hopkins treated *Richard III* as a modern play. Barrymore brought the verse alive with a contemporary vitality and passion. *The New York Call* observed that Barrymore did not use "rhetorical singsong.... [He] lives and thinks and speaks with the sharp enunciation and natural inflections of flesh and blood."[28] Heywood Broun added that Barrymore had "fire and life" and was no longer guilty of "false emphasis," of stressing whatever arbitrarily chosen word suited him.[29] Some critics doubted that a comedian like Barrymore could do a credible job of speaking verse.[30] Nevertheless, a hallmark of Barrymore's Shakespearean work was his intelligent, clear line delivery. Reviewers made much of the fact that they could understand everything he said. Carrington must have been delighted when the critic for the *New York Dramatic Mirror* praised the actor's impeccable diction and delivery and his clear understanding of the lines.[31]

Barrymore's next project with Hopkins and Carrington was the 1922 production of *Hamlet*. This time Hopkins asked Carrington to prepare Barrymore for the role. She agreed on condition that she would have at least a month to work with Barrymore and that the opening date would be set only when she felt he was ready. Barrymore appeared on the doorstep of her Connecticut home one summer's day with an armload of books about *Hamlet*. This visit turned into a stay of two and a half months. They worked tirelessly together, in the gardens and in the woods, six to eight hours a day and sometimes into the night. Just as she had done with *Richard III*, Carrington asked him to treat *Hamlet* as a modern play that had never been performed and to disregard all previous interpretations of the script. They studied only the Temple edition of *Hamlet*. She also asked him not to memorize the part until they had explored every nuance of meaning in the script. Carrington attributed the spontaneous quality of his performance to this method.[32]

At the same time that Barrymore was wrestling with the meaning of the lines, he was continuing his voice training. Carrington wanted to rebuild his voice from the ground up, and he was willing to throw himself into more vowel and breath exercises. The day Carrington felt Barrymore was ready, she notified Hopkins.

---

28 Louis Gardy, "The Stage: Barrymore's 'Richard III'," *New York Call*, 9 March 1920, p. 6.

29 Heywood Broun, *Tribune* (New York), quoted in "Barrymore's Bout with Richard," *Literary Digest*, 65 (April 3, 1920): 37.

30 J. Ranken Towse, *Evening Post* (New York) quoted in "Barrymore's Bout With Richard," *Literary Digest* 65 (April 3, 1920): 36–37.

31 Louis R. Reid, "The New Plays on Broadway: 'Richard III'," *New York Dramatic Mirror*, 13 March 1920, p. 466.

32 Carrington, "The John Barrymore I Knew," 3–4.

Carrington's work did not end with the preliminary coaching; her services were needed during the run of *Hamlet*. Hamlet is a vocally demanding role and when performed eight times a week, as Barrymore had to, a vocally exhausting one. Barrymore's incessant smoking added to the strain of a heavy performance schedule. A trail of half-smoked cigarettes followed him everywhere backstage. He took two or three drags on a cigarette before every entrance. Lark Taylor, who was cast as Bernardo and the First Player in the New York production, noted that Barrymore had vocal problems which plagued him all season: "Paul, his devoted yellow valet, was kept busy with ice-bags and various remedies. Sundays Margaret Carrington worked with him most of the day to get him in good shape for Monday."[33] The work paid off handsomely: "[He] spoke his lines with ease and convincing naturalness, showing he had worked carefully and earnestly. Margaret Carrington had almost entirely obliterated his monotonous delivery and Bowery pronunciation, and his voice had a surprising range and quality."[34]

Hamlet opened in New York on November 16, 1922, and played for 101 performances that season, breaking Edwin Booth's record of 100 performances. The next season Barrymore toured the United States with *Hamlet*, and in 1925 he successfully remounted the production at the Haymarket Theatre in London.

Barrymore's voice and speech came under critical scrutiny again. Critics agreed his voice quality and text delivery continued to improve, giving an impression of greater emotional expressiveness and depth. Walter Prichard Eaton, who had reviewed Barrymore as far back as *The Yellow Ticket* in 1914, commented on the actor's progress in vocal skills and in handling the rhythm.[35] In *Theatre Arts*, Kenneth Macgowan wrote of the "most brilliant Prince of this generation...lovely of voice and poignant with emotion."[36] John Corbin thought Barrymore's deeper, lower pitches now made his voice worthy of tragedy.[37] Heywood Broun praised the actor's vocal skills:

> Somebody ought to write a tale about Barrymore called "The Story of a Voice." It is one of the most amazing adventures in our theatre. Here

[33] J. Lark Taylor, "With Hey Ho!," Unpublished Autobiography. Special Collections, University Archives, The Jean and Alexander Heard Library, Vanderbilt University, Nashville, Tennessee, 339.

[34] Taylor, "With Hey Ho!," 336.

[35] Walter Prichard Eaton, "Mr. Barrymore's Hamlet," *The Freeman* (January,10, 1923): 424. Clipping from the Theatre Arts Collection, Harry Ransom Humanities Research Center, University of Texas, Austin, Texas.

[36] Kenneth Macgowan, "And Again Repertory," *Theatre Arts Magazine* 7 (April 1923): 97.

[37] John Corbin, "The Twentieth Century Hamlet," *New York Times*, 17 December 1922, sec. 7, p. 1.

Has do you deliver verse?

was a peculiarly pinched utterance distinctly marred by slipshod diction. Today it is among the finest voices in the American theatre. We don't mean that it vibrates and rumbles and roars, but that isn't our notion of a fine voice. It is attuned to talking. Hamlet never deafens the members of his family, the audience, or even himself.[38]

All agreed that Barrymore made the meaning of every line clear, but critics parted company on the question of how well he handled the verse. Whitford Kane, who played the Grave Digger, felt that Barrymore was too modern and naturalistic and was better in the prose scenes, especially the scenes with Polonius.[39] Maida Castellun in the *New York Call* found the "splendors of passions and the soaring organ tones of Elizabethan rhetoric" lacking in Barrymore's "colloquial, casual" performance.[40] A lack of rhetorical punch or emotional fire was a charge also leveled by George Bernard Shaw, J. Ranken Towse, Glenn Hughes, and Edmund Wilson. For them, his low-keyed speech and his thoughtful style of delivering soliloquies made the play too long and too tame.[41]

Most reviewers, however, applauded Barrymore's delivery precisely because he eschewed "soaring organ tones" and rant. They found his colloquial style vital and persuasive. Heywood Broun and Alexander Woollcott approved of the way Barrymore seemed to think his way through the part, declaring the soliloquies did not strike the ear as familiar set pieces but rather as the artless expression of a man wrestling with a problem.[42] John Corbin of the *New York Times* described the "flawless" line readings as restoration of a lost art. He liked Barrymore's conversational manner which, in his opinion, served the rhythm of the verse.[43] Stark Young liked the simple honesty of Barrymore's readings, "no idle tricks of the voice."[44] Young did take the actor to task for occasionally stressing a word in a verse line not

---

[38]   Heywood Broun, "Mr. Shakespeare, Meet Mr. Tyson," February 1923, p. 33, Unidentified Clipping in the Theatre Arts Collection. Harry Ransom Humanities Research Center, University of Texas, Austin, Texas.

[39]   Whitford Kane, *Are We All Met?* (London: Elkin Mathews & Marrot, 1931), 232.

[40]   Maida Castellun, "The Stage: John Barrymore is Intelligent and Beautiful as a Hamlet Without Fire," *New York Call*, 18 November 1922, p. 4.

[41]   George Bernard Shaw, quoted in John Barrymore, *Confessions of an Actor*, n.p.; J. Ranken Towse, "'Hamlet' Spectacle and Little Else," *Evening Post* (New York), 17 November 1922, p. 7; Glenn Hughes, "Repressed Acting and Shakespeare," *Drama* 13 (March 1923): 211; Edmund J. Wilson, "The Theatre," *The Dial* 74 (March 1923): 320.

[42]   Broun, "Mr. Shakespeare, Meet Mr. Tyson," 33; Alexander Woollcott, "The Reviewing Stand," *New York Herald*, 17 November 20 1922, p. 8.

[43]   John Corbin, "A New Hamlet," *New York Times*, 17 November 1922, p. 14.

[44]   Stark Young, "Hamlet," *The New Republic* 33 (December 6, 1922): 45.

meant to take the stress. Such misplaced stress disrupted the rhythm of the verse and the continuity of the thought. Barrymore had not entirely renounced his old habit of exploding on "meaningful" words.

Other reviewers felt Barrymore had delivered the verse with entirely too regular a beat, too predictable a stress.[45] This is at odds with those who censured Barrymore for breaking up the rhythm of the line with an indulgence in misplaced stress. Walter Prichard Eaton said that the actor emphasized words "at the end of lines, or just before the caesural pause."[46] By making the audience too conscious of the rhythm he did not allow the music to set the mood. Since *Richard III* is an early play with many end-stopped lines, it is not surprising that reviewers heard a regular beat.

In London, *The Sphere* brought up the point the British found most remarkable, that Barrymore did not have an accent.[47] Rather than sounding American or British he used "unmarked" English. Reviewers extolled the precision of his diction and delivery and his thoughtful readings.[48] Others praised the verse speaking: "The wonderful verse of the poet could not have been delivered with finer intelligence or more charming music."[49]

William Poel believed the way that Barrymore "talked his way through the part and got the other actors to do the same," made the production superior to either Irving's or Forbes-Robertson's.[50] Constance Collier later wrote that "Jack's exquisite diction and lovely voice absolutely overwhelmed the English audience and his triumph was phenomenal."[51] The Bard's own countrymen then accorded the audacious Yankee the tribute of an extended run.

---

[45]   Cuthbert Wright, "Mr. Barrymore's 'Hamlet'," *The Freeman* (January 3, 1923): 401. Clipping from the Theatre Arts Collection, Harry Ransom Humanities Research Center, University of Texas, Austin, Texas.

[46]   Eaton, "Mr. Barrymore's 'Hamlet'," 424.

[47]   Herbert Farjeon, "The Play's the Thing," *The Sphere*, (March 7, 1925): 272.

[48]   James Agate, "Hamlet," *Brief Chronicles: The Contemporary Theatre, 1925* (1926; reprint, New York: Benjamin Blom, 1969), 12; "Barrymore's Hamlet in London," *The Christian Science Monitor*, 10 March 1925, p. 10. Clipping, Theatre Arts Collection, Harry Ransom Humanities Center, University of Texas, Austin, Texas; *The Daily News* (London), quoted in "Barrymore Wins London as Hamlet," *New York Times*, 20 February 1925, p. 20; "Entertainments: A New American Hamlet," *Times* (London), 20 February 1925, p. 12; Desmond McCarthy, "Drama: The New Hamlet," *New Statesman*, 7 March 1925, p. 627; *The Morning Post*, quoted in "John Barrymore Stirs London," *The Literary Digest* 84 (March 28, 1925): 30.

[49]   *The Daily Telegraph*, quoted in "Barrymore Wins London as Hamlet," *New York Times*, 20 February 1925, p. 20.

[50]   William Poel, "Letter to Reginald Pole, 1925" quoted in Robert Speaight, *William Poel and the Elizabethan Revival*, (Cambridge, MA: Harvard University Press, 1954), 27–28.

[51]   Collier, Unpublished Manuscript, 7.

Critics agreed that Barrymore's voice was up to the demands of Shake-speare. The issue of rhythm and stress in his verse was more problematic. Critics who approved of Barrymore's line delivery usually did so on the grounds that he was colloquial, not ranting, not using old-style declamation. Those who disapproved of his delivery generally charged he was too tame and lacked emotional fire.

Evidence from several quarters—fellow actors, a director, and a critic—agree that Barrymore was an erratic performer, very intense and focused one night and lackadaisical other nights. He husbanded his strength in some scenes of *Hamlet* and committed to full energy in other scenes. During the New York run of *Hamlet* Barrymore began to take longer pauses until he had added thirty minutes to the playing time.[52] Low vocal energy and a slow pace could account for the fact some critics heard a tame and lackluster vocal delivery. In other words, the judgment of how well he delivered the verse may have been confounded by variation in vocal energy and rate of speech.

Two great Hamlets of this century commented on Barrymore: Gielgud, who was twenty when he saw Barrymore's production at the Haymarket, and Olivier, who was seventeen. Gielgud said that Barrymore's grace made his "brilliantly intellectual performance classical without being unduly severe." He found it an "enthralling and in some ways ideal production."[53] Olivier acknowledged a debt to Barrymore for his own later Hamlets. Barrymore had breathed life into the part and swept away a poetic languor that had emasculated the role since the days of Irving:

> Everything about him was exciting. He was athletic, he had charisma and, to my young mind, he played the part to perfection. Although American, his English was perfect. He was astonishing.... Some critics knocked him for his verse speaking, as indeed was to happen to me in later years. They were wrong. I know they were wrong. He had a way of choosing a word and then exploding it in a moment of passion. Perhaps you did not always agree with the choice, but it was constantly riveting. He would vary the pace, but never gabble, always understandable. There would be a sudden burst and then again a lull, rather like the wind freshening up before a squall. For my money he really seemed to understand Hamlet.[54]

---

[52]   Hopkins, *To a Lonely Boy*, 231; Taylor, "With Hey Ho!," 344–345; Woollcott, "At 'Richard III'," *New York Times*, 21 March 1920, sec. 6, p. 6; Blanche Yurka, *Bohemian Girl: Blanche Yurka's Theatrical Life* (Athens, Ohio: Ohio University Press, 1970), 100.

[53]   John Gielgud, Notes Inscribed on Program for *Hamlet* at the Theatre Royal, Haymarket, 26 March 1925. The Raymond Mander & Joe Mitchenson Theatre Collection, Beckenham, Kent, courtesy of Dr. Martin F. Norden, University of Massachusetts.

[54]   Lawrence Olivier, *On Acting* (London: Weidenfeld & Nicolson, 1986), 36.

Lionel Barrymore knew it was Margaret Carrington who made Barrymore's success possible: "Jack had gone to Mrs. Carrington to get a rasp out of his throat. He went to her humbly acknowledging his fault, conquered that fault, and emerged stronger in every other department."[55]

The partnership of Barrymore and Carrington was summed up by Hopkins:

> Mrs. Carrington had the kind of derision that Jack appreciated. He took her most merciless barbs and went back for more.
>
> To her, he was the great opportunity that she long had sought.
>
> Just to find one voice that was really worth freeing, to hear just once the grandeur of Shakespeare's lines with unobstructed accompaniment. So, after long perseverance, two dreams were realized — Mrs. Carrington's and Jack's.[56]

A longtime friend of Barrymore's, Gene Fowler, wrote that Margaret Carrington was Barrymore's "principle and only real advisor" when he was preparing to do *Hamlet*.[57] She had worked with him roughly six hours a day for more than two months before rehearsals began. He had memorized his lines and set a great deal of the interpretation before he started rehearsing with Hopkins.[58] Barrymore did experiment with stage business during rehearsal, but he had shaped the basic path he was to follow in the months of work with Carrington.

Barrymore told Mary Astor that Carrington "was a truly great dramatic coach" and he credited her "for the fullness of his own development as an actor."[59] Shortly before his death, Barrymore told Dorothy Gish he was indebted to Margaret Carrington for his theatrical success: "Everything he had done that was worthwhile was because of Margaret Carrington.... Without her, he claimed, he would have been a fifth-rate actor."[60]

This is the story of a collaboration that has slipped out of the pages of history, perhaps because Barrymore took pains to craft a public artistic persona in which he was the sole author of his success. In his memoirs he does not credit Carrington for his amazing new voice. However, during the run of *Hamlet* in New York, he confided to Lark Taylor how much Margaret

---

55   Lionel Barrymore and Shipp, *We Barrymores*, 203, 206.

56   Hopkins, *Reference Point*, 118.

57   Gene Fowler, "Letter to Dr. Harold Thomas Hyman," quoted in Will Fowler, *The Young Man from Denver* (Garden City, NY: Doubleday, 1962), 208.

58   Taylor, "With Hey Ho!," 332, 334; Yurka, *Bohemian Girl*, 98.

59   Mary Astor, *My Story: An Autobiography* (Garden City, NY: Doubleday, 1959), 73.

60   Gish and Pinchot, *Lillian Gish*, 317.

Carrington had helped him.[61] Certainly those close to Barrymore acknowledged the role of this particular coach in the famous actor's career.

Stark Young marked Carrington's passing in 1942 with a salute to

> ...one among the half-dozen most distinguished and brilliant figures of the theatre of the last two decades.... [She was a] teacher and authority and inspiration such as few of our flat, flim-flam stage favorites either perceive or hunger after. She was indeed a gift from heaven for certain actors who had the possibility, as it were, of surpassing themselves.[62]

This was a fitting tribute to the woman who charged Barrymore to speak and enabled him to surpass himself and achieve greatness in his two most important stage roles.

---

[61] Taylor, "With Hey Ho!," 332, 339.

[62] Stark Young, "Distinction and Theatre," *The New Republic* 107 (August 24, 1942): 227.

15

STANDARD SPEECH:
THE ONGOING DEBATE

DUDLEY KNIGHT

Speech training is still a subject about which few people agree. Members of VASTA (Voice and Speech Trainers Association) sometimes ruefully comment that there is not even firm agreement amongst the members on how to pronounce the organizational acronym. It's that annoying first vowel: flat? intermediate? broad?

As the excellent video documentary *American Tongues*[1] amply demonstrates, in the real world of American society we all carry about with us our own set of complex stereotypes about other people's speech patterns. And all of us — ALL of us — somehow manage to stigmatize some other groups. Her Brooklyn accent causes too much distracting attention for the midwest clients of a young business representative, so she seeks the help of an accent-reduction specialist. Southerners think Northerners sound harsh and dismissive. African-Americans hotly debate the value and utility of Black American Speech. A woman with a strong German accent cannot understand why visitors find her "Pennsylvania Dutch" (read *Deutsch*) speech hard to understand, especially those southerners who really have an accent. In these days when sensitivities about language use are particularly acute, when one attorney in the "trial of the century" can accuse another attorney[2] of racist tendencies when a witness suggests the possibility of identifying an African-American by his accent, it is not strange that the more limited issue of speech training for the stage is not immune from these controversies.

---

[1] A video documentary by Louis Alvarez and Andrew Kolker, produced by the Center for New American Media, 1988.

[2] Both of them African-American.

However, for American actors, especially those who wish to act in the classical repertoire, these issues do not seem limited or parochial; they are concerns that find their way into every rehearsal, every performance.

Any real discussion of standards for theatre speech in the future must begin with an awareness of where we are now. And where we are now depends on where we have been.

THE SOURCE

As a child in Australia, growing up in the 1860s and 1870s, William Tilley could not have dreamed that his destiny would be to define the sound of American classical acting for almost a century. For one thing, throughout his life he hated theatre.

Nor did his interests seem to impel him toward the United States. Certainly he could not have imagined that his primary sphere of influence would turn out to be, of all places, New York City. Germany, and German culture, were his models and his home for the study of human language and its sounds. After his university training, his subsequent philological training with Henry Sweet[3] in England and Wilhelm Viëtor in Switzerland, and his membership, one of the first, in the International Phonetic Association during the 1890s, Tilley established a highly successful school in Germany teaching German language and culture to foreigners; its peripatetic existence carried it through several cities until it reached Berlin around 1905 at Gross-Lichterfelde where it became an internationally famous institute. The transplanted Australian — according to his student Bruce Lockhart, noted English author, diplomat, and spy — did "more for Anglo-German friendship than any man living."[4] The school catered mostly to English students who had already been through university in England, another of whom was the young Daniel Jones, whom Tilley introduced to phonetic study. Daniel Jones subsequently became arguably the most influential figure in English speech and dialect study in the first half of this century.

Residence at the Tilley Institute was not for the faint of heart, or brain, for that matter. University graduates who had slid easily through the tutorial system at Oxford or Cambridge were abashed to encounter Tilley's rather more demanding teaching methods. "Tilly ruled them with a rod of iron, and *taught them how to work*; they often didn't like his methods at first, but in the long run most of them came to have unbounded admiration for him," enthused Daniel Jones.[5] By the time Jones wrote this obituary for his friend

---

[3]   The model for G. B. Shaw's Henry Higgins, Sweet was the inventor of "Broad Romic" transcription, the basis of IPA phonetic symbols thereafter.

[4]   *Retreat From Glory* (New York: G. P. Putnam's Sons, 1934), 274.

[5]   In *Le Maître Phonétique*, October 1935 [italics by the author].

and mentor in 1935, Tilley had long since shortened his surname to Tilly. With the focused attention to language sounds that ruled his life, Tilly changed the spelling when he discovered that the "ey" ending was confusing to German postal employees when he went to collect his mail at the post office and told them his name.[6]

Tilly's rigorous pedagogy became the stuff of legend. Marguerite De-Witt, one of his students after Tilly had moved to America, gives what may be Tilly's own picture of his Institute in Berlin:

> In pre-War days on the Continent there was an at-core ultra British Institute, one that was run with the precision, regularity, and energy of the English Navy; one that was always on time, in order and at work. A British historian has said that one never catches the Navy napping! For many a year people came to Professor Tilly so that they might use the science as a means to their various ends. Students, teachers, professors, consuls, diplomats, actors, singers, authors, members of all professions came ... As colleague, friend or acquaintance of leading international scholars in the modern language field, and more especially as a friend and follower of that master philologist, Henry Sweet, Professor Tilly was an enormous drawing card who in his own domain was in a position to turn aside all shirkers and poor workers.[7]

Shortly after the First World War broke out, Tilly's Institute was closed; his family—who worked with him—was dispersed,[8] and Tilly was interned by the German government for a short period of time. He made his way to England and at the close of the war settled in the United States, where in 1918 he found a teaching position at Columbia University in the extension program. Here he remained for the rest of his career; he never joined the regular faculty of the university.

But Tilly attracted students quickly. He began to teach a large number of people who wished to master English as a second language. More and more his innovative methods of teaching phonetics attracted teachers in the public school system of New York City, women (for the most part) who in their view were trying to maintain acceptable standards of English pronunciation within a secondary school curriculum that still allowed for the active

---

[6] They would have expected him to say "till-eye" [tɪlaɪ].

[7] In *Americanadian Euphonetic Notes*, no date, but probably 1926–1928. Marguerite DeWitt, who wrote extensively on speech issues in the 1920s, had a fondness for portmanteau words, as the title of her irregularly published newsletter suggests. In addition to "Americanadian" and "Euphonetic," Miss DeWitt characterized those who lived in the United States but refused to learn the proper pattern of English pronunciation as "Americanots."

[8] According to Marguerite DeWitt (*Notes*), two of Tilly's daughters, Emily and Edith, went to China to teach English in Peking (Beijing).

teaching of speech, rhetoric, and forensics. Marguerite DeWitt described the process:

> Just as Henry Sweet hued [sic] out great blocks of phonetic knowledge so has Professor Tilly taken these blocks and broken them into chips so small that they may in great part be passed on to children. He has done more than any other to promote the practical application of phonetics and has done it on a comparative basis — *using the standard form of a language as the foundation for work.*[9]

William Tilly considered himself a reformer, attempting to clear away the detritus of outworn teaching methods. And he was right. Phonetics itself, during the first three decades of this century, was still defining itself as a separate area of study. A crucial tool of the growing social sciences of anthropology — with its need to notate newly-discovered languages — and linguistics as it evolved out of the historical orientation of philology, phonetics was still searching for the ideal notation form. Tilly believed strongly in Sweet's "Broad Romic" as adopted by the International Phonetic Association, which had been founded in the 1880s by Frenchman Paul Passy.[10]

But Tilly went further. Because his particular area of interest was the proper pronunciation of English, he was a firm advocate of so-called "narrow" phonetic transcription, which essentially means a more detailed and precise form usually defined by numerous diacritic symbols. Anthropologists and most linguists rejected narrow transcription, preferring the "broad" or more general form because their needs did not require such specificity, and because they considered narrow transcription overly laden with detail. In writings critical of Tilly's approach, the word "fussy" appears more than once.

His attention to detail was influential, especially in areas of language study where Phonetics itself was new. But Tilly's chief reform, and the one that was passed down to his followers in theatre, was his attempt to teach the pronunciation of English as a *spoken* language, and not as a written one.

If one listens to the recordings, made in the early 1920s, of E. H. Sothern and Julia Marlowe,[11] the grand American theatrical couple at the turn of the century, one is able to hear a vocal pattern that hearkens back to the elocutionary teachings of William Murdoch, and before him to the founder of elocution, James Rush, in the America of the early nineteenth century.[12] It

---

[9]   *Notes* [italics mine].

[10]   Passy also edited the IPA's journal *Le Maître Phonétique*, "The Phonetics Teacher."

[11]   Early recordings of Sothern and Marlowe, and many other famous actors from the late nineteenth century on, are available in the Crest Cassette series "Traditions of Acting," produced by the Creegan Company, Steubenville, Ohio.

[12]   Sothern studied with Murdoch, who had studied with Rush.

was a pattern that mandated the extreme extension of vowel sounds often with a tremulous dying fall of intonation when a word is to be emphasized, so that the lines were more sung than spoken; a pattern that required syllables — which in ordinary conversation are unstressed — to be stressed with discrete vowel sounds, as though one were reading the written word out of a book and paying attention only to the word as spelled (the "book word"), not to the spoken utterance (so that "ocean" becomes "owe-see-yun"); a pattern that insisted upon a heavy glottal attack on words beginning with vowels as a sign of vocal vigor: the active explosion of the vocal folds into an open orotund vowel sound.[13]

This was the hallmark of elocution in its late and somewhat decadent form, where every inflection, every gesture, every pronunciation was predetermined in the textbooks. One can easily imagine this prescriptive progression through the decades in nineteenth-century America where oratory emerged as the popular form of entertainment. In a growing nation in which professional theatrical performance was not easily available to large segments of the rural population, oratory satisfied the theatrical needs of the country. While acting genius could not be directly taught to the general public, oratorical techniques certainly could. Speakers who needed to be persuasive in large halls, or in open spaces, adopted dynamic if unsubtle vocal styles. So the trilled "R" flourished, along with the heavy glottal attack and the book-word pronunciations.

But William Tilly perceived that in American oratory, and also in speech education generally, verbal form had become a parody of practical function. It was time for a more scientific approach which drew its standards from the speech action and not from orthography.

Tilly's two main contributions to speech training were his zealous promotion of the International Phonetic Alphabet, called the IPA like the organization that developed it, and his use of the IPA to teach speakers prescriptive patterns based on the spoken rather than the written word. Speech texts in the United States that were written just after the turn of the century[14] contain few if any attempts at phonetic notation of any sort, which made for unwieldy transliterations to transmit the details of the spoken sounds to the reader of the book. But by the 1930s nearly all texts used phonetics. Much of that rapid change was due to Tilly.

---

[13]   See, for example, John R. Scott, *The Technic of the Speaking Voice* (Columbia, MO: published by the author, 1915), 50–53. Scott had been a protégé of Murdoch.

[14]   A good example is S. S. Curry's *Mind and Voice* (Boston: The Expression Company, 1910). Curry was one of the handful of eminent voice and acting teachers who made Boston the center of voice, speech, oratory, and acting training early in this century. Along with his School of Expression were the Leland Powers School, where Edith Warman (Skinner) studied with Margaret McLean, and Emerson College.

Elocutionists, even into the second decade of this century, rejected the use by speakers of syllabic consonants, such as [sʌdn̩] for "sudden," insisting instead on the intrusion of a vowel between the "b" and the "d" as in [sʌdɛn], with some stress on both syllables, because that corresponded most closely with the word as written. Tilly rightly regarded that practice as nonsense, and devoted his sole written article[15] to the subject of unstressed syllables and weak-form vowels. His insistence on weak-form vowels, the vowel sounds we produce in unstressed syllables, helped to shape a special place for phonetics in speech education, as a notation of spoken sound that was far more useful than the orthography of printed Roman letters.

WORLD-ENGLISH

There was another item on William Tilly's syllabus for his students, however, and it marked the dividing line between Tilly the language scientist and Tilly the passionate advocate. He believed fervently in the inherent superiority of a pattern of English pronunciation which he and his students termed "World English" or sometimes "World Standard English." His disciple Marguerite DeWitt in her writings portmanteaued it into "Euphonetics," while Margaret Prendergast McLean — and later Edith Warman Skinner — always termed it "Good American Speech."[16]

As initially defined by Tilly and those students who put his doctrines into print, World English was a speech pattern that very specifically did not derive from any regional dialect pattern in England or America, although it clearly bears some resemblance to the speech patterns that were spoken in a few areas of New England, and a very considerable resemblance, as we shall see, to the pattern in England which was becoming defined in the 1920s as "RP" or "Received Pronunciation."[17] World English, then, was a creation of speech teachers, and boldly labeled as a class-based accent: the speech of persons variously described as "educated," "cultivated," or "cultured"; the speech of persons who moved in rarified social or intellectual circles and of those who might aspire to do so. Margaret Prendergast McLean asked, "WHAT USAGE is the law and rule of speech?" and answered, "Linguistics scholars and historians have incontestably established the fact that it is the speech of the intelligent, cultivated classes — who have sorted, refined and polished the speech of the masses — which becomes the final law and rule."[18] Sophie Pray, who brought Tilly's teaching into the New York public school

---

15 William Tilly, "The Problem of Pronunciation," in *A Course of Study in Speech Training and Public Speaking for Secondary Schools*, A. Drummond, ed. (New York: 1925).

16 A term which, for obvious reasons, was never reduced to an acronym.

17 "Received" in the sense of "accepted" or "preferred."

18 *Good American Speech* (New York: E. P. Dutton, 1928), 55–56.

system, had a more mystical formulation for this key to upward social mobility: "Good speech signifies the possibility of readier spiritual integration with, and membership in, the cultured group in which most of us want to live as citizens." [19]

What is more, World English was considered by Tilly's followers to be an identifying pattern for cultured coequals among English speakers the world over, precisely because it was not actually spoken by any known regional dialect group. For Margaret McLean, this acted to counter the frequent resistance by American students to learning what — to their untutored ears — was a British accent:

> The author has never met an American who was not willing to accept the standard form of English speech as being the best form when the meaning and significance of 'standard' was clearly explained. When he fully understands that it is the international, world-wide form of cultured usage which he is advised to adopt he does so eagerly and wholeheartedly. It is the *mistaken* idea that he is being advised to adopt some other person's regional or national dialect that arouses his indignation, creates his stubborn prejudices, makes him deaf to reason and blind to truth and keeps him in the linguistic gutter. [20]

However, this concept was a slippery one as used by Tilly's followers. In other contexts it seemed more useful to acknowledge the ties of World English to England. Marguerite DeWitt described the Southern English RP as "practically the equivalent of . . . our own Word-Accepted Standard." [21] One possible reason was that while proponents of RP in England were also promoting it as a class-based accent, not a regional dialect, and while some of them — especially Daniel Jones and Walter Ripman — were in close contact with Tilly and his circle, the English were not making any attempt to assert that RP was influenced by any speech pattern beyond the shores of the sceptred isle. So those Americans who wanted to find common ground for their own "cultured" speech and England's RP needed to make the ideological voyage eastward.

THE PATTERN

World English and RP were different from one another in many details, but they shared important vowel and consonant sounds which, for Americans, were markers for an English accent. World English used the "broad A" or "ah" (phonetically [ɑ]) in many of the same words as RP, such as "pass,"

---

[19]   *Graded Objectives for Teaching Good American Speech* (New York: E. P. Dutton, 1934), 5.

[20]   *Good American Speech*, 77.

[21]   *Our Oral Word, As Social and Economic Factor* (New York: E. P. Dutton, 1928), 127. Clearly the Tilly followers had a friend at E. P. Dutton.

"dance," and "half," but not in the words that did not follow the usual spelling conventions governing "broad A" use, such as "banana," where the American "flat A" [æ] was employed. The RP lip-rounding as a substitution for the American "ah" on words like "hot" and "not" into the phonetic [ɒ][22] was also used, producing a short, open "aw." The first vowel sound in "current" or "worry" was pronounced with an "uh" [ʌ] and the American "short E" of "bet" [ɛ] was raised to the tenser RP [eᴛ]. However, unlike RP, there was little if any diphthongal slide from a mid or front vowel on the "long O" [oŭ]. Weak form vowels were, of course, always used in unstressed syllables.

World English did employ American stress patterns, so that words like "corollary" and "controversy" were always pronounced with a stress on the first syllable, not the second, as in the RP of the period. And World English did not share the English insistence on anglicising all French loanwords, so that "garage" phonetically was pronounced [gəˈɹɑːʒ] not [ˈgæɹɪdʒ].

The most important consonant change — and one defended with singular intensity by Tilly's students — was the elimination of all post-vocalic[23] "R" sounds in words like "car" or "hurt" (what is usually called "R-coloring.") Now, this already was a feature of most East Coast American dialects from Maine to the Carolinas, but its inclusion in a pattern which already had several key RP sounds made it seem even more like an English accent to most American speech teachers who were working in the primary and secondary school systems.

There are many phonetic examples of World English as it was defined by Tilly and his followers. The most prolific recorder of approved speakers of the approved accent was Marguerite DeWitt, who included in her books dozens of "euphonetigraphs," phonetic transcriptions of persons reading from the collected works of Marguerite DeWitt.

In the 1920s the battle over American speech standards was particularly fierce, mirroring a like controversy a decade earlier over RP in England.[24]

---

[22]   Generally, at that time, transcribed as [ɔ] or [ɔᴛ]. The "aw" of "law" or "bought" was transcribed as [ɔː].

[23]   Those occurring after a vowel in a syllable.

[24]   Robert Bridges, then Poet Laureate, had a bitter fight with Daniel Jones over the primacy of Northern Standard *versus* Southern Standard of RP. Bridges wrote, "We have only to recognize the superiority of the northern pronunciation and encourage it against London vulgarity, instead of assisting London jargon to overwhelm the older tradition, *which is quite as living*." From *A Tract On the Present State of English Pronunciation* rev. edn. (Oxford: Clarendon Press, 1913). This was mild in comparison to the Scottish Dr. J. Y. T. Greig, who called RP "the most slovenly of all the ways of speaking English...that silliest and dwabliest of all the English Dialects, P.S.S. [Public School Speech]." From "Breaking Priscian's Head" quoted in John Burbank, *What Is Standard English Speech?* (Tokyo: Shijo Shobo, 1934), 72.

The issue centered not on speech for the stage, but on speech as it should be taught in public schools, or used by speakers in public life. When Professor John Kenyon first published his influential textbook *American Pronunciation*[25] he came out firmly against the primacy of any one speech standard in the United States, especially one that was based on class and not on the way any actual Americans spoke:

> The author has tried to avoid dogmatism with regard to preferable pronunciations. No attempt is made to set up or even to imply a standard of correctness based on the usage of any part of America. He believes that the state of cultivated pronunciation does not warrant the more prescriptive method used by Professor Daniel Jones and Mr. Walter Ripman in standard pronunciation in England. Whether there is ever to be a single standard in America or not, the time is not ripe for it.[26]

Kenyon then announced that he would use as his model his own locality, the Western Reserve of Ohio.

The response by Tilly's disciples was instantaneous. Windsor P. Daggett, in the pages of *Theatre Arts Monthly*, belittled Professor Kenyon as "the boy from Ohio," in a lengthy article on speech standards.[27] And this was by no means the only barrage. By the time Kenyon wrote the preface to his fourth edition, a few years later, he was clearly on the defensive:

> Certain criticisms . . . make it necessary to affirm again that the author does not advocate this [General American] or any one type as the sole standard for America. To help students escape from such a point of view was one of the objects of this book. The author admits no rivalry in his admiration of that clear, intelligent pronunciation of the best types of Southern and Northern British, of Scottish standard English, of Eastern, Southern, and General American, which is the best index of personality, that most interesting of facts. But apparently this does

---

[25]   Ann Arbor: George Wahr, vi.

[26]   It should be noted that use of words such as "cultivated" were not the sole precinct of the Tilly group, as demonstrated by this quotation. The difference, though, is that with Tilly's followers, the class-based focus was an active and central part of their ideology, not merely an obeisance (as with Kenyon) to the biases of the age.

[27]   In *Theatre Arts Monthly*, September, 1925, 604. In the July 25, 1925 issue of *The Billboard*, the weekly show-business newspaper, Daggett devoted an entire column to a scathing critique of Kenyon. A few years before (September 23, 1922) in the same weekly, Daggett had been even rougher on a letter-writer named "Gene," a teacher who had criticized the Tilly standard on the post-vocalic "R"; Daggett asserted that Gene's ideas "ought to dismiss you from any position you hold as a teacher of English." Addressing Gene as "you poor nut," he suggested that "you ought to be handcuffed to Olga Petrova [a vaudeville performer with a dubious Russian accent] and forced to listen to her uvula-r for the rest of your life."

not satisfy such critics. One must not describe or even speak respect-fully of the traditional speech of ninety million people. Some of the astonishing specimens of neither fish nor flesh nor good red herring that greet the radio listener appear to be prophetic of what we may ex-pect from a continued fostering of the naïve assumption that only one form of speech can be correct.[28]

In this campaign the Tilly followers showed enormous solidarity and dedication. In 1933 a call had gone out in *Le Maître Phonétique*[29] (the jour-nal of the International Phonetic Association) for some descriptive tran-scriptions of American speech, and Tilly's students responded immediately. Everything in that journal is written phonetically, and for two successive is-sues the Tilly model was represented by, among others, Sophie Pray, Margaret McLean, Letitia Raubicheck, Alice Hermes, and Edith Warman (not yet Edith Warman Skinner). All the phonetic transcriptions from these several donors were absolutely identical in their speech patterns. Even their sometime ally Daniel Jones, then editor, had to demur:

> We have received numerous letters from American colleagues sug-gesting that the pronunciation shown in the specimens collected by Miss Pray represent a theoretical standard and not what is actually heard in any part of America. As an outside observer who endeavors to be impartial I would say that the pronunciation shown in those texts appears to me to be rare in America, though I have heard it from three American speakers, including one of the contributors to those texts.[30]

If even Daniel Jones observed that World English was "rare in America," it must have seemed obvious to Tilly's followers that their missionary efforts needed to be redoubled.

The war was waged for almost three decades — until the mid-1940s — in the pages of professional journals like *American Speech* and *The Quarterly Journal of Speech Education*. Marguerite DeWitt, Windsor P. Daggett, Letitia Raubicheck, Sophie Pray, and occasionally Margaret Prendergast McLean were the chief warriors for the Tilly group. C. K. Thomas of Cornell Uni-versity, John Kenyon of Hiram College, and phoneticians Giles Gray and Claude Merton Wise were frequent critics of World English. The renowned philologist George Philip Krapp, who like Tilly taught at Columbia, had been claimed through very selective quotation of his influential 1921 book *The English Language in America*[31] to be one of the Tilly camp, despite his hav-

---

28 *American Pronunciation* (4th edn.), vii–viii.

29 By Jaime De Angulo (January, 1933), 12.

30 September 1933, 19.

31 2 vols. (New York: Century Company). See also Krapp's earlier *The Pronunciation of Standard English in America* (Oxford University Press, American Branch, 1919).

ing coined the term "General American" to describe the accent pattern of the mid-west and western states, i.e., most of the country. But after the publication in 1924 of Marguerite DeWitt's *EuphonEnglish in America*, Krapp's apparently scathing rejection of the Tilly standards in a review in the *New York Tribune* caused the indefatigable DeWitt to devote an entire chapter in her next book[32] to answering him.

We know already that the level of invective on the Tilly side was high, and it was often matched by its critics. Gray and Wise condemned the Tilly followers for "fanaticism,"[33] and C. K. Thomas referred to them as a "cult."[34] When Thomas published the results of a survey of phoneticians and speech professors around the country which roundly rejected World English in *Quarterly Journal of Speech*,[35] Tillyite Letitia Raubicheck did a counter-poll for the same journal, confining it to New York City colleges and schools where World English was still taught by many instructors and adding Margaret McLean (who by this time had moved to California) to the list for good measure; the results[36] were predictable.

The accusations of cult status, while perhaps extreme,[37] were understandable, given the overwhelming zeal and determination of Tilly's students. World English for them was not an option, it was a mission. The very rigor of Tilly's system, no doubt deriving more from the pedagogy of German philology than from the British navy as DeWitt had speculated, set him apart from other teachers. A student who began study with William Tilly was embarking on a years-long apprenticeship; most of his students — including Edith Skinner — studied with him for at least five years, and some for over a decade, even after establishing active careers in the field themselves. Tilly demanded that students arrive at his classes with precisely six well-sharpened number two pencils at the ready, the better to transcribe the tiniest defining diacritic. The class dynamic was censorious and hierarchical: students sat, row on row, in the order of Tilly's estimation of their abil-

---

[32]   *Our Oral Word, As Social and Economic Factor* (New York: E. P. Dutton, 1928), 142–169. DeWitt cited Krapp's review as "Phonetics and People," *New York Tribune*, 7 June, 1926. However, I have been unable to find it in the issue cited, and 1926 is two years after the publication of *EuphonEnglish in America*. DeWitt tried to characterize Professor Krapp as playing both sides of the issue, but he had co-written a speech improvement textbook in 1922 with Anna I. Birmingham, *First Lessons in Speech Improvement* (New York: Charles Scribner's Sons) that favors the General American pattern, not World English.

[33]   *The Bases of Speech*, 199.

[34]   *QJS*, October 1945, 326.

[35]   *QJS*, October 1945, 318–327.

[36]   *QJS*, April 1946, 51–54.

[37]   Even allowing that the word "cult" is a much more ominous word today than in 1945.

ities. Margaret McLean always occupied the place of honor, "first chair" in the front row as Tilly's assistant, and the less favored labored to slowly work their way up to the front. Edith Skinner prized the fact that after several years, she found herself sitting next to McLean.

Other factors isolated Tilly and his followers from the rest of their colleagues, their use of narrow transcription, for example. Most speech teachers and linguists tried to keep their phonetic transcription as simple as possible so as not to confuse their students or burden them with unnecessary detail. But Tilly positively reveled in phonetic minutiae, with subscript diacritics depending down from other subscript diacritics in nearly every word, gently—compulsively—tweaking the sounds this way and that.

More idiosyncratic is the fact that none of this bounty was spent on truly descriptive transcriptions of the way people actually talked. While Tilly pioneered the use of nonsense dictation as a teaching tool, and phonetic transcription using foreign languages which the transcriber did not know, he always adhered to a rigid standard of pronunciation in any language, and his students' transcription of his phonetic patterns became almost ritualistic in their sameness; this had the effect of countering any potential advantages of narrow transcription. An examination of a page from Edith Skinner's notebooks while she was studying with Tilly shows that ostensibly descriptive details, such as onset of vocalization in initial D's, ossify into rules which must be repeated every time the sound is transcribed.[38] Little wonder that the valuable *A History of Speech Education in America* describes Tilly's "cumbrous diacritics" as "symbols of orthodoxy rather than tools of fine distinction."[39]

Tilly and his students also used a non-connected cursive phonetic script in their transcription, even though most other phoneticians had started to use printed symbols exclusively, and some of Tilly's symbols were quite unlike those being used by others in the field, so the sense of detachment from the mainstream of phonetic study was enhanced by the very mechanics of the work.

LEADING THE WAY

William Tilly, in spite of—or perhaps because of—his stern teaching methods and grudging approbation, exerted an almost mystical hold on his students, who felt that he was showing them something truly unique and irreplaceable, a standard of language use that they could carry to the rest of the nation. Windsor P. Daggett gives a quaint, if condescending, picture of Tilly's students during his prime in America:

---

[38] My deep appreciation to Timothy Monich for giving me access to Skinner's notes.

[39] Karl Wallace et al. eds. (New York: Appleton-Century-Crofts, 1954), 338.

When William Tilly steps out of his phonetic classroom at Columbia University to go a-visiting he puts on his prettiest coat and a wing collar, brushes his fatherly locks into a boyish combback, and looks like a financier on Fifth Avenue for Easter parade. He carries in his head such a bankful of certified checks on the sound of "r" that he defies anyone to look him out of countenance or to call him a fabricator. All the school teachers follow after Tilly when he goes a-visiting, and when he has been announced to speak on the letter "r" the auditorium of Hunter College isn't large enough to hold the schoolmarms who follow their Pied Piper into the mountain of "Silent Letters." . . . Tilly told his audience, mostly women, that he was not sorry that there were only three men in sight. If the women take hold of this question we shall have nothing to fear in the progress of cultured speech. Tilly gave several readings of English "as it should be spoken." There was no interruption until the janitor shouted "Six o'clock!" The teachers swear by Tilly, and they are going to knock the "r" out of New "York" and several other places.[40]

The book dedications to Tilly show a similar respect, indeed an awe. Marguerite DeWitt acknowledged "Professor William Tilly, than whom there are no other world-scholars who may fairly claim to have done more to promote and develop the practical application of Phonetics and especially Euphonetics."[41]

Margaret Prendergast McLean's acknowledgement was even more reverent:

> I should not presume to undertake this task if I had not had the guidance of Professor William Tilly of Columbia University, with whom I have had the privilege of working for the past five years, and to whom I am indebted for my knowledge of the science of phonetics and its application to spoken English, and other languages. All of the charts, tables, terminology, and general methods of procedure used in the text have been given to me by Professor Tilly, either directly or indirectly.
>
> I most gratefully acknowledge my indebtedness to him for these and countless other favors; for his great courtesy and kindness; for his patient and constant help and encouragement; and for the inspiration which his wide vision, high culture, and noble ideals have given, and will continue to give me. Like Plato's cave men, I was groping in the dark and he showed me the light.[42]

When Tilly passed away, his grieving students formed the William Tilly Phonetic Association. Their Resolutions, adopted only two weeks after his

---

[40]   *The Billboard* (May 5, 1923), 39, 43.

[41]   *EuphonEnglish in America*, 158.

[42]   *Good American Speech* (New York: E. P. Dutton, 1928), vii.

death, sum up their attitude toward their mentor better than any interpretation. This is its summation, in part:

> The voice of a Master of the Spoken Word has been silenced in death, the stout heart of a leader has been stilled in its labors. Those who knew William Tilly as a teacher of teachers, realize the great loss the schools have suffered in the passing of one who had the gift of kindling ardor, of calling forth devotion to a worthy cause, of infusing courage into his followers to persevere in the face of difficulties and opposition...
>
> In his effort to achieve this splendid goal, he received the accolade of greatness — misunderstanding, opposition and, at times, hostility. These, however, did not daunt his sturdy spirit but engendered a loftier consecration, a more exalted enthusiasm.
>
> His work is done; his death ends an epoch. His devoted followers across the chasm of separation salute his gentle spirit and rededicate themselves to the unfinished task of training the young to the use of good oral English. William Tilly, though dead, speaks to ears receptive to his message:
>
> "Be Strong!
>> *It matters not how hard the battle goes, the day how long,*
>> *Faint not, fight on! Tomorrow comes the song.*"[43]

A call to arms: the thing that further separated the Tilly group from its colleagues. For not only did they possess an ideal and a hero, they also had an enemy.

THE CAUSE

Margaret Prendergast McLean once remarked to fellow voice teacher Robert Parks that a reasonable prediction for American speech was that everyone would be using the "schwa" (a very relaxed, neutral "uh" sound, phonetically [ə]) as their only vowel in a few years.[44] This was probably a somewhat facetious comment, but it describes a vision of a kind of linguistic entropy afflicting verbal discourse in this country that was at the core of the Tilly rhetoric. Without that thin brave line of speech teachers preserving the standards of articulation, American speech would soon deteriorate into one dull groan through articulators indisposed to, or incapable of, any movement at all. (Of course this dire prediction did not come to pass. Nor will it: speech within any dialect group finds the level of sound differentia-

---

[43]   "Resolutions Adopted By The William Tilly Association, October 11, 1935, New York. Columbiana Collection, Columbia University Library.

[44]   In conversation, 1989. For many years Parks was the voice instructor at Carnegie-Mellon (formerly Carnegie Tech), the same training program where Edith Skinner spent most of her career as speech teacher.

tion that effectively serves communication within that group, but no more than that. There is no need to produce sound differentiations that do not contribute to improved comprehension by the listener.)

As Marguerite DeWitt's book title *EuphonEnglish* suggests, the pattern espoused by Tilly was supposed to represent not only clarity, but also euphony. Throughout the writings of the group, it was asserted again and again that these sounds were quite literally more beautiful than the lesser regional dialects and foreign accents they were meant to supplant. Much of this ideology came from their prime source for English language history, Henry Cecil Wyld, whose campaign on behalf of RP in England had been unceasing. Wyld was given to such pronouncements as "We must consider that a dialect which has no [ā][45] is under a grave disability as a sonorous form of speech . . . This sound [æ] is neither as sonorous nor as beautiful as [ā]."[46]

So the Tilly followers were grappling with the forces of verbal ugliness, represented by every form of speech that was not this particular ornate artifice of speech teachers — those forms of speech, in short, which almost all Americans actually spoke.

Within only a few miles' radius from Columbia University, the embattled speech teachers could find millions of people whose speech showed the influences of these malign forces: the hordes of foreign-born who had immigrated in recent decades, the African-Americans who were moving more and more into the cities of the north, the many other Americans who rejected the "fahncy speech"[47] of World English in the street and on the stage for patriotic reasons and who felt — like H. L. Mencken — the growing identity of an "American language," the growing numbers of American socialists and communists who rejected any class-based standard of speech and harkened back instead to Thorstein Veblen's dictum that "great purity of speech is presumptive evidence of several successive lives spent in other than vulgarly useful occupations."[48]

Tilly's followers, in striking back, did not stop at ridiculing the sounds of a polyglot United States; they attacked the people who spoke them also. "Ignorance may be condoned," Sophie Pray warned, "lack of dexterity may be excused, but faulty speech and foreign accent are indelible signs of social inferiority."[49] Marguerite DeWitt went further, devoting a section of *Euphon-*

---

[45]   In modern phonetics [ɑ], the "Broad A."

[46]   "The Best English: A Claim for the Superiority of Received Standard English." In *Proper English?* ed. Tony Crowley (London: Routledge, 1991), 213.

[47]   Especially derisive because English RP doesn't use the "Broad A" in pronouncing "fancy."

[48]   *The Theory of the Leisure Class* (New York: MacMillan, 1899), 399.

[49]   *Graded Objectives,* 6.

English to an urgent plea for a more restrictive immigration policy. This is the ideology of World English stripped of the euphemisms that often surrounded it:

> Because a nation may have passed through an obligatory stage of increase from without it is not bound, morally or otherwise, to a life-long policy of non–exclusion. Arriving at a certain stage of progress, prosperity, international recognition and influence and almost unlimited future opportunity makes it a national danger to follow an unrestricted and, above all, non-selective immigration policy.... Neither for these nor any other reasons can a nation afford to de–racialize its nucleal self, and no nation that has developed a moderate race-consciousness will tend toward, or persist in tending toward, an eventually suicidal policy...
>
> The innumerable poverty-stricken, unfortunate, but self-respecting, law-abiding foreigners who came to our shores in past generations with a genuine desire to become an integral part of our national existence — who, however lowly, came here with a background of ideals — were an entirely different proposition from THE FAR TOO UN-LIMITED INFLUX OF THOSE ALIENS[50] who are in great part racially opposed to us, or those who are but the unlamented dregs of Europe, relieving the nations that they desert, and who vitally injure whatever nation they descend upon.
>
> To squander national vitality and money on that which will but cause biological disintegration of a nation is not philanthropy; to infuse into a body politic blood that destroys the racial blood of a nation is not the deed of a rational healer; to foster the growth of parasites on a national tree of education and knowledge is not the work of an advanced sociologist.[51]

Overt racism and ethnocentric bias were hardly unknown in American academic writing of the 1920s, and were fairly common before then; but the important point is that DeWitt's view is crucial to the class basis of World English, not merely a peripheral issue. As an American, living in a country that made much of denying the existence of classes (at least on a formal cultural basis), she was arguing on behalf of a social elite: one founded not on noble birth, but on a presumed nobility of thought, ideal, and purpose, as defined by predictable standards and in predictable terms — cultured, cultivated, and so on. Of course, from the standpoint of social science (actually, from any informed perspective) the imposition through incessant drill of a homogeneous accent contrived by speech teachers and actually spoken by no one would have precisely the opposite effect of sucking any cultural identity out of verbal discourse. World English is, in a very real sense, a consciously decultured accent.

---

[50]   Emphasis by the author.

[51]   35–36.

Certainly too, DeWitt's opinions on the subject of race are not in themselves proof that others in the Tilly circle thought precisely as she did, but
none of her friends and colleagues ever rejected these views in writing. To
the contrary, every major writer in the group — Tilly himself, Daggett,
Raubicheck, Pray, and McLean — either praised *EuphonEnglish* in print, or
quoted approvingly from it, or both.

As America moved through the Great Depression, the Tillyite ideal of a
smooth upward social mobility borne on the wings of World English for
those immigrants possessed of the proper values and the proper skin color
must have seemed a cruel joke, as millions of workers became unemployed
and even some people with the most refined accents explored their own
downward mobility from the windows of buildings. By the time Tilly died,
just short of his seventy-fifth birthday on September 29, 1935,[52] his work had
been rejected by practically all American speech teachers, leaving the field —
in prescriptive speech education — to the "General American" (or Inland
Northern) of John S. Kenyon and George Philip Krapp. His fellow phoneticians had rejected his system also. The hastily formed William Tilly
Phonetic Association seems to have expired sometime in the early 1940s, and
it was only in the New York City Schools that World English was still taught
by a few stalwart Tilly followers for a few more years. By 1950 William
Tilly's influence on the speech patterns of Americans had finally ended.

Almost.

A LIFE IN THE THEATRE

At the beginning of the twentieth century, American actors in classical
plays all spoke with English accents, which were still considered the norm of
"elevated" diction. In *The American Language* H. L. Mencken recalled "There
was a time when all American actors of any pretensions employed a dialect
that was a heavy imitation of the dialect of the West End actors of London.
It was taught in all the American dramatic schools, and at the beginning of
the present century it was so prevalent on the American stage that a flat *a* had
a melodramatic effect almost equal to that of *damn*."[53] So the application of
World English to the stage was not a difficult task, even when World English was being rejected as a pattern for the American populace at large.

The aesthetics of classical stage performance at the time further enabled
World English to flourish onstage while it languished within the audience.
Most people considered that characters in classical plays were truly larger
than life, and that the poetic language which emerged from the mouths of

---

[52]   According to Margaret McLean, in a letter to Edith Skinner, his last words were to
       tell Sophie Pray to shut up. Conversation with Timothy Monich, 1991.

[53]   4th edition (New York: Alfred A. Knopf, 1936), 331.

such characters needed to be expressed in an idealized "elevated" diction; the standards for real people were not the standards for Romeo or Juliet. Charles Henry Woolbert, a professor at the University of Illinois, decried the use of "stage speech" in real life, but added that "the stage is irrevocably tied down to the necessity of being different from everyday life. Everything that appears on the stage is in some way an exaggeration of the life it portrays: lights, costumes, makeup, stage sets, action, dialog, and pronunciation...Everything on the stage is illusion, including pronunciation."[54] This perception meant that even the most vigorous opponents of the Tilly pattern in real life reserved their opposition when it came to matters of stage speech.

While Tilly himself had no interest in the theatre, his direct influence on stage diction began only a few years after his arrival in America, through the efforts of a young student of his, Windsor P. Daggett. In 1921 Daggett began to write a lengthy column titled "The Spoken Word" in every weekly issue of *The Billboard*. Today *Billboard* covers the music industry almost exclusively, but in Daggett's day it was a formidable national tabloid for the entire entertainment industry: theatre, film, records, radio (in its infancy), vaudeville (nearing its dotage), opera, operetta, minstrel shows, the circus, carnivals, magic shows. For six years — through 1926 — Daggett was able to write at length on the voice and speech work of the stars of Broadway, and his columns, taken together, are an impressive, detailed, and often very perceptive record of the period. The enterprising Daggett, who had more or less cornered the New York market in theatre speech improvement, ran his own speech school for clients onstage and off, and founded Spoken Word Records, a label that lasted for some years; by the mid-twenties Daggett could offer a complete course in World English on records, as well as dramatic recitations by well-known actors of whom Daggett approved.

As we have already seen, Daggett had his biases. He vigorously disliked the acting of Alfred Lunt, because of Lunt's overly conversational vocal delivery on stage and his slurred consonants.[55] Daggett's ideal classical actor at the time was Walter Hampden, who had his own company and produced Shakespeare regularly, not to mention introducing *Cyrano de Bergerac* to American audiences in 1923. Daggett made extensive phonograph recordings of Hampden both in Shakespearean roles and in modern plays (e.g., Ibsen). But Hampden, though an American, spoke with a marked English accent. Like many talented American actors, Hampden first appeared onstage in England, working first with Frank Benson's repertory company, and later at the Adelphi Theatre in London. Only when his reputation was es-

---

[54]   In a paper delivered at the Annual Convention of the National Association of Teachers of Speech, New York City, December 29, 1925.

[55]   For example, in *The Billboard* of February 13, 1926, Daggett speaks of Lunt's being "exceedingly negligent of words." 37.

tablished did he return to the United States in 1907.[56] Once again, for Daggett, World English and RP would seem to be conflated into essentially the same pattern.

Daggett's column was the perfect place for him to campaign on behalf of World English, and to fulminate against its foes. His battle cry, extracted from a letter to him by Harvard philologist C. H. Grandgent, was "The best speech in America is heard on the stage," and it was taken up by other Tilly followers as well.[57] The stage, then, was to serve as a model for the speech of Americans generally. And to those who opposed World English, Daggett's limitless store of contempt was at the ready:

> During the holidays I dropped into a meeting of the Modern Language Association in session at Columbia University. I didn't stay very long and I didn't hear very much, but what I heard was enough.
>
> Up stands a stalwart educator, a Ph.D., no doubt, and a professor of influence in some parts of the country. There was a militant strength in his "inverted r-sounds" on which his tongue curled back with sufficient energy to crack a nut. "We ar-err the people who know," he said. "but we ar-err being ignor-err-d. We must inter- err-fer-err with the new speech depar-err-tments in our-err schools and their-err ar-err-tificial standar-err-ds of cultur-err. We must save Amer-err-ican speech from the ar-err-tificial. We ar-err the exper-err-ts and ar-err-biter-errs of the spoken wor-err-d."
>
> God save the mark! [58]

"God save the mark," indeed. When it came to the defense of World English, Hotspur (who uses this expletive in Shakespeare's *Henry IV, Part One*) was not a bad exemplar for Daggett's intemperance, though not a likely model for his speech.[59]

But given these biases, Daggett had an acute sense of how speech issues fit into the rest of the acting process. He was even capable of criticizing his own: in 1925 he reviewed Margaret Prendergast McLean's platform reading from *Les Miserables*, and while—not surprisingly—he praised her "beautiful voice and perfect diction," he also faulted her for staying "outside" the material she was reading, and of being overly conscious of form: "She is not of it and with it in that intimate, sensitive participation which gives the final spark of universal experience and contact with the spiritual foundations of life." [60]

---

[56]   See *The Oxford Companion to the Theatre* (Phyllis Hartnoll, ed. 4th edn.), 368.

[57]   Especially Marguerite DeWitt.

[58]   *The Billboard*, January 17, 1925, 41.

[59]   Since Hotspur is often played as having a speech impediment.

[60]   *The Billboard*, May 9, 1925, 41.

Daggett continued to write about World English in speech periodicals and in *Theatre Arts Monthly* for several years, even after "The Spoken Word" was dropped from *The Billboard* in late 1926.

MCLEAN AND SKINNER

Margaret Prendergast McLean was Tilly's assistant for a decade, and by the late 1920s was one of the most influential speech teachers for actors on the east coast. She was Head of the Department of English Diction at the prestigious Leland Powers School in Boston, and was also teaching at Richard Boleslavsky's American Laboratory Theatre in New York. Her textbook *Good American Speech* was published in 1928, and sold widely.

Edith Warman (later Edith Warman Skinner) was McLean's star pupil at the Powers School, and they remained close lifelong friends. When Skinner came to New York City, she began immediately to study with William Tilly; her notebooks from these classes suggest that she began working with Tilly in 1928 or 1929, and continued with him for at least five years.

Skinner had trained as an actress at the Powers School, so it was only natural that her interest in speech training focused on its theatrical application. McLean had brought Skinner in to work with her at the American Laboratory Theatre, and soon after, Skinner became the speech instructor at Carnegie Tech's theatre training program. At Carnegie, Skinner gradually established her reputation as the most eminent theatre speech trainer in America, not only because of the many well-known actors she worked with over the years, but also because of the many speech teachers she trained. Shortly before her retirement from Carnegie, Skinner was brought in by John Houseman to be a founding member of the faculty in the new theatre program at the Juilliard School; here Skinner trained a whole new generation of American classical actors.

In a way, it is arguable that McLean exerted an even greater influence on Skinner's formulation of World English (now called Good American Speech) than did Tilly. Good American Speech followed Tilly closely in most respects, but had a few differences. The most important of these was the use of the "intermediate A" [a] in place of the "Broad A" [ɑ] as used in English RP, in the so-called "ask-list" of words—grass, path, half, past, command, and the like. This change mediated the vowel sounds closer to the General American pronunciation, although to most American ears it still sounded English. McLean followed Tilly's treatment of the "short E" sound in words like "bet" or "tell" (in General American [ɛ]) representing it phonetically as a closed, linguistically tense sound [eˑ] much like the English pronunciation. Skinner, perhaps to simplify, took the change even further,[61] using the unlowered form [e], which has the phonetic disadvantage of being indistinguishable from the French E *accent aigu* of words like "été."

There was a third Tilly follower who had a major influence on speech for the stage. Alice Hermes taught for many years at the HB Studio in New York City, and there trained a huge number of actors and several noted speech teachers.

After the diction doldrums of the 1950s, marked by the ascendency of "method" acting on stage and in film, Skinner's influence on American speech training revived with the growth of the regional theatre movement in the 1960s. There was a sudden demand for actors with skills in the classical repertoire. Regional theatres became sites for professional training, and simultaneously the number of M.F.A. acting training programs at universities began to multiply. Many of the founders of regional theatres were Carnegie graduates[62] and most of the speech instructors in the training programs were Skinner students.

But Skinner was not the only theatre speech teacher in America, and not all American speech teachers used the World English model. Why did Skinner's approach prevail? At least part of the answer lies in Skinner's embrace of the Tilly pedagogy in her own teaching. Like Tilly, Skinner ruled her classes with the proverbial rod of iron. Like Tilly, she seated students in order of their skills in Good American Speech, and progression to the front of the class became a sought-after goal. Like Tilly she favored narrow, rather than broad, phonetic transcription. Like Tilly, she used phonetics primarily as a tool to inculcate Good American Speech, not as a means of defining sound distinction in itself. Like Tilly she relied heavily on incessant drill exercises. Like Tilly, she used an unconnected cursive phonetic transcription, with a strong emphasis on writing the symbols beautifully. Like Tilly, she insisted on Good American Speech as a speech pattern for life as much as for art.

And like Tilly, Edith Skinner imparted a sense of mission to her students. Skinner made it clear that she was engaging in a long struggle to mold the cacophony of her students' regional accents into the euphony of Good American Speech. Gaining her approbation was not easy for her students, and once won, it was all the more cherished. The lengthy agony of learning Good American Speech was something very akin to a conversion process for many Skinner students who went on to teach speech, having entered Carnegie (or

---

[61]   In her book *Speak With Distinction*. This most influential textbook, which grew out of Skinner's classroom materials at Carnegie Tech, was first put out in book form in the early 1940s. *Speak With Distinction* is currently available in a considerably revised version edited by Lilene Mansell, with new material by Mansell and Timothy Monich (New York: Applause, 1990).

[62]   Ellis Rabb at APA Phoenix, and William Ball at the American Conservatory Theatre are just two examples.

Juilliard) with their regional accents betraying their cultural deprivation, and leaving with the audible imprint of cultural achievement.

Of course, it didn't always work. Actor Charles Grodin recalled:

> Edith Skinner, a tall, thin, austere woman with glasses, who was one of the foremost teachers and authorities on "good American speech" came over from Carnegie Tech. Her dedication to having everyone master "good American speech" was as intense as that of a scientist trying to rid the world of a dread disease, which was how she saw "bad American speech" — something from which I evidently suffered in abundance. "Good American speech" to me, on the other hand, sounded like an English accent. Many of Carnegie Tech's drama majors graduated sounding like Englishmen, which didn't lead to a heck of a lot of work in America. I would say a few sentences for Miss Skinner, and she would write furiously, page after page of notes of criticism for just my few sentences of "bad American speech." Finally, she said, "How can you ever expect people to pay money to see you as an actor, given how you speak? Nobody should speak like that; it's just not good American speech, it's terrible." [63]

Late in her career Skinner, by all accounts, moderated her condemnation of regionalisms, although in an instructional videotape made in her last years she still described as "atrocious" the pronunciation of "horrible" as [hɔɚˈləbḷ].[64]

Similarly, many Skinner-trained teachers today have quietly backed away from use of the "Intermediate A" in the "Ask-list," or the use of [ɒ] in words like "not" or "hot," despite their veneration for their great teacher. Some will even allow a little "R-coloring" to hang on the ends of appropriate diphthongs. But in this general retreat much of the World English pedagogy still remains. I hear Skinner teachers today still requiring that their students use Good American Speech in their daily lives as well as on stage; I hear Skinner teachers still deriding the "Broad A" as an intrinsically ugly sound when used in place of the [ɔ] in words like "caught" or "fall," however sonorous Henry Cecil Wyld (or William Tilly) might have thought it in other contexts; I hear Skinner teachers recoil from the intrinsic ugliness of the raised nasalized "Short A" [æ̃ᵻ], an assessment that might offend the speaker of classical French. Most Skinner teachers still use unconnected cursive phonetic symbols and Tilly's application of vowel symbols — both rejected by linguists for over fifty years. Most of them still rely on lengthy rote word drill as the primary teaching technique to effect sound change in actors' speech.

---

[63]   *It would Be So Nice If You Weren't Here* (New York: William Morrow, 1989), 38–39.

[64]   "Seven Points of Good Speech in Classic Plays" (Mill Valley, CA: Performance Skills).

WORLD ENGLISH TODAY

McLean and Skinner labeled it "Good American Speech." Speech it is, most certainly, and for better or worse it has shaped generations of American actors. But its definition as "Good" is mired in a self-serving and archaic notion of Euphony, and in a model of class, ethnic, and racial hierarchy that is irrelevant to the acting of classical texts and repellent to the sensibilities of most theatre artists.

Its pedigree as "American" has already been shown to be open to serious question, especially since its earliest advocates bragged that its chief quality was that no Americans actually spoke it unless educated to do so, thus marking it as a badge of a self-defined cultural elite. But neither does one like to speak with an accent from nowhere, however "cultured." So a number of other terms for this pattern developed: Stage Standard, Stage Diction, etc., limiting its *locus* to the magic area inhabited by the player; in the larger world the most common term was the geographic oddity "Mid-Atlantic"[65] (the ocean, not the states), which had, at least, the advantage of paying obeisance to the magnetism of those English vowel sounds that so captivated Tilly and his followers.

Even Edith Skinner and Alice Hermes[66] seemed occasionally to confuse Good American Speech with the English Received Pronunciation (RP). When Skinner was guest-teaching at the American Conservatory Theatre in the 1970s, a young voice teaching colleague attended the classes, hoping to learn a good American accent. But every time that she spoke a sentence, Skinner told her that her sounds were perfect Good American Speech. Raised in Ireland and trained at London's Central School of Speech and Drama, Catherine Fitzmaurice was slightly puzzled by this praise.[67]

What, then, should be the fate of this World English speech training, this pattern codified early in this century and passed down, virtually unaltered, to the American actors of today through a combination of zealous instruction, collective acquiescence, and sheer happenstance? Unquestionably, actors trained in this pattern have the ability to perform complex classical

---

[65] And its more travel-conscious companion "Transatlantic." See Robert Hobbs, *Teach Yourself Transatlantic* [Palo Alto: Mayfield, 1986). Hobbs's recommended speech pattern, it should be noted, differs somewhat from Good American Speech/World English.

[66] While Hermes herself provided no direct evidence of this, I recall vividly sitting in a class conducted by one of her protegées, in which the teacher informed a young Puerto Rican actress with a strong "Nuyorican" accent, that if she worked really hard she might be able to "sound like Greer Garson." Aside from the fact that Garson's illustrious film career peaked in the late 1940s, the statement also glosses over the reality that Garson, Irish-born, always sounded English in her films.

[67] In conversation, 1992.

text with denotative clarity and with an often admirable muscularity of articulation. But a price is paid.

Actors using this pattern usually sound somewhat British but not fully so. The effect is to place them (if not in the mid-Atlantic) into a kind of nether-world of Theatre Speech which is often defended as being "neutral" but which is actually merely anonymous. It is reasonable to assert that a particular regional American accent (West Texas, let's say) might clash with a specific Shakespearean production concept. But the same could be said of any specific dialect, whether English or American, including RP. Certainly there are ways to provide a more general American accent that does not limit locale obtrusively, but which yet provides some linguistic tie to the American audience that is being addressed. There might be some distraction — in a given production — in Hamlet sounding like he was from St. Louis, but it seems reasonable to expect that he might just speak with a dialect pattern indigenous to planet Earth.

Even more problematic is the normative practice of combining beginning instruction in phonetics with instruction in World English, as though the former exists only as a vehicle for conveying the latter. The imposition of a prescriptive pattern at the start of phonetics instruction means that the student is not focusing on identifying sound change (and registering it as a physical action), but instead is focusing on working her or his way into that required pattern. As a result, training in World English necessitates lengthy repetitive rote drill in class or in tutorial. (Or, as we have noted, inclusion in daily life.) Which means in turn that mastering World English becomes very time-consuming and difficult for most young actors — a self-fulfilling prophecy by its instructors, since the students are required to produce a patterned "product" before they have been allowed to learn the perceptual and articulatory skills necessary for them to do so easily. And the end result is that young American actors often come out of such training regimens burdened with a self-conscious uniformity of speech sounds, having lost whatever instinct they may have had to find the unique voice of the characters they are playing, carefully measuring out their vocal passion lest it sully the perfection of their Good American Speech.

William Tilly was a visionary and a reformer. Margaret Prendergast McLean, Alice Hermes, and — especially — Edith Skinner, were all exceptional teachers who trained many noted actors whose artistry confutes all of the dire assessments listed above. And yet ... the past of World English still pervades the present of Good American Speech. Cut off from the forces that might have naturally changed it, reified in its isolation as the only true standard for theatre speech improvement, this strange artifact of the Edwardian Era still exists, little-changed, as we approach the year 2000.

Speech training for American actors whose careers will take them into the next millennium requires a radically new formulation if speech training is to exist at all. And in doing so, if only to approach the entire issue afresh, we must let go of our nostalgic grasp on the entire structure that called itself World English or Good American Speech: let go of its pattern of sounds, let go of its formulation of phonetics, let go of its instructional approach, let go of the vestiges of its ideology. Most poignantly perhaps, we will have to turn away from those last putative native speakers of "Mid-Atlantic," huddled together in their dinghy bobbing in the swells somewhere off the Azores, calling for help — faintly, but very very clearly.

WHAT THEN?

Why then teach speech to actors at all?

In the 1960s and 1970s, there developed a strong reaction among many voice teachers and actors against the rigidity of the Good American Speech training; these trainers and actors took the opposite extreme, asserting that all speech training for actors has a negative effect, and should perhaps be abolished. There are two main thrusts to the argument. The first is that all prescriptive patterning of articulation inevitably leads to stiff and homogeneous speech production. The second is that training an actor's own speech into a different pattern robs that actor of linguistic heritage and racial or ethnic identity.

Both points were based on valid observation and experience, and both can be true in individual cases. The question really is whether either one must be true all the time, and the answer is no. For decades the Good American Speech pattern was the only game around, and set — for good or ill — the standards for phonetic rigor and speech pedagogy for actors.[68] So a young actor from an ethnic or racial minority sitting week after week in classes that try to drill into her or him the habits of "good" speech, with the further injunction that one take this "good" speech into one's daily life, might very well consider that any prescriptive patterning of speech is invasive of one's cultural essence. Were we to think so, though, we would have to believe also that learning any new dialect, or adopting a character voice for a role, or for that matter going through the complete physical, vocal, and instinctual alterations that any actor has to do to play any role at all would serve to rob the actor of cultural identity. Acting is, after all, largely about becoming someone else, albeit through the vehicle of one's own personality and awareness. Learning a new dance step, or remembering one's blocking on stage, or hitting one's marks in film, or picking up a cue, or coping fluently with complex and archaic sentence structure in classical text, are all prescriptive requirements,

---

[68] Robert Barton and Rocco Dal Vera, in their useful book *Voice: Onstage and Off* (Fort Worth: Harcourt Brace College Publishers, 1995), insist that "no other system can take the boy from the 'hood' and make him the prince in his palace like [Skinner's] can . . . This work can achieve levels of of speech ability simply not available . . ." 285.

and actors learn to meet them every day without losing their spontaneity or their sense of personal identity. What that student might really have been objecting to is the repetitive ideology that one speech pattern is "good" and all other speech patterns therefore less so, and the inculcation of this ideology through the use of lengthy rote drill on discrete sound change, which increases self-consciousness about the form of articulation separated wholly from its content and the physicality of its production.

Ideology and pedagogy are also the real culprits that gave rise to the first part of the argument. It was observed that many actors who came through the Good American Speech regimen not only spoke almost exactly the same as one another, they also seemed less available to verbal impulse, cut off from the immediate passionate verbal response because everything seemed filtered through the requirement to observe a particular form. On the contrary, it was asserted, if an actor could simply make the articulators available to impulse through release of inhibitory tensions, and then think the text clearly, specifically, and passionately, then sloppiness of articulation would disappear.

There is great truth in this insight. But like many great truths it carries with it a handy portable pitfall. To suggest, as Louis Colaianni does, that a "limiting regional accent is merely the by-product of patterns of tension frozen into the vocal tract"[69] is to suggest that all American regional dialects would be released magically if only those residual tensions could be released. But released into what? Lurking within this generous pronouncement is the same hierarchical view of speech clarity that reformers like Colaianni would seek to supplant. If a person has grown up speaking a dialect that habitually eliminates a consonant from a consonant cluster,[70] for example, will freedom of articulation plus intensity of thought actually cause that hitherto unused consonant to magically reappear, without the intervention of any prescriptive model? Is there some strange shared "deep dialect" hidden within all of us to which we all aspire? If so, then Tilly had a powerful argument.

Every dialect has its own complex set of muscular tensions (and relaxations too), but none of them are inhibitory to communication within the dialect group (or they would already have been modified), and releasing these held tensions will not in itself usually increase communication with dialect groups outside. Instead there needs to be an active model for the new muscular action that forms any new dialect or accent, and if it does not come from somewhere deep in our collective psyche, it then will have to come from careful listening to native speakers or instructors, combined with the skill to match the new articulatory pattern, and the ability to

---

[69]   In *The Joy of Phonetics and Accents* (New York: Drama Book Publishers, 1994), 57. Colaianni's book is otherwise excellent.

[70]   An example would be saying mus' instead of must.

hear — and feel — sound change. Prescriptive (and even proscriptive) training of a physical action does not in itself cause a lessening of spontaneity, as long as an actor does the preparatory work of mastering these skills of action before the prescriptive pattern is introduced, and as long as rote drill is minimized. Relaxation of unneeded tension is a crucial part of this preparation, but it is not responsible for the actively patterned sound change.

FOR THE FUTURE

It is a shared assumption of all speech teaching, and most language instruction as well, that if a speaker uses more of the available linguistic elements in a word, the word will be more readily understandable to all persons who speak the language, regardless of their accent. With this in mind, it becomes obvious that a model for such linguistic detail would be highly useful to the actor of classic texts, where the audience must be able easily to understand dialogue with archaic words or modern words with archaic meanings, as well as a much more complex sentence structure than we find in contemporary conversation.

Based on our awareness of what speech training for actors has been in the past, we can now look to what speech training might consist of in the future. I can suggest at least some general guidelines for a program on a two- to three-year arc of training.

1. *The ability to physically experience and isolate sound change in speech must precede learning any prescriptive pattern.* If an actor learns the physical skills of speech production, if s/he gains flexibility of articulation combined with muscularity of action, and if that actor can learn to perceive subtle gradations of sound change and feel where these are focused in the vocal tract and in the rest of the body, then the process of learning a "detail model" or the prescriptive pattern of any accent will become very easy and take a relatively short period of instruction, thus obviating the need for lengthy rote drill on the "correct" pronunciation of words and sentences. Drill, to the degree that it needs to take place, should be focused on the muscular isolation of specific sounds.

2. *Phonetic training should be descriptive before it is prescriptive.* Actors proceed very quickly if they learn acuity of perception through hearing what makes a speech pattern unique. The ability to notate what one is actually hearing is the basic objective skill for all dialect acquisition. Reliance on the unstable crutch of "illustrative words" to teach individual sounds, while perhaps unavoidable altogether, can easily be minimized.

3. *Phonetic training should include all the sounds of the world's languages, not just the ones used in a single form of American English.* Most of these speech sounds outside the repertoire of American English have direct applica-

tion in acquiring dialects or foreign accents, and even those sounds that do not will still provide a strong physical awareness of the variety of sounds possible in the production of human language.

4. *Actors should learn Narrow[71] Phonetic Transcription.* Broad transcription is appropriate for most language-learning, but actors need to learn dialects and accents in much greater detail.[72]

5. *Actors should learn phonetic printing, not phonetic script.* Printing is the standard in all other practical applications of phonetics.

6. *The Detail Model.* This is a model, not a mandate; one possible formulation of an American accent for use in speaking situations where listener comprehension of unfamiliar vocabulary or syntax is more demanding than in normal conversation. Actors may use all of it, or part of it, or none of it, depending on the speech requirements of the individual dramatic character. It does not need to be held together as one structured sound pattern, but rather is a model for detailed physical action of the articulators.

The sole criterion for the inclusion of vowel and consonant sounds in the model is linguistic detail, providing for the hearer as much linguistic information as possible from the speaker. While the detail model would enhance what would usually be called clarity of articulation, we should not make clarity, as such, the goal of a model, since our biases can easily enter into such a definition.

The detail model might take various forms, but for American actors it should always be based on patterns (especially with vowels) found in a large number of American speakers. The pattern still often (mis)termed "General American" or "Broadcast Speech" is based on "Inland Northern," the dialect found in a narrow band of northern states; since it is my own dialect I find it crystal clear in its articulation, wonderfully euphonious, and altogether the ideal dialect model.[73] Speakers of other general dialect areas, such as North or South Midland, might have other ideas.

---

[71]   That is, more detailed.

[72]   In this, Tilly had the right idea. Where he went wrong was in valuing rules over observation, a failing that continued into *Good American Speech.*

[73]   For an extreme opposite view, see Timothy C. Frazer, "The Language of Yankee Imperialism: Pioneer Ideology and 'General American,'" in *"Heartland" English,* Timothy C. Frazer, ed. (Tuscaloosa: The University of Alabama Press, 1993). Frazer sees Inland Northern as a Puritan power play effected by serried ranks of grim westward marching New Englanders, foisting their dialect on innocent southerners who had wandered out to Kentucky and Missouri, presumably to commune with nature. Ironically—within the context that we have been considering—Frazer's chief villains are John Kenyon and George Philip Krapp. Frazer ends by suggesting Inland Northern's complicity in the U.S. military interventions in Southeast Asia and Latin America in recent decades. This does seem to be an overstatement.

Because the detail model is not a monolith, parts of it may be combined with any other dialect or accent, to widen the dialect's comprehensibility to speakers of other dialects in a theatrical setting.

Learning the skills of flexible, active articulation, and a complete repertoire of speech sounds through descriptive, experiential phonetic training does take time in itself. But the time expended is more than made up for by the increased capacity to learn any dialect, from the detail model to Tangier Island, in a matter of days or weeks, rather than the full year that was customarily used to learn Good American Speech. Good American Speech itself is still a very useful dialect when playing actors or social aspirants of yesteryear,[74] and like any dialect it can be readily available to any actor who has gained the skills of making sound distinctions easily.

7. *Rejoining the world.* Perhaps most important of all, speech training for actors—so long frozen in time and isolated in pedagogy—must reestablish the ties with allied disciplines that it forswore so many decades ago. The fields of articulatory phonetics, acoustic phonetics, and dialectology have valuable resources in their research for actors and theatre speech teachers. I would submit, too, that theatre speech and dialect training has much to offer these disciplines in the development of pedagogy, since its laboratory is the mind and body of the performer; this requires a physically-based approach, and a unity of precise speech skills with freedom of voice production. Performance dialects also require great detail and accuracy of transcription and replication, yet are regularly taught in rehearsal settings where time and attention spans are at a minimum, and therefore may provide teaching methods useful to our colleagues in allied non-theatre areas.

There are many hopeful signs that this emergence into the world of today is already happening, in large part spurred by the dialogue among theatre voice and speech teachers that began with the founding of the Voice and Speech Trainers Association.

Speech training for actors will always be a subject for debate because human speech patterns are always subject to change, and these changes will always be measured against the need for full and easy understanding in the theatre environment.

---

74 The famed monologist Ruth Draper created a wonderful portrait of a New York "society lady" in the 1930s, in her monologue "The Italian Lesson," using the World English/Good American Speech pattern.

16

THE ROY HART THEATRE:
TEACHING THE TOTALITY OF SELF

LAURA C. KALO
WITH
GEORGE WHITESIDE AND IVAN MIDDERIGH

The Roy Hart Theatre is renowned for going beyond the vocal limits of what is considered acceptable sound. Alfred Wolfsohn, whose vocal investigations beginning in the 1930s led to the eventual emergence of the Theatre and its unique way of working with the voice, was among the first people in the West to recognize the profound value of "unacceptable" human sound. His focus was the experiential research of what the human voice is capable of. Man has for many centuries failed to appreciate his voice; he has underestimated it and neglected it and allowed it to waste away; he has virtually strangled it, chained it up and confined it in a straitjacket. As he has so often done before, man has once again turned his sinning against nature into dogma, the dogma of tightly restricted, neatly labeled categories: male and female voices, high and low voices, children's voices and adult voices. The dogma that maintains that every human being has been assigned a particular register from birth, or at least from the moment the voice breaks, that covers no more than around two octaves: soprano, mezzo-soprano, and alto for women, and tenor, baritone, and bass for men. The truth is that the natural human voice, freed from all artificial restrictions, is able to embrace all these categories and registers; indeed, it is able to go much further.[1]

The vocal "method" of the Roy Hart Theatre is based on an extended vocal range able to reach beyond the normal musical concepts of bel canto

---

[1]   Alfred Wolfsohn, cited in Eric Weiser, "Stimme Ohne Fessel," *Die Wellwoche*, 30 Sept. 1955.

singing, and into the experimental realm of vocal production. This extended range is explored through sounds not typically heard in everyday experience: bird-like chirps, belly growls, nasal cries, bright screams, dark moans, tender melodies, and chorded sounds involving the simultaneous production of overtones. All sounds are explored; no aspect of human experience is excluded. Simply put, the focus is on singing the totality of the self.

Yet no manual exists to pass down the techniques that the Theatre has discovered. What have been passed down are a limited number of unpublished essays and speeches by the Theatre's original members and, more significantly, an ethic, an approach to living the voice rather than merely using it, which has been passed in direct and intimate contact from person to person. It is basically an aural tradition, defying codification as a simple set of rules or exercises.

There are currently thirty or so members of the Theatre teaching. Their teaching styles are highly improvisational and intuitive, as diverse as the personalities of the teachers themselves; they have no one way of guiding a student. What they share, however, is the legacy of the pioneering vocal work of Wolfsohn and his student Roy Hart.

The story of Wolfsohn's life is the key to understanding the evolution of the Roy Hart Theatre and the way its work has been passed on and developed (since his death). Born in Berlin of Jewish descent in 1896, Wolfsohn was eighteen when he was conscripted into the army to fight in the First World War. During his third year of service, something happened which altered his life forever:

> The year was 1917. We were entrenched somewhere at the front — we did not know where — under heavy bombardment. At long last came the relay. Heavy rain had turned the trenches into swamps of mud and in a short while I became trapped in it. I called to my comrades for help, but no one heard, and soon I was quite alone. Hour after hour, inch by inch, I crawled back. After a while I heard a voice nearby moaning incessantly, "Help, help, help." I fought a terrible struggle with myself: should I try to crawl to him or not? I did not do it. After an agony of more than twenty hours I reached a reserve dugout. I do not remember what happened after that, except that I learned later I had been hit and buried by a grenade and that I awoke the next morning in the cellar of a house in St. Quentin, amongst a heap of corpses.[2]

Like thousands of other war veterans, Wolfsohn suffered from an illness then known as "war neurosis," or shell shock, exacerbated in his case by the

---

[2]   Alfred Wolfsohn, "Orpheus, or the Way to a Mask," trans. Marita Gunther, unpublished manuscript written in Berlin, 1936–38, held at the Jewish Historical Museum, Amsterdam.

guilt of leaving his comrade, though had he crawled to him, both would surely have perished. Marita Gunther, a founding member of the Theatre, has written: "Intellectually, he accepted the argument but emotionally he was powerless to change his conviction that he had forfeited his claim to that which he had held to be the purest and highest in him: the aim to realize in himself the concept of a human being."[3]

Years of treatment with physicians and psychiatrists failed to exorcise Wolfsohn's memory of the wounded soldier's haunting cries. Eventually, on his own, he began to seek relief by reproducing the very sounds he had heard in the trenches. What Wolfsohn discovered was that making audible these hidden or wounded areas of his soul actually led him to the inner healing he sought. He began to accept pupils and to apply what he had discovered in his own vocal development to them. This marked the start of Wolfsohn's career as a voice teacher.

Wolfsohn fled Hitler's Germany just before World War II, taking refuge in London. There he again began to accept vocal students, many of whom had vocal problems. Gunther, one of Wolfsohn's first students, has written, "Their voices had become sick because they too had suffered psychic damage, and no progress, no result could be achieved if it was not possible to heal this damage, to restore their confidence and to transfer his belief and strength to them."[4] Much of his research was influenced by the theories of Freud and Jung, particularly Jung's archetypes, which Wolfsohn believed exist in the body of every person and can be reached, even brought to life, through sound. Roy Hart later wrote, "We were in close contact with Jung, who told us that although what we did profoundly interested him, he could no longer interest himself in us because he was not a musician."[5]

Wolfsohn's growing group of pupils, realizing with him that it would take years of study to develop their voices fully, undertook a pilgrimage into an uncharted territory of vocal range, color, and sound exploration. Wolfsohn wrote:

> Here I want to stress once more that when I speak of singing, I do not consider this to be an artistic exercise but the possibility and the means to recognize oneself and to transform this recognition into conscious life. Singing is, however, the primeval field of application of music, the gift bestowed on everyone by nature in order to express himself. For the communication between men takes place through the

---

[3]   Marita Gunther, "The Human Voice and Alfred Wolfsohn," Spring: *A Journal of Archetype and Culture* 55 (1990): 66.

[4]   Wolfsohn, cited in Gunther, "The Human Voice," 68.

[5]   Roy Hart, "Let There Be Consciousness Tonight and Forever," interview by Jose Monlean and Ricardo Domenech, Madrid, 4 March 1971.

language which does not just consist of neutral combinations of sounds but is used in an up and down of musical movement. In my attempt to discover the secret of singing, nothing has compensated me more for all my searching and worrying than the discovery that that which I had onesidedly understood as "expression" in its symbolic and spiritual sense, had to be taken in its literal meaning. I found that the sound of the human voice gained its fullest expression exactly at the point where the singing person—having found the right balance on concentration and tension—could express it bodily. However simple it may sound, important are only three factors which constitute the elements of singing: CONCENTRATION, INTENSITY, and as a result thereof, EXPRESSION. Whoever is convinced like me that exactly the simplest things in life contain the most complicated problems also knows that the mastery thereof leads to the desired goal.[6]

As Wolfsohn's work became more widely known, critics expressed apprehension that the multi-octave sounds might damage the vocal chords. Wolfsohn never doubted that the sounds his students were producing were healing and true. Nevertheless, in 1956, he sent two of his students, Roy Hart and Jenny Johnson, to be examined by Professor R. Luchsinger of the Zurich Otolaryngological Clinic, using X-ray, stroboscope, and high-speed film while the students sang in their extended range. Luchsinger found no abnormality in the larynx, which remained relaxed even on the highest of notes and appeared healthy and normal. This provided empirical evidence that an extended vocal range did not cause damage to the vocal cords and larynx.

Roy Hart was one of Wolfsohn's most promising pupils. Born in Johannesburg, South Africa, in 1926, Hart studied psychology and English at Witzwaterand University in his native country. He came to London in 1946 on a scholarship to the Royal Academy of Dramatic Art, where he quickly emerged as a gifted actor with a brilliant future. However, Hart quickly became disillusioned with his training. It was at this point that he met Alfred Wolfsohn through an acquaintance and began to train with him. Hart wrote:

> I was becoming more and more convinced that there was a serious philosophical flaw in the approach to Theatre in the Drama schools in those days. I was interested in the relationship between the actor and his personal life. I became concerned with the relationship between voice and personality, especially as this manifested itself in a spectrum of energy production varying from apathy to intensity...
>
> I had thought of myself as an artist, and an actor in the making. But because I took that Art deadly seriously, it had led me elsewhere.[7]

---

6   Wolfsohn, cited in Gunther, "The Human Voice," 70.

7   Roy Hart, "How a Voice Gave Me a Conscience," Seventh International Congress of Psychotherapy, Wiesbaden, Germany, August 1967: 2.

Once he had experienced the profound impact of Wolfsohn's training on his own life, Hart stopped performing on the stage, relinquishing a promising "West-End" theatre career, to dedicate himself to the study of the human voice. He remained Wolfsohn's protégé for sixteen years.

When Wolfsohn's health began to fail, Hart himself started teaching some of Wolfsohn's students. Alfred Wolfsohn died in 1962. Roy Hart took over the leadership of a core group of Wolfsohn's students, and soon began expanding Wolfsohn's essentially therapeutic vocal research to include artistic expression and, eventually, performance.

The group persevered and evolved. Gunther explained:

> What had been, in the beginning, exclusively a teacher-pupil relationship developed into a cohesive group with a family spirit. What had begun with small voice-demonstrations slowly took the shape of theatrical performances. The idea of a multi-octave voice which had come about as one man's [Wolfsohn's] psychological need to find answers concerning his own voice and which had developed into a good therapeutic/ artistic tool — making audible the possible integration of the personality — now underwent a careful change in bias: from the therapeutic/ artistic studies to the artistic/therapeutic application. This is a subtle point because using the voice as we do — and teaching someone to discover or develop his voice — of necessity touches upon psychic forces which must be understood and sometimes have to be dealt with. As new ground in the voice is opened up, great surprises await us — joy, satisfaction, and unexpected feelings and sensations — but also the light is let in on certain psychological problems.[8]

Where the members of the group had learned from Wolfsohn to practice singing as a "redemption of the body,"[9] Hart's journey in sound now led the group toward what Hart called an "eight-octave approach to life," the belief that every person has the potential to sing across eight octaves.[10] Their vocal research was influenced as much by the organic development of the company members' individual lives as by the continued expansion of their vocal range. They began meeting not only to sing and explore their voices but also to share their daily experiences and nightly dreams. The telling and interpreting of dreams in particular became more integral to their work together. As those discussions progressed, they found that they were becoming students not only of voice, but of life. They began to speak of "living the voice,"[11] the notion that if only all possible human feelings can be expressed

---

[8]   Gunther, "The Human Voice," 73.

[9]   Hart, "How a Voice," 3.

[10]   Hart, "How a Voice," 3.

[11]   Roy Hart, personal interview with Ivan Miderigh, 1974

vocally, without judgment, one can live consciously without being controlled by one's feelings. The group began calling itself the Roy Hart Theatre. "The result of my work on my voice," Hart wrote, "is that I have established a new kind of community living—a body of people who have chosen to call themselves Roy Hart Theatre. I did not personally aim to establish a theatre. It grew involuntarily out of my work, and perhaps in time it will come to be known as "Theatre of the Heart." [12] In 1967, the Theatre began work on its first full-length production, a pre-verbal version of Euripides' *The Bacchae* done in sound rather than spoken text. After a full year of rehearsal, they performed the work at their studio in London to invited audiences. Response was favorable, and the company was invited to perform the piece at the 1969 World University Festival of Theatre in Nancy, France.

The emerging company faced the perennial artist's challenge. Roy Hart wrote of this period:

> We all earned our livings in different ways, so we are neither exclusively a theatrical group nor a set of monastic mystics...Shortage of time—shortage of money—these challenge our values. Each of us knows that he has to make room in his life for what he values, no matter how poor he is, or how rich he is, or how prolific or loving a parent he is...We are not escapists from family or business commitments, if we limit both to allow for the growth of understanding. One of our most bitter battle-fronts is the clash between this work and the demands of family and bread-winning. We watch to see where these clashes can be prevented or eased, for such work as we do, such concrete prayer, needs a recognized place in the daily scramble. [13]

They worked out of a building in London called The Abraxas Club. Their definition of abraxas was "the creative synthesis of opposites." [14] It was a working gym and sports club with squash courts, exercise equipment, and a restaurant which members of the theatre managed. The club also served as their meeting house, rehearsal space, movement studio, and second home. Here they gave demonstrations of their work, attracting the attention of renowned musicians, theatre directors, and psychoanalysts. Many composers were also interested in the work but did not know how to utilize it.

During this period Hart lectured at the Jung Institute, the International Congress for Psychotherapy in London, the Seventh International Congress for Psychotherapy in Wiesbaden, and the Third International Congress for Psychodrama in Vienna. During one lecture, Hart said:

---

[12] Roy Hart, "The Objective Voice," Seventh International Congress of Psychodrama, Tokyo, 1972: 6.

[13] Hart, "How a Voice," 5-6.

[14] Hart, "Objective Voice," 3.

One of the most pressing problems of our day is to redefine the whole meaning of art and artistic gifts. Has the creative impulse only to be considered the possession of a hierarchy of gifted people, musicians, painters and so on? Or must we reconsider the intrinsic common factor behind the creative impulse? Many so-called untalented people, factory hands, office workers or manual laborers, have been demoralized out of all sense of their own creative potential; and the diffidence thus imposed on them results in serious misuse of their leisure hours... In primitive society, the creative, artistic urge was shared by all and given dignity... When we learn to value the clumsiest creativity of our human acquaintances, and honor their most tentative gropings, they become our friends.

My family [the Roy Hart Theatre] believes that the greatest contributing force to mental breakdown is the lack of outlet for truthful self-expression, tolerance of this expression by others, and courage to persevere in it for oneself. The medium we have chosen can safely contain the variety of man's emotions without crushing him.[15]

Roy Hart himself began to perform publicly again in 1969 with the world premiere of "Versuch uber Schweine," a work specially composed for Hart's voice by Hans Werner Henze, performed with the English Chamber Orchestra at Queen Elizabeth Hall in London. This was followed by "Eight Songs for a Mad King," also composed for his voice, this time by Peter Maxwell-Davies, with the Pierrot Players at Queen Elizabeth Hall; and "Spirale" written by Karlheinz Stockhausen, performed at St. Paul de Vence, France under the auspices of The Foundation Maeght.

After a concert in Hamburg, Germany where Hart performed "Eight Songs for a Mad King," a critic wrote:

Roy Hart is an artist who commands not only all the voices of the human registers—ranging from deepest bass to the highest soprano, but also (incredibly enough) is able to produce several sounds simultaneously, added to which he gives an acting performance, which stretches from the most tender allusion to the most macabre realism. All this was (banal as the formulation may sound) simply phenomenal, unique, sensational. Yet it lay beyond all "sensation." It was so deeply stamped by immediate experience, it was the art of presentation which, at every minute, used the means available in a conscious way, and yet never transgressed the borderline that leads to trash... the solo part is specifically written for Roy Hart. No other artist could probably realize this part so penetratingly.[16]

Hart's performances were not always this well received or understood.

---

[15] Hart, "How a Voice," 6.

[16] Heinz Jochaim, *Die Welt*, review of "Eight Songs for a Mad King," Hamburg, Germany, 20 October 1969.

There were those who could not accept his pioneering break from classical Western music; they were not able to "hear" him. To this Hart responded, "I have often referred to my art as 'Conscious Schizophrenia,' a conscious bringing together of the many parts into which Western man usually likes to divide and subdivide himself."[17] For Hart, one's art and one's humanity were inextricably bound. Hart went on to say:

> People have asked why I am so obsessed with the voice — what about all the other important means of expression? I have found that full development of the voice, that is connecting all its tones of expression to embodied feeling, includes everything else, and forms a vital bridge between head and body, the conscious and unconscious. It is because I have aimed to sing eight octaves or more, using my whole body, will and imagination to do so, that my acting performance appears as immediate and embracing. To educate my voice to produce at will a great variety of timbres and nuances that relate to immediate experience rather than to a clever, intellectually acted simulation of experience, I had to gain in my body the knowledge of my comprehensive humanity.
>
> My life's work has been to give bodily expression to the totality of myself. This means bringing an enormous unconscious territory into consciousness, with the help of the dream world and the unbiased observations of co-students of many conscious gestures, words, actions. Some of the sounds which I and my colleagues make seem identical to many to be heard in any psychiatric ward, and at my concerts several people have found my sounds disturbing and have had hysterical reactions, but, for those who can hear without fear, it is clear that these sounds are consciously, detachedly "produced," "commanded" to come forth, and because I and my fellow students choose where, how and when to make them, we are not forced to become alienated from society, as are those in the psychiatric wards, who seem to be making similar sounds.[18]

The English theatre director and author Peter Brook visited the Roy Hart Theatre's London studio a number of times and described the work as "full of pith and moment." Brook supported their work by writing on behalf of the company in their efforts to secure a research grant. He wrote, "What they are doing deserves encouragement and support and could certainly be of interest and value culturally and educationally to the English theatre as a whole. There are no other groups with such aspirations."[19] Brook invited the

---

[17]   Hart, "Objective Voice," 2.

[18]   Hart, "Objective Voice," 2.

[19]   Peter Brook, cited in "Voice: the Roy Hart Theatre Journal," edited by Ivan Midderigh, unpublished, November 1985: 7.

Polish theatre director Jerzy Grotowski to a demonstration of the company's work. Much later, in 1979, Grotowski publicly acknowledged his debt to Wolfsohn's research. Another supporter of the Roy Hart Theatre was Jean-Louis Barrault who, in 1972, invited them to perform along with Brook's company at a festival organized by the Theatres des Nations in Paris.

Critics in France were much more receptive to the Theatre's performances than those in England. This welcome embrace by the French led the company to relocate to the south of France in July of 1974. With loans and personal savings, the members made the first payment on a crumbling twelfth-century chateau called Malerargues in the Cevennes region. The move was full of hardship. It took months of grueling repairs to the chateau to prepare it for habitation; the last of the forty-odd member company arrived from London nine months later in March 1975. Ian Magilton, a company member, describes it thus:

> Practical and financial steps were taken to create an independent and self-sufficient theatrical community at Malerargues, ranging from large scale international transactions on one hand, to a campaign to earn a maximum through part-time jobs on the other. This campaign was first christened "The Vision" and subsequently "L' Impossible." [20]

Roy Hart and two of the company's principal actresses, Dorothy Hart and Vivienne Young, died in a car accident while en route to Spain for a theatrical tour, on May 18, 1975. Without their leader, the next few years were to be the company's most difficult. Magilton wrote:

> The deaths...came as an unbelievably crushing blow, which no one who has not been a part of Roy's theatre will ever be able to measure. As well as being a personal, artistic and inspirational loss, their deaths had merciless financial implications. So that time when we needed to draw together and nurse our terrible wounds, and to create the future of our Theatre, was one of extreme poverty. [21]

Everyone contributed as they could to the collective survival of the company. Various members went to work in nearby towns to support a core group that toured with performances. Members gathered regularly for group and private singing lessons, to maintain the discipline of the vocal exploration. They barely survived these early years. At times, people from the surrounding communities would bring gifts of bread and vegetables. Company member Orlanda Cook recalled, "They knew we were starving. Even though they did not 'understand' our work, they understood its importance and they supported our efforts. We would not have made it through that first winter af-

---

[20]   Ian Magilton, "How Do We Live?" unpublished essay, 1976: 1.

[21]   Magilton, "How Do We Live?" 1.

ter Roy's death had it not been for their generosity."[22] The company gave free performances in the villages to show their gratitude.

Marita Gunther writes of this time:

> As well as losing very loved friends, colleagues, and teachers, we faced the question once again: were these unique ideas totally dependent on the strong personality of one man, or had they been rooted enough in order to live and continue evolving?
>
> Not one but several of us formed a kind of inner council. What had been a group of amateurs began to develop into a small society. New fields of responsibility were formed. There were the artistic leadership, the teaching body, the financial side. There were the house to be looked after and the administrative work.
>
> Life as a society brought also professionalism. It brought recognition and expansion. Today we perform and teach in many different countries of the world...What has made it possible to stay together is that we have held on—despite or perhaps because of manifold trends—to our work on the voice, the singing-lesson...the confrontation ultimately with oneself, with the voice as a probe and as a mirror. We are learning to explore life to its fullest and to transform it into theatre. Ours is a philosophy which contains as one of its basic principles the bridging of the gap between life and art.[23]

The connection between life and art sustained their work. Over time, Gunther writes, they found that they were not "dependent on the strong personality of one man."[24] Though the style of performance changed as various company members took over the direction of new productions where previously they had been directed by Roy Hart, it was still the continuing investigation of their own voices that gave the Roy Hart Theatre—as it continued to call itself—identity and purpose. The "professionalism" that life brought the company came in the form of an Obie Award for the four-person production of *Pagliacci—Insights into an Opera*, performed at La Mama in New York in 1985. The *Village Voice* critic, Eileen Blumenthal, wrote:

> The Roy Hart Theatre's daring and virtuosic "Pagliacci," one-and-a-half-hour version for four performers, piano, and triangle, is called "insights into an opera"...But while Leoncavallo refined his elements into bel canto, the Roy Hart Theatre uses the same elements to express raw, unrefined feelings—from secret desperate love, to misery, to commedia fun, to rage and terror. The sounds of this "Pagliacci" are rarely beautiful. There is a range of gasps, screams, and howls.

---

[22]   Orlanda Cook, personal interview, 17 August 1988.

[23]   Gunther, "The Human Voice," 74-75.

[24]   Gunther, "The Human Voice," 74.

When the performers do (more or less) sing from the original score, they are approximate about their pitch, and their timbre is usually more hollow than honeyed...As the work goes on, it becomes increasingly clear that the voice quality is being precisely modulated for precise, sometimes stunning effects. For example, a lyrical duet between lovers transforms its tone subtly but totally into a wail. Performers harmonize (hitting the pitches exactly as they want to), sometimes singing duets, sometimes turning one voice into an accompaniment for another. As performers vocalize creaks, chirps, and moans that one usually hears only from synthesizers, they give those noises the charged expressiveness that makes the difference between any live versus synthesized voice.[25]

The mission of the theatre slowly broadened beyond performance. Smaller groups within the theatre began to form, concentrating on various interests such as myth, opera, storytelling, and commedia dell'arte. Theatre members began to direct workshops and take on private students. The teaching methodology depended on the particular focus and personality of each teacher. Long-time company member Paul Silber wrote:

I have no formulas, there is no technique. The only "technique" is listen to what you're hearing, and hear what you're listening to, stand where you're standing, see what you're looking at. That's the technique. But then, that's a very demanding technique. It means that somebody, Roy Hart...has enabled you to see a little bit better than you did before, hear a little bit better, think, feel...there's no structure which can be guaranteed from one person to another. There's basically only work: effort, trial, success, failure. That is the journey. There is no end; that is when you're put in the box and put away forever. The journey is what lasts, the moment...Be where you are when you're there.[26]

Magilton explains the vocal work as

...complex and not easily defined: it is a singing technique; it is a therapeutic work to activate, express and discipline the totality of being; it is an instrument for unveiling, investigating and quantifying profound psychological realities; it is the harnessing of these possibilities for the theatre.[27]

In essence, one teaches how to free the soul so that one may sing it. For the student, the goal is to realize and draw forth the music of the entirety of one's being and sing it without fear. Company member Kaya Anderson notes:

[25]   Eileen Blumenthal, "Artful Commedia," review of "Pagliacci — Insights into an Opera," *The Village Voice*, 19 Feb. 1985.

[26]   Paul Silber, personal interview, 11 August 1988.

[27]   Ian Magilton, "What Does the Roy Hart Theatre Teach?" unpublished, 1979.

> The voice is the muscle of the soul and it can unite the body with the soul. That is, if the searcher is able to feel, to hear and recognize the great sources of energy and psychic inspiration which the voice can evoke. And if the searcher is making efforts to evolve towards the integration of his personality.[28]

The pathways to this goal are as varied as the individuals who seek it.

How then are the accumulated years of intensive research to be passed on to a new generation? It is a question many of the members have been struggling with for some time: how to pass on what is essentially a living method and body of work, rather than something that can be "taught" in a single workshop or lesson. As Silber has written, "What is being offered is what has always been offered, starting with Alfred Wolfsohn, that the work is in fact a life-time's discipline."[29] The work can be arduous, and "results" are not automatic. Magilton says: "We cannot give understanding. We can give glimpses of a way of working that offers possibilities for growth. For those whose work is not ours, we can offer an approach to work and life that can feed the one that they have chosen. The immediate practical results can be: a voice less restricted, strengthened, and deepened; and contact with more objective sources of imagination and means of expression."[30] Company member Barrie Coghlan has written:

> I needed a way to survive the torture and agony that the individual experiences when the mode of life is no longer in keeping with the reality of the whole of the psyche. One is living a lie, or else life is felt to be without value or meaning; and it becomes necessary to examine every aspect of being, painful though that examination may be . . . for myself, of the various means by which we express ourselves, the voice is by far the most intimate revelation of our essential self. It is rooted in the very depths of our primitive being and yet aspires to the height of spiritual awareness. It encompasses every instinct, emotion, feeling and mood which we can experience, and it expresses them all with the most subtle modulations.[31]

The centerpiece of the Theatre's teaching "method," used by all of the members without exception, is the singing lesson — the teacher working one-on-one with the student. Using only a piano, the teacher guides the

---

[28] Kaya Anderson, "Voice My Soul," The Phoenix Theatre, program notes, San Francisco, 19 January 1990: 1.

[29] Paul Silber, letter to the author, 16 September 1994.

[30] Magilton, "What Does the Roy Hart Theatre Teach?"

[31] Barrie Coghlan, "The Human Voice and the Aural Vision of the Soul," First International Conference on Scientific Aspects in Theatre, Karpaczi, Poland, September 1979: 8.

student in vocal exploration, allowing any and all sounds as they come. The intent of the singing lesson, as Silber describes it, "is self-discovery; therefore, in some degree, extending the range. I want them [the students] to come out of the limits they normally impose on themselves . . . to move them out of their habits . . . especially the limits of their own thinking regarding their own voice." [32] The teacher's responsibility is to allow the student to re-connect to the voice, as well as to the sounds of the unconscious. Silber continues, "There is a risk in every single note; every request and every response contains a risk, an unknown factor . . . people are beginning to understand that what we are engaged in is promoting themselves to their most potential selves." [33] It is a transformative pedagogy, a way to reunite body and soul by confronting the realities contained in one's own voice. As Wolfsohn wrote:

> My first concern is to free my pupils from the fear of heights and the fear of depths conditioned in their voices by tradition. The baby, not yet acquainted with these fears, screams with all his might using the whole of his body as a resonating chamber. But alongside the fear of heights and the fear of depths, each individual is variously prey to a whole host of psychic inhibitions and conflicts, anxieties and complexes, the elimination of which leads to the opening out of the personality and the voice.
>
> But none of these has anything to do with the mystical, it is a completely natural process . . . I am neither a sorcerer nor a hypnotist. I can only help my students to overcome their inner tensions and difficulties, and through this easing of tension to loosen the inhibitions which hold their personalities as well as their voices in chains. But the bulk of the work they must do themselves. [34]

In such an approach to the voice, a basic trust is allowed to develop. Magilton speaks of the teacher-student relationship as a key factor in the unveiling of a voice:

> Understanding, growth and artistic sensibility are not acquired easily; they can only be gained by the student, and cannot simply be given by a teacher . . . The aim is to search for the strongest possible links between the voice and the singer: to begin the slow process of reconnecting with the deep body sources of each voice. Thus in our classes we begin by discovering the voice as it is. As an educative principle, we do not force pupils into areas that they are not willing or ready to enter. The relationship between the teacher and pupil is para-

---

[32]   Paul Silber, personal interview, 9 August 1991.

[33]   Paul Silber, personal interview, 11 August 1988.

[34]   Wolfsohn, "Stimme Ohne Fessel."

mount, and as trust in this relationship grows, so the investigation of the limits of the voice can begin. We work on the widening of these limits for two principal reasons: to touch on as yet unlived aspects of being; and to inform and strengthen the normal range. The extension of limits applies in the sense of height and depth, in strength, quality and expression, and in finding "new" voices within the range. Each teacher in the Roy Hart Theatre is also a pupil and knows intimately what he or she is asking for in a lesson.[35]

What must the teacher do to assist the process of unfolding a voice? The Roy Hart Theatre members place tremendous importance on listening, on attuning oneself to the sounds one hears coming forth out of the unconscious. Gunther writes:

> Great importance is given to the art of listening: listening to each other, listening to our own voice, listening above all to the infinite shades of what lies behind the voice. It is the stretching of our aural sensitivity which is so important in our teaching and being taught.[36]

The premise is that only as a teacher listens can he or she truthfully guide the pupil through the vast labyrinth of vocal expression.

Noah Pikes describes his experience as a teacher:

> When I teach, I do not feel that I am a therapist; I feel myself to be involved with a process that is to do with faith, the opposite of therapy. As if both the student and I are working in submission to a deeper authority than that which gave rise to the 2–3 octave view of the voice.[37]

Anderson describes her experience similarly:

> When I am teaching, my listening to the pupils is physically and mentally attuned. The pupil's voice, look, attitude, gestures, as well as my own, allow me to estimate our states of being. At times, these are so subtle that the method, or tactic of guiding the pupil varies enormously. From just breathing deeply, making very easy, gentle sounds, or working on a song, text, poem, to getting big energy going, big voice, breaking sounds, pushing the limits. When a state of grace emerges in a lesson — those worked for, awaited and listened for wonderful moments, then the pupil is freed from mere determination and can allow his voice and being to flow, because he is moved. This is the worked for miracle.[38]

---

35 Magilton, "What Does the Roy Hart Theatre Teach?"

36 Gunther, "The Human Voice," 73–74.

37 Noah Pikes, "Singing — Is It Prayer Or Therapy?" unpublished, June 1979: 1.

38 Anderson, "Voice My Soul," 2.

The Roy Hart Theatre still maintains its headquarters, now known as the "Centre Artistique International Roy Hart," at the Chateau de Malerargues in southern France. Many members live and teach all over the world: Ireland, Spain, England, Italy, Switzerland, Holland, Germany, Sweden, Denmark, Norway, Poland, Israel, Canada, South America, and the U.S.

"Whether they [students] know it or not," Silber says, "their unconscious hears the word voix and it knows (since the unconscious is the dustbin where all that is disowned by the conscious brain dwells) that the word voix and imagination are intimately linked... when anyone really uses their voice to the full capacity of their body, then voice, body and imagination become one."[39]

---

[39]   Paul Silber, "What Shall We Do When The Workshop Is Over?" unpublished, 1980–81.

NB: Several of the unpublished sources above are available through the Centre. Mailing address: Centre Artistique International Roy Hart Chateau de Malerargues — Thoiras 30140 Anduze, France.

IV

THE VOICE AND CURRENT PRACTICE

17

A CONSUMER'S GUIDE TO VOICE AND SPEECH TRAINING

BONNIE N. RAPHAEL*

In the pursuit of greater excellence, more and more stage, film, and television actors as well as public speakers of all kinds are seeking means of improving their voice and speech skills. Despite their best intentions, many find themselves confused or overwhelmed by the great diversity in training available. This general survey is an attempt to provide an introduction to the most widely used and easily accessible types of voice and speech training and rehabilitation available in the United States at the present time, in the belief that informed consumers will make better choices about how to best meet their respective needs.

AN OVERVIEW OF THE POSSIBILITIES

In addition to having individual vocal needs or agendas, different people find themselves more receptive to one mode of learning than to another and to one style of presentation than to another. Because voice training involves behavior modification, it is quite useful for the prospective student to have an idea of which mode of learning and which presentation style are most productive for him or her. Certain speakers, for example, do best when information is auditory. Systems based on listening to a model and then making the necessary adjustments in one's own sound are quite helpful to auditory learners. Other speakers do best when they can obtain information visually—by observing a particular facial posture or shoulder relaxation technique and then duplicating it as best they can while observing themselves in a mirror. Still

* Reprinted with permission of the *New England Theatre Journal.*
    The author wishes to thank Dr. Jeffrey Martin for suggesting the subject for this article.

other speakers thrive when the information they receive is kinesthetic, when they can learn by being either physically touched or told what they might experience in their own breathing or postural or facial muscles and then seeing whether they can voluntarily produce the desired kinesthetic sensation.

Obviously, there can be no such thing as a learning mode which is purely auditory or visual or kinesthetic; virtually all behavioral modification techniques involve stimulation and information provided in all three modes, but one or another might be more prominent and therefore more useful to a particular individual. Similarly, certain actors might be most comfortable working with a teacher or coach on an individual basis on an ongoing level, while others would feel more comfortable as a member of a small class which might meet two or three times per week for a number of months or a semester. Some speakers choose to work with a speech therapist specializing in voice rehabilitation while others might seek to improve breathing, relaxation, resonation, and range by learning how to sing. If the professional voice user is willing to do a bit of investigative work and to interview a number of candidates, then he or she is likely to obtain the best match between type of training and specific needs.

If the voice is relatively normal, basically free of problems which might be referred to as clinical (e.g. vocal nodes or polyps, contact ulcers, vocal fold trauma or paralysis, chronic laryngitis, and the like), then most actors and other public speakers might consider one of the four basic types of training described in this survey: traditional, Skinner, Linklater, or Lessac. If, on the other hand, there are any organic problems or issues of chronic pain or recurring voice loss, then the process of vocal rehabilitation should begin with a medical examination followed by a series of sessions with a speech therapist specializing in voice.

VOICE REMEDIATION THROUGH SPEECH THERAPY

Speech therapists who specialize in voice remediation can most often restore a damaged or impaired voice through a series of individual therapy sessions if the client is attentive, compliant and willing to take responsibility for his or her improvement. After a thorough physical and behavioral examination by an otolaryngologist (a medical doctor who specializes in ear, nose, and throat pathology and treatment), the speaker will most often be referred to a voice therapist for eight or twelve or more sessions which typically run about an hour in length and quite frequently are covered by medical insurance. Speech therapists have completed both undergraduate and graduate-level courses in anatomy and physiology of voice, basic acoustics, speech disorders, clinical practice, speech science, and related subjects. Ideally, they should be clinically certified as well, which means they have completed at least a year of supervised therapy in a hospital or clinic.

Sessions with a speech therapist will be structured to the needs of the individual, based on information provided by the examining physician and on a history provided by the client. Typically, these sessions will take place either in a hospital voice clinic or in the therapist's private office. To remediate problems related to vocal nodules or chronic laryngitis or vocal fatigue, for example, exercises might well include work on dynamic relaxation, on breathing and alignment, on avoidance of hard glottal initiation (which occurs when the vocal folds bang together abruptly when voice is initiated), and on vocal warmup and support (i.e., maintaining a healthy and dynamic relationship between the breath and the voice). Some speech therapists will terminate their work when the original complaint has been resolved, referring the speaker, if further training is warranted, to a qualified voice teacher, vocal coach, or singing teacher. Other therapists are trained and experienced enough to do continued work with the speaker — on range extension or projection in large spaces, for example. However, medical insurance may not cover this extended work.

Other speakers might consult a speech therapist specializing in accent reduction or elimination if this is their chief concern. Through a process of ear training and articulation practice, foreign or regional accents can be reduced significantly in many cases.

Advocates of the therapeutic approach to voice remediation cite the clinicians' intimate knowledge of anatomy and physiology, speech science, and the medical ramifications of both their complaints and their treatment. They like as well the one-on-one interaction and the use of objective measures to confirm and validate progress. Critics of speech therapy are frequently put off by a hospital setting and by the profusion of medical and scientific terminology. They prefer working with a teacher or coach on acquiring new skills rather than being treated like a patient with a pathology that needs to be fixed. Some actors observe that many therapists have very limited knowledge of what goes on in the theatre, resisting well-meant suggestions from a therapist to refuse roles in which they are asked to cough or scream, for example. Nonetheless, if there is an organic or related medical problem present at the outset of voice training, then the recommended course of remediation begins with a medical examination and referral to a qualified speech therapist.

Many practicing otolaryngologists, especially those affiliated with the Voice Foundation[1], work in collaboration with one or more speech therapists. A prospective client would do well to interview a few speech therapists in order to discover whether a particular practitioner has had experience with performers and is capable of providing information and skills in a way which

---

[1]   The Voice Foundation is an international organization of physicians, voice scientists, speech therapists, teachers, and coaches, all of whom deal with professional voice users; Foundation offices are located at 1721 Pine Street, Philadelphia, PA 19103 [telephone (215) 735-7999].

is attractive and accessible. Those wishing more information about speech therapists practicing in their geographical areas can contact the American Speech, Language and Hearing Association.[2]

TRADITIONAL APPROACHES TO TRAINING

It is understandably difficult to categorize any individual voice and speech teacher or coach. Each has undergone a particular sequence of education, training, and practical experience which has involved diverse influences. Those traditionally trained, for example, may have completed undergraduate and graduate-level course work in the anatomy and physiology of speech, in speech education, in phonetics, in oral interpretation, and perhaps in communication. For those seeking traditional training, many colleges and universities as well as some theatre conservatories offer an introductory-level course in voice and speech which may be open to non-matriculated students. Typically, in a period of ten or fifteen weeks, students are introduced to the basic anatomy and operation of the voice mechanism, to techniques fostering the elimination of stage fright, to the development of a warm-up routine, to the acquisition of techniques for better breathing and the development of individual vocal dynamics (i.e., pitch, rate, loudness, quality), and to the elimination of some sub-clinical problems common to many speakers — hypernasality, insufficient loudness, and mumbling, for example.

If the course is offered through a speech or communication department, then performance experiences provided might consist of speeches presented to other class members or readings of poetry or prose. If the course is offered through a theatre department or conservatory (a number of which use Evangeline Machlin's excellent text, *Speech for the Stage*[3]), then performance experiences might consist of dramatic poetry and monologues or even scenes from dramatic literature.

A number of public speakers find introductory courses such as these all they need in order to acquire enough basic information and skills to both speak and perform with greater effectiveness. Advocates enjoy the straightforward, easily understandable presentation of basic information and skills and feel that, by the end of a good introductory course, they know how to continue to build vocal technique by working on their own. Many have their appetites whetted by an introductory course and decide to develop further skills by enrolling in more advanced voice and speech courses, such as oral interpretation, text analysis, stage dialects, voice-over technique, or even singing. Critics of some traditional approaches find them too academic or

---

[2]   There are currently 335 members of the Voice and Voice Disorders Special Interest Division of ASHA, whose national office is located at 10801 Rockville Pike, Rockville, Maryland 20852 [consumer help line: (800) 638-8255].

[3]   Evangeline Machlin, *Speech for the Stage* (New York: Theatre Arts Books, 1966).

cerebral, deficient in the area of getting knowledge and skills beyond the brain and down into gut level where they are more useful for performers.

THE WORK OF EDITH SKINNER

Edith Skinner was one of the most famous students of the noted Australian phonetician William Tilly, who came to America to teach his work in the early part of this century. After learning the International Phonetic Alphabet and techniques of sound transcription, Skinner applied them to the speech training of actors, teaching for a great many years at Carnegie-Mellon and then at Juilliard, producing a considerable number of actors and teachers highly proficient in what she called "Good American Speech." In her work, a carefully defined and prescribed series of rules for pronunciation is applied to speaking, reading, and acting by students who have been taught the International Phonetic Alphabet and phonetic transcription. After intensive articulation drill and practice, these pronunciation standards are then applied to a wide variety of materials in performance until they become more habitual.

Proponents of Skinner's work observe that a great number of judgments are made about people on the basis of how they speak and that acquiring Good American Speech will help those who wish to sound more cultured or better educated. It is also true that several sounds acquired through this training carry more easily in large performance spaces and are more easily understood by listeners from different parts of the United States or even those for whom English is a second language. Critics note that what is identified as Good American Speech is not a neutral American but rather a somewhat affected sound, based on a Southern British model rather than on native American speech and also based on a white and singular cultural standard. They feel it eradicates or undervalues the great diversity of speech patterns characteristic of different areas and cultures present in this country and smacks of an older generation of American stage and film actors. Nonetheless, Skinner's work produces speakers with excellent ears and beautifully precise speech. Her training is used in a large number of highly-regarded theatre programs throughout this country. Good American Speech (or American Stage Speech or Mid-Atlantic Speech as it is also called) is used in a number of professional productions of classical plays and also of plays in translation.

Edith Skinner wrote a training manual for use by her students while she taught at Carnegie-Mellon.[4] She and Timothy Monich also produced an audio cassette tape with an accompanying manual which is commercially available.[5] And in the last few years, a revised version of her manual with an

---

[4]   Edith Skinner, *Speak with Distinction*, 6th ed., (New Brunswick, New Jersey, 1965), published by the author.

[5]   Edith Skinner, *Good Speech for the American Actor* (New York: Drama Book Specialists, 1980).

accompanying audio cassette tape has been published.[6] Skinner-trained teachers are presently offering courses based on her work all over this country.

THE LINKLATER METHOD

Kristin Linklater was trained as an actress at the London Academy of Music and Dramatic Art in England. She received her voice and speech training under the eminent master teacher, Iris Warren, whom she later assisted. In 1963, she introduced Iris Warren's work to this country by training a select number of American and Canadian teachers and coaches for an extended period of time. She continues teaching and coaching actors throughout the world to this day.

Linklater's work begins with the proposition that each of us has a beautifully functioning, natural voice with which many of us interfere (because of insidious tension and habitual inhibition) as we attempt to communicate our thoughts and feelings. Her approach, as best described in her book, *Freeing the Natural Voice,* involves a process of freeing the vocal channel from habitual physical and psychological impediments which may prevent the voice from emerging in its most expressive, unadulterated form.[7]

Linklater's work begins with and never abandons a connection with breath and impulse to speak from deep within the body. Exercises deal with allowing the free passage of this breath, especially when dealing with emotionally-charged material; with freeing up the vocal channel via loosening the shoulders, the neck, the jaw, the tongue, and the lips; with developing greater vocal range through contact with and exploration of a series of resonators; and with immersing oneself in the intricacies and subtleties and implications and layers of the language itself, of the text being spoken.

Advocates of Linklater's work cite the actors' connection with their selves, their emotions, and their text, and cite the wonderful simplicity, honesty, and lack of self-consciousness in their delivery. Critics of Linklater's work describe it as a long and detailed warm-up process that shortchanges both attention to clear articulation and the development of the actor's ability to characterize vocally; they say that those trained solely in Linklater work do very fine and compelling acting, but only in their own personae.

Linklater has trained a great number of teachers, directors, actors, and public speakers in her approach — through a month-long intensive workshop she taught for years at Shakespeare & Company, through the courses she now teaches to undergraduates at Emerson College in Boston, and through

---

[6]   Edith Skinner, *Speak with Distinction,* ed. Lilene Mansell, rev. with new materials added by Timothy Monich and Lilene Mansell, (New York: Applause Theatre Book Publishers, 1990).

[7]   Kristin Linklater, *Freeing the Natural Voice* (New York: Drama Book Specialists, 1976).

the private workshops she continues to offer in the Boston area and elsewhere.[8] She has written two excellent texts which are widely used and available, either through their publisher or through a number of drama book shops throughout this country.[9] In addition to training a number of people who base their own teaching on her work, she has intensively trained and certified a select number of teachers whom she feels are most qualified to pass on the essence of her technique and philosophy. So a performer or public speaker seeking to undergo Linklater training should inquire of any potential teacher about the exact nature of his or her training and qualifications.

THE LESSAC SYSTEM

Arthur Lessac began his own training as a singer at the Eastman School of Music in Rochester, New York. As his interest in the workings of the human voice developed, he supplemented his musical training with course work in the anatomy and physiology of the voice and then, later on, to the workings of the human body in general. He began to develop his system of behavior modification in a search for something organically American rather than derived or adapted from late nineteenth- and early twentieth-century British acting schools. He has been investigating, experimenting, and evolving a detailed system for the use and training of the human voice for at least forty years in this country. During the past twenty years or so, he has expanded his consideration of voice and speech to encompass detailed work on the actor's body as well.

Lessac's work is based on the proposition that the speaker must eliminate all anesthetic, deadening habits in his or her communicative behavior and replace them with an ongoing state of habitual awareness. Awareness is a matter of being present and conscious on a moment-to-moment basis as one breathes, produces voice, and speaks. Instead of seeking to imitate or to duplicate any other models, each speaker uses kinesthetic awareness in order to rediscover and enjoy sounds which are healthy, aesthetically pleasing, and based on natural behavior.

In the voice area of his work, Lessac approaches this rediscovery through the acquisition of three complementary vocal actions. In structural action, the speaker uses the natural forward structure of the face and oral cavity to produce vowels which are rich, full, and free of restricting habitual tensions. In tonal action, the speaker becomes aware of and learns to produce buzzing and ringing vibrations on the hard palate and up into the top front quarter

---

[8]   Located at The Mount, Lenox, MA 02140 [(413) 637-1197]. Month-long workshops in acting, voice, movement, and text have been offered in both January and June of each year. Linklater's voice work is being very ably taught at these workshops by a number of teachers whom she has trained.

[9]   Linklater, op cit. See also Kristin Linklater, *Freeing Shakespeare's Voice*, (New York: Theatre Communications Group, Publishers, 1992).

of the skull in order to focus the tone in such a way that it will project effortlessly and protect the speaker from any vocal injury or discomfort, even when speaking in inhospitable vocal environments. In consonant action, the speaker treats each of the consonants as a musical instrument, learning to taste its particular identifying vibrations, to explore its particular range, to communicate emotional feelings and connections, and to incorporate this new-found vibratory and rhythmic awareness into spoken language.

By "leading" with one vocal action or another, the actor learns to surface different colors, interpretations, or readings of dramatic material and to adapt effortlessly to different playing spaces. By learning to explore while performing memorized materials, the actor learns to truly be in the present moment and to allow performance to be a discovery rather than a reproduction of what has been rehearsed in the past.

Advocates of Lessac's system cite its ability to heal and strengthen voices which have, in the past, suffered from hyperfunction and strain, and its ability to produce speech sounds which are clear and communicative and beautiful, even in actors who dislike articulation exercises and drill sheets. Some critics are put off by Lessac's untraditional terminology. Others observe that until students can fully understand and internalize or own their training, they may look and sound forced or uncomfortable as they speak and that when taught incompletely or incorrectly, the system might produce a way of speaking which is self-conscious or even pretentious.

For many years, Lessac and a small number of his master teachers taught the voice and body work each summer at intensive, four- to six-week workshops — at the State University of New York in Binghamton, at Southern Methodist University, and on other campuses in Iowa, in California, and in various other parts of the United States. His system and philosophy are described in detail in his two major books, *The Use and Training of the Human Voice* and *Body Wisdom: The Use and Training of the Human Body*.[10] A number of teachers who trained by taking one or a series of his summer workshops or a specific course of study at the State University of New York at Binghamton are presently teaching in different locations throughout the country. Information about their location and qualifications can be obtained by contacting either Arthur Lessac or Sue Ann Park.[11]

---

[10]   Arthur Lessac, *The Use and Training of the Human Voice*, 2nd ed., rev. (Mt. View, California: Mayfield Publishing Company, 1967); Arthur Lessac, *Body Wisdom: The Use and Training of the Human Body*, Originally published by the author in 1978 and currently distributed by Tom Leabhart, Theatre Department, Pomona College, Claremont, CA 91711, [(714) 621-8186].

[11]   Lessac Research and Training Institute, 826 Second Street, #306, Santa Monica, CA 90403, or Sue Ann Park, White Horse Village, 535 Gradyville Road, Apt. G111, Newtowne Square, PA 19073.

Other Options

The intent of this article has been to introduce an interested but relatively uninformed reader to the different types of voice training available in this country. Some generalization and superficiality are unavoidable in an undertaking such as this. Furthermore, in order not to obscure the general information provided in this article, the decision was made to confine descriptions to major systems of training and remediation available in this country. However, in actuality, there are several other excellent approaches to training as well which deserve at least a brief mention.

Several excellent voice and speech teachers base their work on the writings and teachings of Cicely Berry, Clifford Turner, and Patsy Rodenburg in England.[12] A number of actors and public speakers have found great value in the work of teachers connected with the Roy Hart Theatre in France.[13] Other actors or speakers who feel that limitations or restrictions in their voices are absolutely and undeniably physically based have benefitted greatly from work with an Alexander teacher, a Feldenkrais practitioner, or a physical therapist.[14] Several speakers really enjoy or have always wanted to learn to sing and discover that there is a very strong connection between singing training and significant development of many facets of the speaking voice. To find qualified singing teachers, many speakers and actors contact a school of music or conservatory nearby for referrals or inquire of the National Association of Teachers of Singing (NATS) as to the location of singing teachers who are members in good standing.[15]

In truth, there are as many methods or approaches as there are teachers, so the wise consumer will shop around. This might mean reading or at

---

[12] Cicely Berry, *The Actor and His Text* (London: George G. Harrap & Company, Ltd., 1987); Cicely Berry, *Voice and the Actor* (London: George C. Harrap & Company, Ltd., 1973);Clifford Turner, *Voice and Speech in the Theatre*, 3rd ed., rev. by Malcolm Morrison (London: Pitman, Ltd., 1977); Patsy Rodenburg, *The Need for Words* (London: Methuen Drama, 1993); Patsy Rodenburg, *The Right to Speak* (London: Methuen Drama, 1992).

[13] Roy Hart Theatre, Malerargues, Thoiras, 30140, Anduze, France; several residential workshops are offered each year, and several Roy Hart affiliated teachers work in this country as well.

[14] Certified Alexander teachers in a particular geographical area can be located by writing The North American Society of Teachers of Alexander Technique (NASTAT), P.O. Box 112484, Tacoma, WA 98411-2484 or by telephoning (800) 473-0620 or (206) 627-3766. Qualified Feldenkrais practitioners can be located through The Feldenkrais Guild, 706 Ellsworth Street, P.O. Box 489, Albany, Oregon 97321-0143 or by telephoning (503) 926-0981 or (800) 775-2118.

[15] The main NATS office is at 2800 University Boulevard North, JU Station, Jacksonville, FL 32211.

least browsing through a number of currently available textbooks in order to identify approaches which seem most compatible with personal preferences or style. This might mean interviewing a number of prospective teachers or coaches and perhaps observing or participating in a few classes before any long-term commitment is made. Many of the most knowledgeable and most qualified voice and speech teachers and coaches in this country are members of the Voice and Speech Trainers Association, so the VASTA membership directory might provide an excellent place to start.[16]

The speaker or actor who wishes to embark on a program of personal vocal growth should expect no miracles, no quick fixes, no magic pills, but must be willing to commit to consistent and ongoing training over a period of at least three months. A year would be far more productive; true practitioners know that the pursuit of vocal excellence is a life-long process. In actuality, it is probably less important that a particular system of training is undertaken than that the speaker is in fact working steadily and consistently on his or her mechanism and technique via some form or other over a significant period of time. Ultimately, many of these seemingly diverse methods are in fact providing different doors into the same room. Finding the most interesting or accessible or productive door and moving through it into a place where one feels comfortable, confident, grounded, present, and continually in process is an exhilarating, empowering experience which will be unique to each speaker.

SELECTED BIBLIOGRAPHY IN VOICE AND SPEECH TRAINING

Anderson, Virgil. *Training the Speaking Voice.* 3rd ed., New York: Oxford University Press, 1977.

Berry, Cicely. *The Actor and His Text.* London: George G. Harrap & Company, Ltd., 1987.

———. *Voice and the Actor.* London: George G. Harrap & Company, Ltd., 1973.

Brodnitz, Friedrich S. *Keep Your Voice Healthy.* 2nd ed., Boston: Little, Brown & Co., 1988.

---

[16]   Write Professor Barry Kur, Past-President, Voice and Speech Trainers Association, c/o Department of Theatre, 103 Arts Building, Pennsylvania State University, University Park, PA 16802 or telephone (814) 865-7586.

Eisenson, Jon. *Voice and Diction: A Program for Improvement.* 5th ed., New York: Macmillan Company, Publishers, 1985.

Fisher, Hilda B. *Improving Voice and Articulation.* 2nd ed., rev., Boston: Houghton Mifflin Company, 1975.

Lessac, Arthur. *Body Wisdom: The Use and Training of the Human Body.* Originally published by the author in 1978 and currently distributed by Tom Leabhart, Theatre Department, Pomona College, Claremont CA 91711 [(714)-621-8186].

———. *The Use and Training of the Human Voice.* 2nd ed., rev., Mt. View, California: Mayfield Publishing Company, 1967.

Linklater, Kristin. *Freeing the Natural Voice.* New York: Drama Book Specialists, 1976.

———. *Freeing Shakespeare's Voice.* New York: Theatre Communications Group, Publishers, 1992.

Machlin, Evangeline. *Speech for the Stage.* New York: Theatre Arts Books, 1966.

Proctor, Donald F. *Breathing, Speech and Song.* New York: Springer-Verlag Wein, 1980.

Punt, Norman A. *The Singer's and Actor's Throat.* 3rd ed., rev., London: William Heinemann Medical Books, Ltd., 1979.

Rodenburg, Patsy. *The Need for Words.* London: Methuen Drama, 1993.

———. *The Right to Speak.* London: Methuen Drama, 1992.

Skinner, Edith. *Speak with Distinction.* ed. by Lilene Mansell, rev. with new materials added by Timothy Monich and Lilene Mansell, New York: Applause Theatre Book Publishers, 1990 (accompanying audio cassette tape available).

Stemple, Joseph C. ed., *Voice Therapy: Clinical Studies.* St. Louis: Mosby-Year Book, Inc., 1993.

Turner, James Clifford. *Voice and Speech in the Theatre.* 3rd ed., rev. by Malcolm Morrison, London: Pitman, Ltd., 1977.

Wilder, Lilyan. *Professionally Speaking.* New York: Simon & Schuster, 1986.

18

VOICE COACHING IN PRIVATE PRACTICE

Lucille Schutmaat Rubin

T HE BIG LEAP

My first day on the job teaching in a theater school, I turned to pick up my papers after class and was surprised to hear the sound of applause. This was a new experience, and unlike any I had in university teaching. The students' reception to the work inspired me, and bridged my move from university teaching into private practice.

Yet, I had been trained not only in theater but also speech. Speech, at the time I received my degrees, meant public speaking and communication arts. So here I was with two fields of endeavor and I loved them both. While teaching at the university, I began to respond to personal and corporate requests to privately coach actors and speakers. I began to coach these private clients after hours in a rented space in New York city. That first step "hooked" me.

It was a leap moving from university teaching to private practice. One does not make job changes without a sense of sure footing. This story is about just that — making decisions about doing the work I wanted to do.

The practice grew. My clients were highly motivated but seeking short-term help to meet particular vocal needs. This was quite different from the long term training afforded me in teaching actors and speakers in a university setting. In private practice there was not the luxury of time. I had to learn to spot clients' immediate needs and provide solutions within limited time frames. The following pages highlight my approach to coaching in private practice.

THE DEMANDS OF PRIVATE PRACTICE

Voice coaching used to be simple. Actors wanted coaching for stage and film, and speakers wanted training in public speaking. Actors today request voice training for musicals, video, radio, television, voice-overs, commercials, soaps, looping, cartoons, character voices, and comedy routines. Speakers today want to know how to deal with stage fright, sound credible, present with ease, maintain audience interest, dismiss vocal fatigue, eliminate accents, find their best phone voice, develop voice appeal, extend communication skills, master on-camera behaviors, and make use of the new technology tools in their presentations. Because the needs have changed, so have the nature and scope of coaching offered in the voice business.

CONTRIBUTIONS OF MEDICINE, SCIENCE, AND THERAPY

Anyone who wants to offer the best in private voice coaching needs to keep abreast of current contributions from voice medicine, voice science, and voice therapy; they also will want to stay in touch with voice professionals in these fields. The coach today needs sophisticated knowledge of vocal anatomy and physiology, ring and registers, and modern biofeedback technology.

Because some of my clients are referred to me by otolaryngologists, I need to be able to translate their diagnoses into viable voice coaching programs. Sharing our findings frequently encourages ongoing dialogues. One ENT told me he had received my consultation findings on his patient, and that those findings helped him better understand how his patients feel and sense their voices. Soon he was borrowing some of my coaching lingo, and I was borrowing some of his medical terms.

Working in partnership with otolaryngologists makes my job easier. For example, an ENT cleared up a sinus infection in one actor, and removed a nasal polyp in another. Because these actors could now feel mask vibrations and breathe through their noses, I could effectively develop their mask resonance and dismiss their denasality. Training time for these clients was shortened with the help of a medical colleague.

Staying up with the contributions from the vocal scientists presents a different set of challenges. Scientific studies on vocal fatigue, registers, tract shaping, resonance, ring, appropriate pitch levels, and laryngeal positioning have revolutionized training methods. One way I stay on top of these new studies and in touch with these professionals is to make a trip to their voice labs. Sometimes I take my clients with me. Here they gain basic acoustical information, see their voice sonograms, and figure out how to adjust vocal fold closure time for "screaming" safely.

Voice therapists continue to find new ways to see, hear, and assess the

voice with state of the art technologies. Much of this technology is cost pro-
hibitive to the coach in private practice, so I book in sessions at a voice center with my clients. Here, with the help of a therapist, my client and I explore
the use of biofeedback as a training tool. In a recent visit, I took a client, an
opera singer, who lacked ring in his speaking voice. After the therapist
demonstrated the use of the spectrograph, my client picked up the mike and
sang. He was thrilled to see the ring in his singing voice on the monitor.
Now it was time for him to get the same sensations with his speaking voice.
It took him six attempts before he admitted, "This isn't easy, you know," and
two more attempts before he located the ring in his speaking voice. Getting
this client to connect his speaking voice to his singing voice was visually and
aurally supported with bio-feedback technology. It was easy to reinforce this
new-found skill with my client during follow up sessions in my studio.

Networking with professional colleagues in the above fields helps me
develop a comprehensive approach to my coaching, and provides my clients
with the assurance that caretakers, rehabilitators and coaches are working
together as a unified support team.

THE STUDIO

Having equipment that supports my professional practice is essential. I
cannot do without the following: video camera with monitor for playback;
VCR to view clients' video tapes; high quality audio recording equipment
and cassette tapes for taking voice samples; microphone for live amplification of vocal habits; presentation board; podium; slide and transparency
projectors; flip chart; computer with monitor and printer, CD-ROM and
speakers; and piano. A fax machine, answering services, and E-mail help me
stay in touch with my clients.

Software programs help clients dismiss accents and sibilancy. Speakers
use software that livens up their presentations with attractive graphs and
graphics. To selected clients I show video films and photos that help them
understand how their voice works, and how to phonate optimally. An incen-
tive spirometer encourages flow phonation and discourages the use of glottal attacks and holding patterns. The Picture-Tel for clients mastering
video-conferencing skills, and Teleprompter for on-camera broadcasters and
politicians are important tools for speakers. This high-cost equipment can be
rented for rehearsal use on either my business site or the dealer's studio.

Providing a conducive environment for coaching is also important. Car-
peting, soft lighting, acoustical life in the room, temperature control, appropriate humidity level, comfortable seating, fragrance-free flowers, and fresh
water contribute to a rewarding coaching session. Selecting a location that is
geographically close to the clients I serve, and one that can be reached safely
by private or public transportation are also important considerations.

STAFF AND CONSULTANT SUPPORT

As a private practitioner, I need staff support beyond secretarial and answering services. Business, legal, and financial consultants are essential. Establishing these relationships early on helped me manage the business more effectively and today provides me with more coaching time. Professional help assures me that a mailing will go out on time, my business plan is solid, my copyrights and trademarks are honored, and contracts properly drawn. The business of running a business is as important as knowing how to be a top coach. If you are a top coach and have limited business skills, you will always feel overworked and underpaid. If you have great business skills but have not updated your coaching skills and equipment, you may have a limited client base.

"WHAT IS IT YOU DO?"

This is a frequent question, so I am ready with a sound bite that details my expertise and services. Those clients requesting coaching in areas outside my expertise, I refer to appropriate professionals from an updated referral list. It is tempting to try to solve all vocal concerns that reach the studio, but doing so prevents me from capitalizing on my real talents. One strategic coach's advice is to focus on strengths, and delegate weaknesses.

I follow up on all inquiries about my services with brochures, current company newsletters, and a cover letter that recapitulates the client's stated needs. The brochures detail the services offered and carry my mission statement. Using one clarifies and distinguishes my services from those of other voice coaches.

COACHING ON-SITE

The demand for on site training is rising in the business world with many courses and private coaching sessions held on the client's premises. This can be helpful to some clients as it prepares them for the real thing. I recall a client I was coaching privately on his company's site. He was the main speaker at a stockholder's meeting and suffered from stage fright. I urged him to get to the meeting early and greet people as they came in the door. I suggested he pretend this was his home, these were his invited guests, and that it was his job to make them feel comfortable. When it came time for him to speak, I could see and hear that he had found a new "comfort zone" and clearly enjoyed speaking to his guests.

Coaching on a corporate site helps me see and sense business clients' environment and company culture. With this new information, I am better able to design future coaching programs for the client, and recommend training programs to the corporation at large.

Actors request that I work with them on stage. There, they become aware of the acoustics of the space, and through exercises I have designed can make vocal choices that help their voices carry with ease. What may have worked for them vocally in a rehearsal space may not work for them on stage. By testing out their vocal choices the actors hear and feel what is working for them. Rehearsing with these new choices on stage gives them the confidence to use them in performance.

Actors appearing in "soaps" or commercials bring in their video tapes. They serve as documentation of their "live" performances. The actor and I together view the tapes, identify our concerns, and address those concerns during that session and, if necessary, future sessions. Receiving a tape in advance of a proposed session is helpful to me as coach; however, viewing the tape together lets me know that we both hear and see the same vocal concerns.

Rehearsing on site is especially helpful to the client, but seeing a "live" performance is especially helpful to the coach. Choices made during one-on-one rehearsals may not serve the actor in the presence of an audience. The acoustics of the room change as do the artistic demands in performance. I like to see stage shows while they are in previews because line readings are not likely to be "set." During the performance I take notes and share them with the actor before the next performance. I avoid giving notes backstage after a performance as I have found this is an inappropriate time for most actors.

Seeing speakers in performance is more difficult because they frequently present a particular speech one time and out of town. If I cannot catch a "live" speech, I review audio or video tapes of their presentations, and together we decide what is working and how to extend those choices. Working on a "gotta fix" list is a lifetime job so I prefer to extend skills that are working and to find new ones.

NEEDS AND SOLUTIONS

Most clients are clear about their vocal goals, but unsure of their vocal needs. I can quickly identify needs and offer solutions with the help of my vocal history and vocal profile forms. The history alerts me to any special medical concerns and the profile documents vocal behaviors and options. Together we select areas we want to change, prioritize those areas, and agree on a time frame. I then design a coaching program indicating the number of sessions needed to meet the client's needs and the specific training offered at each session. Designing the program together helps the client invest in the process. This consultation is essentially a goal-establishing session concluding with a direct plan on how to achieve those goals.

In designing the program, there is always a temptation to offer extensive, in depth training because, of course, it all helps. However, one of the biggest jobs for the voice coach in private practice is to *limit* the training. Most training programs consist of nine to twelve sessions, with serious clients asking for twenty-four sessions. Ongoing clients contract yearly and come in for coaching one or two times a month. This latter group tends to be self-motivated, goal oriented, and specific about their needs. One such business client outlined his own coaching program for the year. It included updating his current presentation, incorporating multi-media tools, a speech tune-up, rehearsing conference call formats, and putting vocal skills to use on the phone to achieve business objectives.

Another business client, who needed a minimum of twelve sessions of training, was limited to three by her employer. In order to meet her immediate goals, I did more coaching than training. For example, I selected three major vocal needs and worked on one in each session using her press release for text. The first ten minutes of each session was spent introducing a skill and the remainder of the one hour session, applying the skill. I gave her skill maintenance exercises for at home practice and a clear plan on how to use her new skills on the job.

The coach in private practice has to be able to quickly spot the needs, to focus the coaching, and apply the new skills to the job or profession. By using my phone-in service, clients leave a daily message indicating what they are working on and then read or speak for three minutes, using their new skills.

In my practice, I find there are few clients with common needs, and consequently I must find uncommon solutions. Uncommon needs include those of an actress who was directed "to speak on an inhale," an actor whose character needed "a voice of steel," and a trial lawyer who wanted "energy" in his voice in order to keep the judge awake. The professions that present common concerns include singers with poor speaking technique, speakers with performance anxiety, Broadway belters with tired throats, voice-over artists with excessive sibilance, and commodity traders with vocal misuse.

The professional demands made on the voices of my clients direct and focus the design of their coaching programs. Perhaps one of my clients, a Wall Street trader, illustrates this point. This trader, who kept losing his voice in the pit, told me he was worth a million dollars with his voice, and worth nothing without it. Hearing this "need," I paid an on-site visit and observed his voice and body behaviors in the pit. After hearing the clamor, I gained a clear idea of his vocal needs and how I could offer him immediate help.

Identifying needs and finding solutions are two important steps in the coaching process. These unlike skills need mastering and honing by the coach in private practice. Having a focused plan and a clear process are mandatory; however, I know that *how* I coach is more important than *what*

I coach. The crux of my coaching can perhaps be summed up as follows: I coach the person, not the voice.

Records and Documentation

Keeping accurate records, sending findings to referring professionals, writing coaching proposals, audio and video taping, and preparing statements are just some of the tasks the private practitioner must perform. Four important record taking tasks in my work are taking the vocal history, recording the voice, preparing the voice profile, and writing the coaching program.

The vocal history form, filled out by the client at the first visit, provides me with the physical history of his/her voice, previous voice training, and vocal goals. Upon completion, I ask the client to speak into the microphone and informally discuss that information with me. I tape segments of that information. Next I ask for a "live" sample of his/her voice as s/he uses it in his/her professional life. This could be a monologue, business presentation, phone pitch, voice-over, speech, business presentation, or a rundown of the days' activities. I record two minutes of that sample. Finally, I ask him/her to read a selection that addresses his/her vocal concerns from my book, *The Voice Handbook.* I record two minutes of that reading. Total recording time is six to eight minutes.

Together we replay the tape and complete the vocal profile form. I design the coaching program and prepare a written copy for the client for our next working session. That session and all future sessions will be audio or video taped.

The voice tape, the history and profile forms, and the written coaching program provide me with documentation that I can refer to at any time. A comparison of the initial and final voice samples charts and documents the progress for both client and coach. The tapes, forms, and coaching program also serve as a point of reference for the client returning sometime in the future. The professional coach needs more than a great memory and a finely tuned ear. Documentation of the training process is essential.

Clients frequently ask me to share the basic design of the coaching program with their singing coaches and voice-over instructors. If the client has been referred by an ENT, I send a copy of the vocal profile to that doctor. Communicating with the clients' professional trainers supports specific optimum behaviors, prevents repetition of training, and helps clients integrate their studies. Coaching that makes me feel part of a team works best for me.

Professional Behaviors

Private coaching demands adopting codes of behaviors that build mutual respect and trust. Here are some guidelines:

1. Use appropriate language, gesture, and vocal tone. Verbalize messages rather than physically touching the client to explain a process. Document each session p ith a video or audio tape.

2. Respect the client's time: Make necessary preparations in advance of the appointment time. Lay out materials and set up equipment. Start and end coaching sessions on time. Honor the time frame agreed upon in the coaching program.

3. Maintain confidentiality.

4. Limit discussion to the work at hand. Lay out specific goals and an agenda for each session for the client to see how the session time will be allocated.

5. Recognize former training and whenever appropriate, integrate it into the coaching program. Offer training at the client's level of expertise.

6. Dress appropriately. Respect the dress codes of clients especially when coaching on their sites.

Staying Alive in Today's Market

Here are some guidelines for voice specialists who are thinking about setting up their own voice business:

Stay visible. You can do this by publishing, presenting, performing, and making media appearances. Engage in coaching activities that take you out of the studio. Keep your brochures and services up to date. Offer what the market or client needs rather than what you want to teach. Continue to study and extend your own skills by taking classes, keeping up with the current literature, speaking to groups, and performing professionally.

Build a strong client base. Focus on clients for whom you know you can bring about outstanding results. Selecting six clients who demand the best of your coaching talents will do more to improve your level of expertise than coaching twenty-five clients who have extensive vocal needs and may never put them to work professionally. Decide whether you want to coach highly motivated clients who demand high level skill training and your best creative energies, or clients who are less motivated and less advanced in their careers. High profile clients are likely to recommend you to other high profile clients. Your client selection to some degree determines the nature of your practice.

Familiarize yourself with your client's company or profession. For business clients, get to know about their jobs, responsibilities, and corporations. Pick up on their "buzz" words. Read some of the books and magazines that your client reads. If you work with performers, take some acting or singing training. By experiencing the artistic demands of performance, you will have a better understanding of the performer's needs. I found that my training in acting, singing, body work, combat, dance, speech, television, and public speaking help me in coaching both actors and speakers.

LOOKING AHEAD

Changes will affect the private coaching profession. There will be new job openings in unusual places. Hospitals and speech communication centers will offer voice training as part of their community outreach programs to both public and targeted audiences. Theater schools will open their doors to the non-actor with classes in singing, voice and speech for the business professional, and voice-over skills. Health clubs now offering classes in The Alexander Technique will perhaps be adding classes in vocal fitness to their roster. Corporations will be asking for more coaches to train more of their executives to be skilled speakers. More speakers will need coaching in motivating and inspiring their audiences.

There will be a proliferation of new training methodologies here and abroad. Voice coaches will design their own methods and rely less on the one or two methods in which they were trained. My Russian-born friend and director, Alan Schneider, once remarked to me after I had finished raving about the Polish director Jerzy Grotowski: "Americans are always looking for the next Messiah!" Maybe we are, but by the year 2000 the American coaches who want to stay on the cutting edge of the voice business will not be teaching anybody's method but their own.

WORKS CITED

Berry, Cicely. *The Actor and His Text*. London: Harrup Ltd, 1987.

Barton, Robert and Rocco Dal Vera. *Voice: Onstage and Off*. New York: Harcourt Brace & Co., 1995.

Blu, Susan, and Molly Ann Mullin. *Word of Mouth*. London: Pomegranate Press, Ltd.,1992.

Grotowski, Jerzy. *Towards a Poor Theatre*. Holstebro: Christian Christensen & Co., 1968.

Leech, Thomas. *How to Prepare, Stage, & Deliver Winning Presentations*. New York: AMACOM, 1993.

Rubin, Lucille S., ed. *Movement for the Actor.* New York: Drama Book Specialists, 1980.

Saxon, Keith G., M.D. and Carole Schneider, M.D. *Vocal Exercise Physiology.* San Diego: Singular Publishing Group, Inc., 1995.

Video

Sullivan, Dan. *The Strategic Coach Program.* Toronto: The Strategic Coach Inc., 1994.

19

INTERFACE BETWEEN THEATRE VOICE AND SPEECH TRAINER AND SPEECH-LANGUAGE PATHOLOGIST

KATHERINE VERDOLINI

How might the theatre voice and speech trainer and the speech-language pathologist interact? In the case of an acting student with a voice or speech problem, a classic scenario has been that the theatre trainer refers the student to the speech pathologist, who works with the student until the problem is resolved and the student is once again "normal." Then the speech pathologist sends the student back to the theatre trainer for continued artistic development.

This type of interface essentially amounts to handing the proverbial stick from one practitioner to the other (hopefully not treating the student like an incidental piece of baggage in the process). Although there is an interface in this case, there is actually little interaction between the practitioners. Are there better ways to think about interactions? Might the mutual enrichment be greater — and the care of the student be better — if we could think more creatively? That is the topic of this essay: creative thinking about the ways in which theatre voice and speech trainers (further abbreviated as "theatre trainers") and speech-language pathologists (further abbreviated as "speech pathologists") might interact.

We will do some thinking about the historical relations between the practitioners, we will think about what theatre trainers might get from speech pathologists and what speech pathologists might get from theatre trainers, what the benefits of reciprocal interactions might be, and where theatre trainers can turn for contact with speech pathologists. We will also point out some cautions in interacting across disciplines.

HISTORICAL AND PHILOSOPHICAL BACKGROUND

Historically, theatre trainers and speech pathologists have interacted preciously little. There are probably at least two major reasons. First, theatre and speech pathology people have tended to focus on different issues in training. Theatre trainers have usually focused on the development of aesthetic and expressive capabilities across a very wide range of human emotions and situations. Speech pathologists have usually focused on restoring impaired voice and speech to normal status, for a comparatively limited repertoire of tasks. With these different goals, it is easy to see how theatre and speech pathology trainers might not have found much to talk about or share.

I think that there is also another and perhaps more significant reason why theatre and speech pathology trainers have interacted little historically. We tend to talk different languages. That is, we tend to approach training with fundamentally different thought-tools. Although the distinction is not absolute by any means, it is probably safe to say that the theatre trainer's tools are often predominantly intuitive, whereas the speech pathologist's tools are often predominantly analytical. In many cases, this type of difference might make communicating quite a challenge.

In thinking about this a bit further, what do we actually mean by "intuitive" versus "analytical" tools? I define intuitive processes as those that heavily rely on non-conscious mental operations, whereby the intuitions are the surface (or conscious) manifestations of such operations. The advantage of this approach is that non-conscious operations are carried out by an enormous capacity mental processor that is equipped to handle formidable amounts of information all at once. The solutions that emerge might be truly powerful ones because they are based on so much information. Analytical thinking, as I am thinking about it in this context, involves the slow, deliberate, and rational assembly of individual thought elements in consciousness. The results can be inspected and described verbally. The advantage is that this type of thinking is flexible; it can extricate itself to a degree from old habits that are run off automatically, allowing for novel solutions. (The interested reader is referred to Kahneman, 1973, and Posner & Snyder, 1975, for a discussion of conscious and non-conscious information processing.)

How might such considerations affect interactions between theatre trainers and speech pathologists in a positive way? This question is the focus of the next sections.

WHAT CAN THEATRE VOICE TRAINERS LEARN FROM SPEECH PATHOLOGISTS?

Theatre trainers can learn a lot of techniques and facts from speech pathologists. Among the many, many examples, it might be useful for the theatre trainer to know that an important aspect of injury prevention and treatment is probably vocal fold adduction, or "pressing" (see, for example, Hillman, Holmberg, Perkell, Walsh, & Vaughn, 1989; Jiang & Titze, in press; Peterson, Verdolini-Marston, Barkmeier, & Hoffman, in press; Verdolini, Druker, Palmer, & Samawi, submitted; Verdolini, Berry, & Titze, submitted; Verdolini-Marston, Burke, Lessac, Glaze, & Caldwell, in press). Theatre practitioners have suspected this conclusion for a long time, but it is nice to have confirmations from controlled experiments. Technical information of this type is undoubtedly useful. However, I think that the real benefit of interacting with speech pathologists goes well beyond the reception of technical information. I think that a more important benefit is the exposure to a way of thinking that is not necessarily salient in theatre traditions — the analytical mode. The point is not that the analytical mode is superior to the intuitive one, but rather that exposure to a new thinking mode, whatever that mode may be, provides an opportunity to expand one's thought repertoire. And how can theatre people reject exposure to any experience of this type, interested as they are in the range of human experiences?

With an analytical thinking mode as we have described it here, theatre trainers might learn to combine rational information in a new way, generating new solutions to novel or old problems. The solutions might be the same as the ones generated by speech pathologists, or they might be different. The point is that well-supported analytical thinking, in which speech pathologists have considerable training, produces flexibility. New training systems can be devised to fit individual cases, old systems can be altered, and the effectiveness of training systems in general can be evaluated in a way that minimizes the trainer's own bias.

If the theatre trainer further becomes involved in the research side of speech pathology, yet other benefits can be expected. Yes, technical information can be gained from scientific work that might be useful in training. However, again, I think that the real benefit of an involvement with research is the exposure to a somewhat peculiar philosophy, on which contemporary science is based. According to this thinking, one can never "prove" something to be true. One can only falsify a hypothesis, leaving other hypotheses available as possibilities. In fact, to assert that some fact is "scientifically proven" is completely oxymoronic. The basic protocol is to successively *disprove* a series of hypotheses, theoretically with some final product left available as a *possibility*. The underlying idea is that "truth" is fundamentally elusive. It cannot be touched nor handled nor seen. It can only be inferred. This philosophy explains why some speech pathologists, who have exposure to scientific methodology, may be more tentative than theatre trainers about what works in training. Properly understood, the scientific philosophy illuminates new possibilities for thinking and discovery that might be exciting and stimulating for many theatre people.

WHAT SPEECH PATHOLOGISTS CAN LEARN FROM VOICE TRAINERS

Speech pathologists have a tremendous amount to learn from theatre trainers. Theatre approaches to voice and speech have evolved over decades, if not centuries, emerging from ponderous "field-testing" in real-life situations. A theatre approach simply will not survive if its trainees are not getting — and keeping — jobs in demanding performance situations. The ultimate result is a robust voice and speech production approach that actually works in *lots* of situations. Being constrained by such tough ecological considerations, most approaches to voice and speech in theatre are physiologically more complex, expressively more rich, and pedagogically more sound than many approaches in speech pathology. Theatre trainers may not know *why* (they might learn why by working with speech pathologists), and they may not be able to *adapt* the techniques for individual situations (they might learn to do so by being exposed to speech pathologists' analytical thinking processes), but I do think it is true that theatre systems are more complex and in some ways, more sound. Let me give a few examples. Theatre trainers tend to consider breathing, phonation, speech, and postural factors all together in training, leading to complex physiological acts that are coordinated across physiological systems (see for example, Lessac, 1967). Speech pathologists tend to train component voice and speech parts separately, and, depending on the disorder, may never combine them all into a cohesive whole. Theatre trainers address a wide range of human emotions and vocal expressions (sorrow and ecstasy, whispers and screams), rendering their work exquisitely expressive. Speech pathologists, on the other hand, tend to address relatively quiet voice and speech in controlled environments. And, by tradition, theatre trainers have tended to emphasize sensory (perceptual) experience in training, consistent with what I consider sound pedagogical principles (see my other essay in this text), as compared with speech pathologists, who have tended to emphasize rational and verbal explanations in training.

From these considerations, it is easy to see how speech pathologists could benefit from exposure to theatre trainers' voice and speech techniques. But as we have already discussed, an even greater benefit might be exposure to a mode of thinking that is not particularly prominent in speech pathology, that involves a generally intuitive approach to training. This is not to say that the speech pathologist would abandon analytical thinking — hardly! However, by learning to trust intuitive elements in training, even more than he or she already does, and by incorporating more of such elements in the training repertoire, the speech pathologist might greatly enrich his or her training style. In theatre, the intuitive approach includes detecting and responding to very subtle aspects of voice and speech production in pre-verbal, spontaneous ways, "moment to moment." The speech pathologist who is exposed to this mode might incorporate it in therapy, resulting in therapy sessions that are more relevant to the learner, with more powerful (encompassing) solutions than those that are sometimes achieved with the predominantly analytical mode that is common to speech pathology.

AND NOW, WHAT ABOUT ACTUAL RECIPROCAL INTERACTIONS?

To this point, we have talked as if theatre trainers might learn from speech pathologists, and speech pathologists might learn from theatre trainers, as if in independent moments. The theatre trainer might take formal courses in speech pathology, and the speech pathologist might receive some formal training in theatre. These solutions would undoubtedly contribute to reciprocal learning, and are discussed in the next section. But what about a truly integrated *interaction*? What might that look like?

Integrated interaction between theatre trainers and speech pathologists might take place in a theatre training room, or in a speech pathology clinic, where actual learners are involved. Let us say, for example, that the theatre trainer wants to institute a prevention program as a part of the training curriculum. The speech pathologist and theatre trainer might develop a coordinated curriculum, so that theatre approaches and speech pathology approaches are combined into single activities. Or in the case of an acting student with a voice or speech problem, the theatre trainer and speech pathologist might conduct at least some sessions together, so that their approaches are convergent.

The outcome of this type of attempt can be quite interesting. Training sessions tend to take on a new look, that is, not the "theatre" look nor the "speech pathology" look. A new entity emerges from the combination of the two traditions. The entity tends to transcend the historical distinction between *esthetics* and *restoration*. Beauty and health converge. The protocol no longer involves a sequential restoration of injury to normalcy, followed by training in the development of superior skills. Restoration and development become one and the same process.

WHERE MIGHT THE THEATRE TRAINER GO TO FIND A SPEECH PATHOLOGIST WITH WHOM TO INTERACT, OR FOR SPECIFIC TRAINING IN SPEECH PATHOLOGY?

One of the best ways to find a speech pathologist with whom to interact is to determine if there is one in the community with a specific interest (and possibly, expertise) in working with performers. Such persons may still be rare, but they do exist in some communities. Another tack would be to determine if there is a speech pathologist with a particular interest in voice disorders. That speech pathologist might be more willing — and able — to work with a theatre trainer than a speech pathologist who specialized in neurological problems of speech and language due to stroke or disease.

If you want more formal training in speech pathology than collaboration with a single speech pathologist would afford, you might consider doing some coursework in a speech pathology department. There are many courses that might be relevant, including courses in anatomy, physiology, and acoustics of voice and speech, voice disorders, articulation or phonology disorders, and stuttering (many of the same issues seem to arise in fluency disorders as in voice).

A third possibility would be to attend regional or national conferences on voice. Some of the most important ones are listed in Appendix A.

A fourth, much more demanding option would be to enroll in a Master's program in speech pathology, for the purpose of obtaining licensing and certification as a speech-language pathologist. There are many good programs in the country, some of which include a special emphasis in voice — and performing voice — for interested students (see Appendix A).

CAUTIONS

There are some cautions that you might want to consider if you decide to interact with speech pathology. Speech pathologists are not in any way frightening or dangerous people — on the contrary. But one danger is that with ongoing interactions, one or both of you might start to think that you are equally competent in the other's area. You might inadvertently overstep your respective professional boundaries. Even after much work with you or even with some coursework in theatre, a speech pathologist is not a theatre trainer and should not claim to be one. In the same way, unless you complete a Master's degree in speech pathology and other certification and licensing requirements, you cannot claim to independently treat voice and speech disorders. There are legal implications in both directions. What I consider more important are the ethical considerations, which require fair and honest self-appraisal and community representation of ourselves and our abilities.

Another issue may be irrelevant in some cases, but relevant enough in others to be worth mentioning. Theatre people and speech pathologists may have a different interaction style, and typically *do* have a different training style. The differences are occasionally upsetting to some people. *On average* theatre people tend to be exuberant and relatively uninhibited in their expressive style, sometimes using colorful language and what some might consider non-traditional dress. In training, theatre sessions tend to explore a *range* of voice and speech possibilities with mental and physical experiences including floor work and touching. *In general,* therapy sessions in speech pathology tend to involve a narrower range of voice and speech activities, and the tone is relatively more "reserved" and less "emotional." You may react to the speech pathologist's work as restricted, and some speech pathologists might respond to you and your work as, well, shocking. I encourage you to persist. After all, the differences provide the actual impetus for interacting. They are the very source of richness that we seek.

CONCLUSIONS

Theatre voice and speech trainers and speech-language pathologists have much to gain by interacting with each other. There is the potential for the exchange of valuable technical information, as well as exposure to a different way of approaching training in general. I hope that theatre trainers will explore such possibilities by seeking out speech pathologists interested in the performer, and possibly by doing some coursework in speech pathology. By interacting, with time we may see the emergence of a new generation training mode, that crosses traditional boundaries with an integration of health and beauty in training, and of restoration and development.

Teachers of singing and speech pathologists have already considered some of the same issues together, and a joint statement between the National Association of Teachers of Singing (NATS) and the American Speech-Language Hearing Association (ASHA) is provided in Appendix B. The Voice and Speech Trainers' Association (VASTA) is currently seeking to develop a similar joint statement that will hopefully further stimulate our thinking on this important topic.

WORKS CITED

Jiang, J.J., and I.R. Titze. "Measurement of Vocal Fold Intraglottal Pressure and Impact Stress." *Journal of Voice* 8 (June 1994): 132-144.

Hillman, R.E., E. Holmberg, J.S. Perkell, M. Walsh, and C. Vaughn. "Objective Assessment of Vocal Hyperfunction: An Experimental Framework and Initial Results." *Journal of Speech and Hearing Research* 32 (1989): 373-392.

Kahneman, D. *Attention and Effort.* Englewood Cliffs, NJ: Prentice Hall, 1973.

Lessac, Arthur. *The Use and Training of the Human Voice; A Practical Approach to Speech and Voice Dynamics.* New York: Drama Publishers, 1967.

Peterson, K. L., K. Verdolini-Marston, J. M. Barkmeier, and H. T. Hoffman. "Comparison of Aerodynamic and Electroglottographic Parameters in Evaluating Clinically Relevant Voicing Patterns." *Annals of Otology, Rhinology, and Otolaryngology* (in press).

Posner, M. I. and C. R. R. Snyder. "Attention and Cognitive Control." In R. L. Solso, Ed. *Information Processing and Cognition: The Loyola symposium.* Hillsdale, N.J.: Lawrence Erlbaum Associates, 1975.

Verdolini, K., D. A. Berry, and I. R. Titze. "Vocal Efficiency from a Therapeutic Perspective: A Computational Approach." *Journal of the Acoustical Society of America* (submitted).

Verdolini, K., D. G. Druker, P. M. Palmer, and H. Samawi. "Physiological Study of "Resonant Voice." *Journal of Speech and Hearing Research* (submitted).

Verdolini-Marston, K., M. K. Burke, A. Lessac, L. Glaze, and E. Caldwell,. "A Preliminary Study on Two Methods of Treatment for Laryngeal Nodules." *Journal of Voice* 9 (March 1995): 74–85.

APPENDIX A

Conferences including Work on Voice and
Professional Voice in Speech Pathology and Master's
Programs with the Possibility of a Voice Specialization

ANNUAL SYMPOSIA:

Care of the Professional Voice.

Sponsored by The Voice Foundation. Usually held in June each year, in Philadelphia. For more information contact The Voice Foundation, 1721 Pine Street, Philadelphia, PA 19103; Phone (215) 735-7999; Fax (215) 735-9293.

Pacific Voice Conference.

Usually held in October each year, in San Francisco. For further information contact Dr. Krzysztok Izdebski at 350 Parnassus Avenue, Suite 501, San Francisco, CA 94117; Phone (415) 476-2792.

American Speech-Language-Hearing Association Convention.

Sponsored by the American Speech-Language-Hearing Association (ASHA). Usually held the weekend before Thanksgiving, in November. Location changes each year. For information contact ASHA National Office, 10801 Rockville Pike, Rockville, MD 20852; Phone (301) 897-5700; Fax (301) 571-0457. Also ask ASHA office about regional conferences occurring throughout the year.

CLINICAL MASTER'S PROGRAM WITH POSSIBILITY OF A SPECIAL EMPHASIS IN VOICE DISORDERS:

Department of Speech Pathology and Audiology, The University of Iowa, Iowa City, Iowa, 52242. For more information contact Ingo R. Titze, Ph.D. (319) 335-6601, or the department chair, Arnold Small, Ph.D., (319) 335-8718.

APPENDIX B

The Role of the Speech-Language Pathologist and Teacher of Singing in Remediation of Singers with Voice Disorders

ASHA AND NATS JOINT STATEMENT

Since the founding of the American Speech-Language-Hearing Association (ASHA) in 1925 and the founding of the National Association of Teachers of Singing (NATS) in 1944, there has been increasing awareness of (a) the importance of having healthy laryngeal function in both speech and singing, and (b) the existence of a connection between optimal vocal usage in speech and optimal vocal usage in singing. The fundamental mechanism for healthy phonation is essentially the same for both singing and speaking. Therefore, it is recognized by both ASHA and NATS that the etiology of a voice disorder can be related to improper singing as well as to improper speaking technique.

Historically, development of the speaking voice related to disorders of laryngeal maturation and function has been the province of qualified speech-language pathologists. Similarly, development of the voice to its maximum function for use in singing has been the province of teachers of singing. The speech-language pathologist has given special attention to remediation of voice disorders to restore and maintain normal voice function. The singing teacher has given special attention to the development of full pitch and dynamic range, artistic quality, and vocal endurance of the singing voice. This has resulted in separate and independent work and in a serial approach to the remediation of voice disorders in singers.

In recent years, there has been increasing awareness within both ASHA and NATS that this dichotomous approach may not be in the best interest of singers with voice disorders. Rather, both organizations acknowledge that the most effective path to vocal recovery will often include an integrated approach to optimal voice care and production that addresses both speech and singing tasks. ASHA and NATS therefore affirm the importance of interdisciplinary management of singers with voice disorders, with the management team ideally consisting of, but not restricted to, at least an otolaryngologist, a speech-language pathologist, and a singing teacher.

ASHA and NATS recognize that there are a variety of possible configurations for such teams. Some ASHA-certified speech-language pathologists may also be experienced teachers of singing who are members of NATS. Similarly, there may be some otolaryngologists who hold ASHA certification in speech-language pathology or who are members of NATS. However, both ASHA and NATS recognize that such dual specialization is rare, and that in most cases, the management team will consist of at least three individuals.

Although ASHA and NATS recognize the differences in both professional preparation and in the primary goals of their respective memberships, both organizations acknowledge the need for broader, interdisciplinary training of speech-language pathologists and teachers of singing who plan to work with singers with voice disorders. The following general guidelines are recommended:

(1) The preparation of the teacher of singing needs to be augmented by inclusion of training in anatomy and physiology and in clinical management of voice disorders.

(2) The preparation of the speech-language pathologist who works with singers needs to be augmented in a parallel manner to include instruction in vocal pedagogy (the art and science of teaching voice) and vocal performance.

Both ASHA and NATS affirm that the following areas remain the province of our individual organizations to act upon as desired: (a) to develop more specific training requirements for individual members who elect to work with singers with voice disorders, (b) to develop criteria for evaluation and subsequent recommendation and/or accreditation of training programs, and (c) to develop criteria for identification and/or certification of individual members who obtain the recommended specialty training.

Both ASHA and NATS recognize the existence of state licensure laws that govern delivery of services to persons with communication disorders, including voice disorders. All persons who work with singers with voice disorders are encouraged to become familiar with these laws. ASHA and NATS affirm that it remains the responsibility of the individual practitioner to ensure that his or her work with singers does not violate the scope of practice defined by these laws.

ASHA and NATS encourage their members to cooperate in the development and delivery of interdisciplinary programs and services for singers with voice disorders.

January 21, 1992
New York, NY

This statement was accepted by the American Speech-Language-Hearing Association (ASHA) in March, 1992, and by the National Association of Teachers of Singing (NATS) on July 4, 1992. Members of the Ad Hoc Joint Committee for development of this statement included the ASHA representatives Janet Graves Wright (chair), Reinhardt Heuer, and Stan Dublinske (ex officio), and the NATS representatives Jean Westerman Gregg (chair) and Ingo Titze.

20

THE PROS AND CONS OF VOICE AMPLIFICATION IN THE THEATRE
AND TECHNOLOGY'S EFFECT ON VOICE/SPEECH TRAINING
OR
"IF YOU'RE GONNA SHOVE A MIKE DOWN MY THROAT, AT LEAST DO IT PROPERLY!"

KATE UFEMA AND BILL BRANDWEIN

T HE DEBATE

"Is it live or is it Memorex?" Companies base entire ad campaigns on the premise that there is little perceptive difference between "live" and "canned" (electronically processed) sound. These product pushers actually expect the public to believe that a voice can be recorded, tracked, filtered, mixed, edited, and recycled without altering the voice's quality and its ultimate effect upon its listeners. In the world of high-tech electronics, getting consumers to believe this false premise has turned into a gold mine. In the world of theatre, believing this premise could result in the demise of "live" theatre.

It appears that the natural human quality of the voice is no longer valued and demanded on the American stage. Only live theatre provides the opportunity to experience the immediacy and the intimacy of the human instrument and all the natural creative qualities of expression that are brought to an audience through the voice of a skilled actor. When we study history, we learn that our theatrical heritage includes a love of language. The respect for the ancient Greek and Roman theatrical orators was unsurpassed. A playwright's skill with words was paramount, and an actor's vocal delivery was his calling card. Audiences delighted in the wit, the charm, the romance, the tragedy, the poetry of the language. Storytelling was dominated by the sound of the performer's voice. Thirty years ago, there was no audience desire for reinforced voices. Theatregoers and artists alike valued vocal craft and the skillful delivery of language. Audiences could hear the actors, and there was no confusion between the different media. What you saw was what you heard. Voice and image were one. How sad that we are becoming prisoners of our technology, not only accepting but expecting artists to always include technological extensions as part of their work. With the use of modern technology, sight has replaced sound and special effects often overshadow plot. Mood was originally created by the nuance of the actor's vocal tone and presence. Today, many stage directors rely on changing lights and recorded sounds to establish the mood, and audiences have come to expect the use of vocal sound reinforcement (amplification) in live theatrical productions.

Why do we, as actors and voice and speech trainers, find this amplification trend so offensive, so intrusive, and so threatening to the live theatre experience we treasure? Why do directors, artistic directors, and/or producers feel so obligated to reinforce an actor's voice? Is it because they think theatregoers expect live theatre performances to sound like a movie? Is amplification chosen because audiences claim they cannot hear the actors? Could it be that voice amplification is desirable because acting styles have become smaller and more intimate, resulting in less vocal projection from the actors? Or does the electronic solution simply appear to be the quickest fix to a variety of problems? Finally, how does this pervasive use of voice reinforcement affect the vocal training and the vocal prowess of both working and aspiring actors? These questions are current subjects of concern and debate in the world of theatre and vocal performance. Let us examine the primary reasons given for needing voice reinforcement, and explore some alternatives.

1. *Voice reinforcement is prescribed because the audiences cannot hear the actors.* If so, is amplification the only solution? Consider other options. Maybe the house acoustics are too live or too dead and need some adjustment or change. Sometimes there are interfering masking sounds, emanating from heating or cooling units, that need to be modified or eliminated. Perhaps more acoustical insulation is desirable to keep out external distractions such as airplane, siren, and traffic noises. Maybe the actors require more training and/or encouragement to communicate with additional energy, diction, and vocal support. These alternatives, and others like them, should be explored before voice amplification is deemed the sole solution.

2. *Voice reinforcement is prescribed because "canned" sound is what audiences have come to expect through frequent exposure to radio, TV, and film.* There is no doubt that we have become accustomed to hearing voices processed

through microphones, amplifiers, and loudspeakers: voices that are transmitted through wires, circuits, and computers after being digitized, quantified, synthesized, and sterilized. Natural vocal immediacy and skill are elements that make live theatre special. Opera enthusiasts, who listen to their favorite works and artists on records, tapes, and CD's, would walk out of the opera house booing if singers' voices were miked. They demand that producers and artists maintain the integrity of their treasured art form. As theatre lovers we have the same obligation to cultivate live theatre's vocal uniqueness and keep it "live."

3. *Voice reinforcement is prescribed because acting styles have changed while theatre spaces have not.* With the advent of "method" acting, a performer's vocal prowess has become "smaller" in order to sound more "real." Actors are getting confused as they hop from stage to film, forgetting that vocal choices must change between the various media. We as voice and speech trainers have a major responsibility to train actors to develop the skills and the awareness to perform in any venue.

4. *Voice reinforcement is prescribed, as is most often the case, because it appears to be the easiest solution to any one and/or all of these problems.* Technology is erroneously considered to be quick and efficient. Good sound reinforcement equipment is *very expensive*, needs constant maintenance, and is only as good as its utilization and operation. Additionally, it must be noted that even the finest equipment changes the voice, altering the overtones and the harmonics that are so indicative of expressive, skilled communication.

Clearly, the decision to reinforce an actor's voice is founded in the complexities of our theatre facilities, our audience expectations, and our actor-training methods. But in the actual analysis, voice amplification is most often a *choice* rather than a necessity. The debate is: where does the artistic commitment lie, and how are the play and its live presentation best served? Will live theatre be encouraged to evolve towards the use of technological elements found in other entertainment media? Or will those who make the creative decisions *choose* to keep live theatre "live?"

Theatre is not radio. Theatre is not TV. Theatre is not film. Rather, theatre is its own art form, with its own manner of communication possessing its own charm. If we allow present trends to continue, audiences will become increasingly interested in the results of the technology rather than in the product of the human artistic instrument. They will literally become addicted to the processed sound of an actor's voice, losing all appreciation for "live," unaltered expression.

Many live performance skills are already becoming obsolete and being replaced by technological counterparts. Musicians are being replaced by synthesizers. Miniature ear pieces feeding pre-recorded lines are known substitutes for the memory of the actor. Computer programs are eliminating the need for composers to learn to read music. Microphones and sound reinforcement systems are encouraging lazy vocal deliveries, resulting in poor technique and the lack of performance stamina. And consider that, often, it is not the athlete with the most talent or skill who wins, but, rather, the winning athlete is the one who has had access to the best equipment and training technology.

The well-trained voice of a sensitive actor can be magical, drawing audience members to the edge of their seats. An actor's voice should lead all attention to the stage, to the character's immediate presence and needs, to the message, and to the story. But instead of creating presence, sound reinforcement creates distance, as voices are delivered to the audience through speaker arrays distributed throughout the house. Thus, the communication becomes mediated and divorced from its empathetic vibratory source. And how demoralizing it can become to have, as one colleague phrased it, "the humanity ironed out of the voice." Actors literally lose control of the effect of their expression as their voices are processed by electronics, placing an artificiality between the actor and the audience, almost like an audible scrim. Elaine Stritch, an actress/singer playing the role of Parthy in *Showboat* on Broadway states, "It's not just the actual projection of sound. It's also the art of reaching an audience. A stage whisper isn't a low sound projected necessarily; it's a sound that says you have a secret. Mikes do tend to destroy that kind of projection."[1]

Is all really fair in love, war, art, and technology? Or are there lines that, once crossed, will blemish or even destroy the state of being? Every discipline must progress with the times or face possible extinction or relegation to tradition, and this includes the arts. But every discipline has its boundaries, beyond which the discipline loses its focus and its path, and thereby its identity. The day will soon arrive when sound technology is so sophisticated that it will be capable of presenting theatregoers with a nearly perfect artificial representation of a live performance. Is this progress or extinction?

Currently, as voice and speech trainers, we appear to be caught in a dilemma. Our knowledge and discipline afford those in our charge a veritable wealth of tools, skills, and resources. We *can* impart it all, without question. Yet we are most concerned about how all these wonderful tools, skills, and resources are ultimately manipulated by electronics and technicians in performance.

KNOW WHAT TO DO

Certainly, there are circumstances when an audience might benefit

---

[1]   Vincent Canby, "Look Who's Talking: Microphones", *New York Times*, January 22, 1995.

from the judicious use of voice reinforcement. Voice amplification may indeed be warranted in giant halls, outdoor venues, if a director chooses to project voices over electronic instruments or large orchestras, and in houses with irreparably bad acoustics. If a production uses amplified instruments, there may truly be a need to amplify voices so that they can be heard. The rock musical simply would not exist without the multitudinous sound processing technology that gives the genre its own unique sound. Additionally, the special vocal effects that can be achieved through the use of reverb and digital effect units can be such fun! Ghost voices in *Hamlet, Macbeth,* or *A Christmas Carol;* the plant's voice in *Little Shop of Horrors;* the Giantess of *Into the Woods;* and the Wizard in *The Wiz* are only a few examples in which electronic voice manipulation and amplification can be desirable additions to, and resources for, character development.

The complexities of amplifying an actor's voice are many. When the reinforcement becomes particularly problematic, one or a combination of the following conditions is usually suspect: 1) the sound designer is a sound effects designer and not a sound reinforcement design engineer, 2) the equipment is inappropriate or substandard, 3) the equipment is improperly used, 4) the sound operator is inexperienced or inept, 5) the actors' skills are substandard, 6) the use of sound reinforcement was a low priority within the design process, and it was left to be added in at the last minute, almost as an afterthought.

In today's world of specialization, a sound reinforcement design engineer and a sound effects designer possess different skills and work with different equipment. Therefore, it should never be assumed that the designer of the music and/or the sound effects for a production has the skills or the equipment to reinforce the actors' voices. Live sound amplification and recorded sound playback are different technologies. If the reinforcement is not going well, it just may be that the sound effects designer is trying to do a sound reinforcement design engineer's job by adding a few microphones and speakers to a sound playback system. This is *not* the same as having a skilled sound reinforcement design engineer using a reinforcement system.

Every show's sound reinforcement needs are distinct. Usually, the equipment and setup that worked well for one production are simply inappropriate for another. Often, sound reinforcement is not part of a show's budget or is low on the show's priority list, and the same equipment is expected to accommodate any and all productions within the same house. Any good sound designer will explain that the sound reinforcement design is as unique to a production as are its set or its costumes, both in the type of equipment needed and the equipment's placement. Monitor and reinforcement speakers are often built right into a set. And body mikes and their battery packs have to be carefully incorporated into each individual actor's costume and/or hair/wig. Therefore, if sound reinforcement is needed, specific sound choices must be made early in the design process. The design team must collaborate accordingly, and the show's budget must include support for the agreed-upon choices.

A sound reinforcement design engineer is not a necessary evil, but rather should be an integral part of the design team, as a conscious effort must be made to create a credible vocal presentation. A flick of a switch in the sound booth can totally eliminate voice amplification at any moment if the director so chooses. There is no such switch to instantly *add* reinforcement. Good voice reinforcement requires careful planning and forethought.

Beyond the equipment and the designer, the sound operator (engineer) is crucial. If the operator is not fully skilled in handling the subtleties of the complex equipment, or does not have a sensitive ear, even the best equipment and design will not produce the desired result. The sound reinforcement operator is potentially the single person who can "make or break" the vocal quality of the show. In fact, this operator has become so crucial to performance outcome that the *New York Times* reviewer Vincent Canby has written, "Time was when you worried whether the leading lady had a cold. Today you do better to hope the sound engineer had a good night's sleep."[2] Therefore, these engineers should be listening in at rehearsals as early as possible so they can become familiar with the actors' natural voices *before* the amps and speakers are incorporated into the sound presentation.

Lastly, and perhaps most importantly, a sound reinforcement system can only amplify what already exists. If the performer is not producing a projected, energized, articulate, and supported communication, no operator or equipment can make the delivery better. *Reinforcement cannot enhance quality, it only amplifies the existing quality.* If the actor's vocal skills are substandard or lazy, amplifying them only amplifies the actor's lack of ability and/or energy. In essence, technology will never be a substitute for performance skills.

TRAINING AND PERFORMANCE SKILLS

Regarding performance skills, it would appear that both actor training and performance are being affected by technology. Microphones and loudspeakers often give actors a false sense of themselves both in training and in performance. Many young actors use amplification as an excuse not to learn the vocal skills that involve diction, projection, support, and stamina. They assume the attitude that any phonation beyond an everyday conversational tone is forced, fake, and unnecessary thanks to the use of sound reinforcement. They rely on technology before they attempt to explore the possibil-

---

[2]   Ibid.

ities of their own natural instruments. They become dependent upon a sound system, weakening their desire to develop a power of expression. The result is a weak, tight instrument, devoid of respect for and facility with language. These actors work to sensitize their emotional memories, their sense memories, their images. But they neglect to develop a vocal instrument through which they can artistically express these honed sensitivities.

According to Otts Munderloh, the sound designer on the recent Broadway production of *Passion*, "Actors were better trained in the past. Nowadays, an actor isn't expected to reach the last row. Miking enables people to get away with giving less than their all."[3]

Tony Meola, the sound designer for the recent Broadway revival of *Guys and Dolls*, agrees: "We're producing a generation of non-projectors. My job is to make the non-projector sound like those who do project."[4] He goes on to say that in the old days, such non-projectors simply were not hired.

The human spirit, the human focus, and the striving for excellence through one's own personal resources is the root of all art. Acting teachers, directors, artistic directors, and producers must insist that strong vocal skills be developed and employed. Voice and speech trainers should not be the only advocates of the actors' vocal craft.

The advent of "method" acting has greatly changed the vocal dynamic of American theatre. In her foreword to Don Richardson's *Acting Without Agony: An Alternative to the Method* (1988), Helen Hayes wrote the following regarding actor training and performance:

> In the thirties the Method was born. It spread like measles among the young.
>
> A great many had no idea of what it was all about, but they latched onto the blissful concept that acting is an art, not a craft, that too much training is dangerous, technique destructive to natural gifts — that the true art of acting comes only from within one's own life experience. So was born the Scratch and Mumble School... I have read Stanislavsky and there is much that is useful... but I am sure that the Strasberg version — which has dominated and dampened the spirit of the theatre for the past fifty years — has no relation to the original.
>
> What our theatres and our screens need now is actors with training in stage deportment. We have some and we treasure them, but we need more with knowledge of projection, of clarity, and, oh, please, of *style*. Then our new playwrights can take off and once again write plays with language.[5]

---

[3]   Ibid.

[4]   Ibid.

[5]   2nd Edition, Allyn and Bacon, Inc., 1994, pp. xiii–xiv.

Veteran actors are also getting caught in the trap of sound technology. Stage actors who become film actors and then return to the stage often have difficulty with the readjustment. Their vocal delivery becomes so filmic that, upon return to the stage, they no longer have the projection or the stamina that live theatre demands. And the sound equipment only emphasizes just how out of shape they are.

There is simply no substitute for vigorous and disciplined voice training and maintenance; training that encourages actors to *project* their vocal truth, and maintenance that keeps them vocally strong. Effective training and proper maintenance could very possibly create a path towards ending the excessive use of and/or need for voice amplification.

FINAL ANALYSIS

We must strive to keep live theatre vocally "live" and skillfully honest. We do not have stunt men substituting for principals in the theatre. We do not have TelePrompTers running lines. So why are so many actors' voices being processed through excessive reinforcement? We already over-amplify all of the musicals. How long will it be before we amplify all of the other genres?

In the sixties, there was a fad to project scenery. But the choice to use projections quickly passed, because the resulting scenic illusions were flat and two-dimensional. Presently, there is a fad which uses microphones, electronics, and speakers to project actors' voices. Let us hope that this, too, shall pass, and for the very same reasons.

Yes, every audience member is entitled to hear, but hearing and listening are different. In most cases, with a competent and sensitive sound engineer, reinforcement, in and of itself, is not the enemy. If there are enemies that threaten our art, one is the attitude that vocal strength and craft are no longer important; another is the expectation that live theatre must imitate the other performance media in order to maintain audience acceptance. These are false attitudes and expectations. Most theatregoers come to a live performance because it is different from what they turn on in their homes. Live theatre is personal and public all in the same breath. It is first-hand communication. It is human.

In the final analysis, voice reinforcement is a *choice*. And we believe that to use this technology *selectively and judiciously* is the strongest choice for the truest expression of live theatre. Therefore, as voice directors and voice and speech trainers, it behooves us to train our actors never to rely on sound reinforcement, and to encourage stage directors and producers along the same path. Audiences will not follow where we do not lead. It is the actor's responsibility to project the communication, and the audience's charge to listen. If actors are trained to be skilled vocal artists and audiences are encouraged to listen, live theatre will truly be "a-live" and always a very special experience.

21

BREATHING IS MEANING

BY CATHERINE FITZMAURICE

Roland Barthes [1977: 183–4] writes: "The breath is the *pneuma*, the soul swelling or breaking, and any exclusive art of breathing is likely to be a secretly mystical art."

In studying breathing I have recognized something of its spiritual and transformative potential, but in teaching actors my aim has been to demystify the process whereby presence and power may be achieved, offering pragmatic exercises which may be practiced by anyone. I have looked for information not only to arts technique, but also to science, philosophy, and psychology, as well as esoteric traditions. Here is a brief history and general description of my voice work which has come to be called Destructuring/Restructuring.

In an analysis of the physical components necessary for sound production — power source, oscillator, resonator — breath occupies the most active place in human vocal production: it is the energy impulse that excites the vibration in the vocal folds and the resulting resonance in the body — starting, continuing, and stopping it. Because of the living and therefore infinitely changeable quality of the particular actions and structures that are responsible for this sound vibration, the way in which the human body breathes affects the voice a great deal, much as the hands of a good pianist and a beginner create different sounds with the same instrument. Breathing, then, makes an essential difference in quality of vocal production. By quality I refer not only to timbre, but to the entire range of use of the voice.

Voice is an action. It has no location in the body except when it is in action, sounding. The essential physical structures — diaphragm, intercostal, abdominal and back muscles; larynx; articulators; body form and cavities — are in themselves virtually mute until, with a particular use of the breath and vocal folds, they all interrelate as power source, oscillator, and resonator to create sound. It is for optimal functioning of the breath energy, as power source, that I have searched.

A singer's voice work deals largely with the use of the vocal folds, practicing different pitches, onsets, durations, trills, and cessations, enjoying the bird-like flutter sensations at the throat, and finding, in the added manipulations of the pharynx, jaw, and articulators, delightful variations of phoneme and tone, while using the breath for tone initiation, consistency, pause, and volume. However, for those without musical skills or aspirations, the voice is usually simply a means of direct communication of ideas or feelings, requiring no conscious effort other than some acquisition of language skills. Actors in the theatre are caught between these two poles. Since the speaking voice is not as determined by meter, melody, or tone as a singer's voice, and since an actor's textual interpretation and given circumstances (real and imagined) of place, time, action, and person are constantly varying, the act of speaking is always somewhat improvisatory, based on impulse, and essentially immediate. It is a commitment to the manifest present.

In my thirty years of work with actors' speaking voices I have focused on breath as the vital active ingredient for physical sound-making as well as for the expression of ideas. "Inspiration" denotes both the physical act of breathing in, and the mental act of creating a thought. The expiration (breathing out) or expression of the thought is likewise both physical and mental. It is the harmonizing of these twin aspects of speaking — the physical needs and impulses and the mental thought processes — that I address, and through them the harmonizing of the two functions of the nervous system in the act of breathing for speaking: the autonomic (which is an unconscious response by the diaphragm to a need for oxygen) and the central (which can override autonomic respiratory rhythm through conscious motor control). The diaphragm contains both unstriated and striated muscle and is responsive to both the autonomic and central nervous systems. It is therefore uniquely appropriate as a site to create such harmony, so that the healing of the culturally prevalent body/mind split is not merely a metaphysical, but is actually a physical and obtainable goal which brings impulse and thought together as action.

In searching for models beyond my own empirical experience and my observation of students and actors, the modern and ancient somatic training systems of Bioenergetics, Yoga, and Shiatsu have been most influential. In experimenting with these exercises myself and on others I explored means to most directly affect breathing and vocal sound, and the adaptations of these systems that I use with actors have over the years resulted in a series of exercises and interventions that I call Destructuring.

The Destructuring work consists of a deep exploration into the autonomic nervous system functions: the spontaneous, organic impulses which every actor aspires to incorporate into the acting process. The tendency of the body to vibrate involuntarily as a healing response to a perceived stimulus in the autonomic "fight or flight" mode (as in shivering with cold or fear, trembling with grief, anger, fatigue, or excitement) is replicated by applying induced tremor initially through hyperextension of the body's *extremities only*, thus leaving the *torso muscles* free to respond with a heightened breathing pattern. At the same time a great deal of unaccustomed energy, waves of tremor, and, ultimately, relaxation, flow throughout the body, sensitizing it to vibration and increasing feeling and awareness. The introduction of sound into these positions allows the ensuing physical freedom to be reflected in the voice too, not just the body, because this freedom also naturally affects resonance and laryngeal use, so that pitch range and inflectional melody are improved, as are tone, timing, and rhythm, and even listening and interrelating.

Destructuring affects not only the vocal performance and the daily breathing (and vocal) habits of the actor, but can also radically alter muscle tone and body organization, allowing sound vibrations to extend beyond the conventional resonators of chest and head throughout the body, adding harmonic range and natural volume to the voice. It encourages the breathing (as power source and therefore timing) and the body (as resonator and therefore tone) to respond organically to shifts in mood and idea, thus achieving variety and complexity of meaning and eliminating unintentionally dry, flat delivery.

Since the physical and emotional aspects and the awareness levels of the actor can be deeply affected by this work, the resulting growth of the personality helps create a more mature artist, with increased potential for both sensitivity and proaction. Through self-reflexive contact with the autonomic nervous system the actor acquires not only a more functional vocal instrument but also gains in autonomy, authenticity, and authority, which affect both personal and social behavior, as well as aesthetic choices.

When the autonomic movements of the "Destructured" muscles of respiration are less inhibited it becomes easy to "Restructure" by introducing the traditional European breathing techniques taught to actors in London at the Central School of Speech and Drama by Elsie Fogerty, Gwynneth Thurburn, J. Clifford Turner, and Cicely Berry. As a child I studied with Barbara Bunch, Cicely Berry's teacher, and I was fortunate to have for three formative years Alison Milne, Thurburn, Turner, and Berry as my teachers at the Central School. I returned there to teach before coming to the United States in 1968. It was the lack of ability in most of my students in both countries to isolate, without undue tension, the breathing actions of the vocally efficient rib swing and abdominal support that caused me, not to give up the idea of technique as others have done in response to the perceived difficulty, but to look for methods of reducing body tension in faster and more radical ways than the voice work or the Alexander Technique which I had experienced at the Central School, so that the breathing isolations could become effortless and therefore economical, limber, and effective. The rib swing and abdominal support actions are, in fact, what an uninhibited body does during speaking.

In 1965 in London, David Kozubei introduced me to the work of Dr. Wilhelm Reich. Influenced by Reich, Kozubei had developed a means of reducing muscle tension which he called "Movements," and he founded a group to study Reich's work in a practical way. As a result I began to study Bioenergetics with Dr. Alexander Lowen and later in the United States with several of his trainees, and more recently have worked with Dr. John Pierrakos in Core Energetics. Both Lowen and Pierrakos were students and colleagues of Reich, and all three have written extensively. In 1972 I began to do Yoga. My own adaptation for voice work of bioenergetic tremors and Yoga stretches exists in their combinations and in a focus on a fully relaxed torso to allow maximum spontaneous breathing movement, and, more specifically, *in the use of sound on every outbreath, no matter how the body is breathing, without changing the placement or rhythm of that breathing.* This accustoms the actor to the integration of breath impulse and tone, while it tends to use only semi-approximated vocal folds resulting in "fluffy," released, *feeling* sounds which are very soothing to overused, tense vocal folds, and which can resemble the sounds that, according to Charles Darwin (1969), precede language, and which give individual paralinguistic meaning to speech. Then, after carefully integrating the unconscious (autonomic nervous system) patterns with the conscious (central nervous system) pattern of rib swing/abdominal support, speech sounds and then speech are introduced as an extension and application of the primary breathing function of oxygenation. This is what I call Restructuring. Restructuring gives the actor control over the timing and the variety of delivery choices of pitch, rate, volume, and tone, and allows approximate repeatability without loss of either spontaneity or connection to impulse.

Restructuring, then, is not only the introduction of intercostal and abdominal breath management into the act of speaking, but is also the harmonizing of that pattern with the individual's physical and/or emotional needs for oxygen moment to moment. It requires the ability to isolate particular parts of the abdominal muscle and of the intercostal and back muscles, without interrupting the organic oxygen need. The Restructuring work for the inbreath expands the chest cavity where the lungs are largest, in the lower third of the ribcage, thus bringing in as much air as needed phrase by phrase without undue effort in the upper chest but also without inhibiting any movement that might occur there as a result of physical need or emotional involvement. I do not teach Clifford Turner's "rib reserve," but the actor will find that as the body accustoms itself to the Restructuring the ribs will naturally stay out somewhat longer during speech because the abdominal support movement (as the Restructuring work for the outbreath) becomes the vocal action, replacing the rib-squeeze or neck tension which often seem to recur when the actor only attempts to stay "relaxed" while speaking. Speaking *requires* an *active* use of the outbreath during its role as exciter of vibration.

An awareness of oxygen need on the autonomic level, and a trust in his right to pause, or to breathe in when he has a new thought, are all essential for an actor while learning Restructuring, so that upper chest, shoulder, and neck tension do not develop, and so that hyperventilation does not occur since the lungs may take in much more oxygen than normal at one time. I always work the Restructuring with speech sounds, nonsense, impromptu speaking, and later, text, because there is no need to have control over breathing placement or timing if the actor is not using the voice. One may then practice the breathing pattern with various speech sounds in combination, with varying lengths, speeds, pitches, and volumes of phrases, with and then without pauses, and later again with different styles of texts, character voices, emotional expressions (e.g. laughing, crying, shouting, screaming), and body positions, actions, and interactions, etcetera. I encourage actors finally not to monitor problems nor even the involvement of the breath tract and articulators in the act of speaking, but, with the help of an imaged "focus line" traveling from the dynamic abdominal action on the outbreath around the pelvis to the spine and up into and out from the "third eye" area, to engage fully, from the intuitive, physical (and metaphysical, "Q'i") centre at the abdomen, in the action of meaningful communication with another, which involves receiving as much as sending.

The sometimes physically and/or emotionally painful work on the release of inhibitory tensions in Destructuring, combined with the mastery and application of technique in Restructuring, is a long and often frustrating journey for the actor, but the rewards are great. The emotional and artistic growth which occurs during Destructuring is audible in the tones of voice and the delivery choices; and just as one may take a while to learn to ride a bicycle or drive a stick shift, but later one is only focused on arriving at one's destination, the initially consciously monitored breathing actions of Restructuring become finally an automatic response to an actor's need to communicate meaning effectively. It is at this point that voice work becomes indistinguishable from acting.

An examination of the early development of my Destructuring work can be found in an unpublished 1978 M.F.A. thesis by Penelope Court for the Goodman

School of Drama through the Art Institute of Chicago, and a later look can be found in an unpublished 1993 M.F.A. thesis by Michael Barnes for the National Conservatory, Denver Center for the Performing Arts. Thanks to Dr. Robert Sataloff for his comments on a draft of this article. This article is dedicated to the memory of Penelope Court.

WORKS REFERENCED

Barthes, Roland. *Image, Music, Text.* New York: Hill and Wang, 1977.

Darwin, Charles. *The Expression of the Emotions in Man and Animals.* Reprint. New York: Greenwood Press, 1969.

V
LAST THOUGHTS

22

THE HUMAN VOICE:
BRIDGE OR BATTLEFRONT

MARIAN HAMPTON

The brilliant and compelling anti-war film, *Breaker Morant*, was playing again on one of the networks the other night, and I began musing, as I had on the several occasions I had seen it before, about the powerful performance of Edward Woodward. I was again moved by his exquisite renderings of short passages from Byron and other poets and by how the sonority of those superbly integrated passages gave such transcendent wisdom to the spare, honest film, by pointing up the contrast between the poor but genteel breeding of Harry Morant and the ironic brutalities of war. The overwhelming sadness of the film's ending seemed, somehow, also to remind me that the ability to integrate such heightened speeches into the mundane language of everyday is a skill much treasured by voice professionals but rarely called for in the theatre and films of our postmodern era. Harry Morant knew himself to be a kind of anachronism in his own particular time warp, a human sacrifice to "peace" at the end of the Boer War. To witness the death of so eloquent and well-spoken a character, with poetry in his soul, suddenly had momentous unforeseen implications for the future of language as a tool of human communication and, indeed, for the survival of civilization.

Obviously, so literal a reading of film "deaths" begs the question of the difference between life and art. But some ten to fifteen years since the making of this film, certain societal changes lend a symbolic charge to the message of the decline of civilization under conditions of war which exceeds even its original impact. Bosnia, Croatia, Chechnya, any of the countless wars grinding along, on this poor tired globe — and our own violence-racked cities — all have given testimony to the fact that not only are people not communicating, telling the truth, expressing themselves effectively, but nobody is really listening any more either.

If we think back to what must have been the very beginnings of language, when our primitive ancestors first began making sounds to convey meaning, we can envision a period in which humankind began experimenting with sound, with the sound of the breath over what later became the vocal folds, and then, with sounds we would later call vowels. It must have been miraculous when those pioneer ancestors first began attending to sounds, trying out the clicks and hisses and pops they could add to their voices to make even more sophisticated sound conglomerates, which we would later call words, and which would eventually become spoken and then written language, leading to the development of thoughts and subsequently to language, and languages, and the whole rich panoply of literature, the world over, which has so graced our lives and moved civilization forward, step by step.

The Bible says, in the first line of the Gospel according to John, that "In the beginning was the Word, and the Word was with God, and the Word was God." Was this also the beginning of God? In one reading, it might seem so. Julian Jaynes, in his seminal book, *The Origin of Consciousness in the Breakdown of the Bicameral Mind*, indicates to us that consciousness is based on language, rather than having existed before language. Certainly, consciousness has come to be that which separates what is human from what is not. That being the case, what might become of the human race if the power and beauty of language were to be lost?

The human voice, through the uses of language and tone, has the ability to build nations. The small talk at social gatherings, where many business ventures are decided on the basis of trust and inspiration, as well as the international treaties which bind nations together, are evidence of the power of the uses of language and of tone, bridges between people and between languages to promote growth and peace in the bodies politic.

The eminent voice teacher and international voice facilitator, Cicely Berry, has spoken of the healing power of the language of Shakespeare when uttered by inmates of Long Lartin and Dartmoor in England. Shakespeare's language provides a broad spectrum of human thought and a heightened speech to give expression to the extreme conditions of their mind and behavior. Patsy Rodenburg has said that psychotic killers often begin speaking in verse, even iambic pentameter, when they tell of their grim deeds. Verse and heightened speech, then, are analogous to extreme behavior, and the language of Shakespeare builds a bridge of understanding to other human beings, as well as a bridge of emotional release and communication to human beings on the fringe of society. Indeed, it might be said that there is no place where language cannot go, cannot serve. If language can enable communication for the mentally insane, then obviously it can enable those who are less handicapped.

Dean J. Robert Wills spoke passionately at an Association for Theatre in Higher Education seminar of the bonding experience he had in working with the cast of a production of *Vital Signs* he was directing. Some of the rehearsal sessions were given over to the telling and sharing of personal stories — often previously untold stories — which produced a deep sense of connection between all of the participants of the production. The telling of stories and the being heard, the listening to stories and true hearing of someone else's story, have the power to build bridges and dissolve the differences between people of disparate background and experience.

In preparing Aeronautical Science Engineering students for oral presentations, in recent years, I realized that the Challenger disaster was the result of unsuccessful communication. There was only one line of communication to the top authority on that project, rather than at least two, as is usually recommended. And those responsible at the top of that chain of command did not adequately hear the information that should have prevented that flight. One wonders just how many human failures to communicate, with required clarity and passion, that the O-rings could not handle the stress of the flight, there might also have been along that same line of command. This realization served to connect me with the life-and-death importance of our ability to communicate clearly and honestly. I saw that every airplane we fly is supported not only by mathematical equation but also by language.

In a different sense, the life-and-death value of words, tone, language, and communication became apparent in discussing with one of my private students his work as a news anchor. After a certain point of working on his voice, regularly, over a year, and getting into how to read the text simply, honestly, it was inevitable that we would talk about the image and the self-image of the news correspondent: just what kind of character is this intruder into your living room and mine? Certainly, he needs to be an honestly caring person, not just a sycophantic opportunist who profits at the expense of the suffering human beings he is paid to observe. But, just as certainly, he needs to possess the wisdom afforded by distance, a view of the whole picture — in other words, something like God. I wondered if this could be why the press exert such authority over our lives, and whether they really know more than we do or merely communicate as though they do.

Almost all of us have had experiences in which we have had an overwhelming fear of speaking out, whether it be in an audition or in a heated public meeting or in an unwanted confrontation of some kind. In fact, the fear of speaking in public supersedes the fear of death in this country, as expressed in many statistical surveys. Perhaps this fear relates to the life-and-death importance of speech; or, perhaps, to the fear of loss of self if one is not listened to or really heard. In the latter sense, there is a real death, although not a biological one.

I have come to the conclusion that the vast majority of non-theatre speakers so modulate their pitch range and tone as to have only a couple of operational notes, because they are, consciously or not, intent on creating a sense of trust in their fellow human beings: that is, to not seem histrionic or "flaky." Nowhere is this more demonstrable than in the world of finance, whose practitioners must lull their clients into a state of unruffled calmness in order to create a successful working relationship.

Yet while there are so many ways to build bridges with words, not all of those entirely honest or unself-serving, but all somehow binding of the family of man, there are just as many opportunities for using words to divide, to conquer, to enrage, to militarize our fellow human beings. The history of war is fraught with verbal misunderstandings, whether those wars be fought on the national stage or in the schoolyard. The art of the politician provides an arena for this kind of divisiveness.

The politician must find an issue, or issues, which will inspire or inflame her constituents. It is her task, in a sense, to polarize the community, in order to set off her campaign from that of the other candidate, for one thing, and to galvanize voters to come to the polls in the hope of redressing some wrong, however trivial. It is the triviality of some of the goals which marks certain politicians as being basically dishonest. Here, rhetoric may be made to serve base motives, and language becomes, in the process, debased and untrustworthy.

Such an example is the current buildup of fascist extremism, in the name of patriotism and service to constitutional "rights." I was reminded of the statement of the commanding officer who gave the order to obliterate the hamlet of My Lai during the war in Vietnam, "in order to save it from Communism," when I read the following passage from *The Turner Diaries*, a futurist novel which is the bible of the militia movement, in *The New York Times*, July 5, 1995:

> Hanging from a single overpass only about a mile from here is a group of about 30, each with an identical placard around its neck bearing the printed legend, "I betrayed my race." Two or three of the group had been decked out in academic robes before they were strung up, and the whole batch are apparently faculty members from the nearby UCLA campus... There were many thousands of hanging female corpses like that in this city tonight, all wearing identical placards around their necks ("I defiled my race.") They are the white women married to or living with, blacks, with Jews, or with other nonwhite males.

The writer goes on to hang "...the politicians, the lawyers, the businessmen, the TV newscasters, the newspaper reporters and editors, the judges, the teachers, the school officials, the 'civic leaders,' the bureaucrats, the preachers and all others who, for reasons of career or status or votes or whatever, helped promote or implement the System's racial program." After this carnage, there must be hardly anybody left. Ironically, William Pierce, who wrote this book, is an escapee from the world of academia — so much for the so-called last bastion of free thought.

What leaps off the page to me, in this frightening book, which goes on and on to catalog the horrors of what could only be the destruction of civilization, is just how much the judgment by this marauding band of revolutionaries depends upon *appearance* and *skin color.* Is this not a world entirely based on *visual* criteria — and thus, a world much like the world which preceded the onset of language as a tool of communication? So the final denouement of the history of primitive, warring clans is a return to primitive warring clans, *because of a loss of consciousness, through the loss of language upon which consciousness is based.* We will have become trapped in how we look to others, with a consequent loss of self and responsible self expression. This might form a new definition of the ancient paranoia.

If there were ever a time when words, language, verbal communication were needed, it is now. If there were ever a time when voice teachers were needed, it is now. If there were ever a time when articulate theatre were needed, it is now. Kristin Linklater, in accepting a Lifetime Achievement Award, spoke of how "the eye is eating the ear." She reminded her audience that the ear has many more nerve receptors than the eye, rendering the ear's version of events a much richer one. We might add that the stakes, in this battle for the survival of the values of the ear, are sky-high and beyond, for civilization and even for the planet.

We must find ways to continue to hone our aural skills, even when everything points to the dominance of the visual. I was not always conscious of why I resisted the idea of E-Mail, until I realized that I depended on hearing the voice of the other person, for in it I could hear tone and choices of language and nuance that told me the state of physical and emotional health, point of view, all the aspects of communication which could impel me to action. Or I might just hear some marvelous story that would move me or make me laugh. I might be able to get some of these results in print, but I get a far deeper connection with my communicator if I can hear the voice.

Unable to single out a superb soloist in the Broadway revival of *Showboat,* I realized that, since all of the voices onstage were coming from boxes rather than from singing performers, I was being cheated of seeing the performer sing by the spectacle of the production. What an irony: even our seeing is being abridged by the uses of technology designed to supplant listening.

I submit that we auditory persons, we small band of voice teachers, have a call as never before to ply our trade on behalf of language, of listening, of humanity, of consciousness. And we theatre folk have the necessity of honoring the spoken word, with all our might and main. For the loss of our language and our effective use of language will presage the loss of our very world. It is a life and death matter that we use words to build bridges of understanding rather than dig a "slough of despond;" that we forge structures for acceptance, rather than vehicles for war; and that we treasure our ability to speak and listen and teach others to do likewise; humanity's very survival depends on it.

BIBLIOGRAPHY

Berry, Cicely. *The Voice and How to Use It.* Virgin Books, London, 1994.

Cox, Murray, Editor. *Shakespeare Comes to Broadmoor.* Jessica Kingsley Publishers, London, 1992.

Jaynes, Julian. *The Origin of Consciousness in the Breakdown of the Bicameral Mind.* Houghton Mifflin Company, Boston, 1976.

Rodenburg, Patsy. *The Right to Speak.* Methuen Drama, London, 1992.

———. *The Need for Words.* Routledge, New York, 1993.

VI

ABOUT THE CONTRIBUTORS

Barbara Acker is head of voice for the Department of Theatre at Arizona State University, and held similar positions at the State University of New York at Binghamton, Louisiana State University, Miami University, and Illinois State University, Normal. She was a member of the Hilberry Repertory Theatre for four years. She received a Ph.D. with a minor in speech science from Wayne State University. She has studied with Arthur Lessac, and taken workshops with Cicely Berry and Roy Hart teachers. She has also studied Alexander and Feldenkrais techniques. She is a past president of the Voice and Speech Trainers Association. She has presented at the Voice Foundation Symposium and has published in *The Journal of Voice* and *The Journal of American Drama and Theatre*.

Frankie Armstrong was born in Cumbria and grew up in the Lake District of England. The loss of her sight, in her teen years, intensified her passion for folk singing. She trained as a social worker. Later she combined her interest in folk singing with social work and developed voice therapy workshops. She is co-author, with Kathy Henderson, of *My Song is My Own* and, with Jenny Pearson, of *As Far as the Eye Can Sing: An Autobiography*. She has contributed to *Glancing Fires: An Investigation into Women's Creativity*.

Robert Barton is head of the acting program at the University of Oregon and a certified Neuro-Linguistic Programming Practitioner. He is co-author, with Rocco Dal Vera, of *Voice: Onstage and Off*, and co-author, with Harry Hill, of *A Voice for the Theatre*, and is the author of *Acting: On-*

stage and Off and *Style for Actors*. His professional acting credits include over two-thirds of the plays of Shakespeare, most notably the title role in a PBS presentation of *Hamlet*. His Ph.D. in actor training is from Bowling Green State University. He is recipient of the American College Theatre Association's Outstanding Acting Coach award as well as the Association for Theatre in Higher Education's Best Book Award of 1993.

CICELY BERRY has been the Voice Director of the Royal Shakespeare Company since she joined the company in 1969. She taught at the Central School of Speech and Drama for twenty years and also had a private studio in London. She has worked extensively with educational and outreach workshops and programs and has given workshops in university theatre departments in the United States and with theatre companies in Germany and the former Yugoslavia. Berry is author of *The Voice and the Actor, Your Voice and How to Use It Successfully,* and *The Actor and the Text*. She organized Theatre Voice I and Theatre Voice II, international voice conferences held at the RSC in Stratford.

BILL BRANDWEIN has served as the Technical Supervisor, Facilities Manager, and Resident Sound Designer at the University of Maryland at College Park since 1986. He trained in technical theatre and physics. As a physics lab technician he developed lectures and demonstrations to teach physics to non-majors. He also directed a four-hour videotape series, "Demonstrations in Acoustics." He has designed sound for many productions at the University of Maryland, including Kate Ufema's productions of *Little Shop of Horrors* and *A Midsummer Night's Dream,* both of which were staged in a 1344-seat theatre.

KATE BURKE is head of the voice program at the University of Virginia, and has served in that position at Universities of Iowa, Michigan, Nebraska, and Washington. Her acting credits include roles at the American Conservatory Theatre, the American Repertory Theatre, and the Iowa Playwrights Festival. She has served as vocal director at San Diego's Old Globe Theatre and the Seattle Repertory Theatre. She is conducting a study of vocal nodes as part of a National Institute of Health grant. She has published articles in

The Voice Journal and *The Iowa State Journal of Research*. She is a member of the Board of Directors of the Voice and Speech Trainers Association.

Mary Corrigan is an Emerita Professor of the University of California at San Diego. She has taught voice in major professional actor training programs for the past twenty-two years. Her graduate degree is in Theatre and Psychology. Corrigan was initially trained by Kristin Linklater, and went on to take workshops with Cicely Berry and Arthur Lessac. She has team taught with Evangeline Machlin and Edith Skinner. She has studied singing, taken extensive workshops in the Alexander Method, yoga, Bio-Energetics, Feldenkrais, Rolfing, and Gestalt psychology. She has conducted numerous workshops in England, Egypt, Canada, and major professional actor programs. She has acted in over fifty plays and been awarded three Best Actress Awards. She is chair of the Acting Programs for the British American Drama Academy at Oxford University, England.

Donnalee Dox is currently a guest lecturer at the University of Arizona. She has taught theatre history and criticism at Arizona State University and Kent State University, and acting at the State University of New York at Oneonta. She was visiting scholar at the University of Oregon, Eugene. Dox studied voice at Westminster Choir College and the New England Conservatory and with Nancy Houfek at the University of Minnesota. She has performed in the choruses of the Glimmerglass Opera Company, the Chautauqua Opera Company, and the Baltimore Summer Opera Theatre Company. From 1985 to 1988 she was a salaried member of the resident choir and cantor at the National Shrine in Washington, D.C. She was acting/singing coach for productions at the University of Minnesota and at Kent State University. Dox has an M.A. from The Catholic University of America and a Ph.D. from the University of Minnesota.

Catherine Fitzmaurice is Professor of Theatre at the University of Delaware, where she teaches Acting to undergraduates. She has also taught Voice in advanced and graduate training programs at the Juilliard School, New York University, Circle-in-the-Square, American Conservatory Theatre, University of Southern California, and UCLA. She holds a B.A. in English and an M.A. in Theatre Studies from the University of Michigan, and completed three years training at the Central School of Speech and Drama in London. She has worked as an actress at the American Conservatory Theatre and in Southern California, and has worked extensively as a voice coach for actors in film, television, and theatre.

MARIAN HAMPTON is Head of Acting at Illinois State University, Normal. She has served as Voice Specialist for the Department of Theatre and Dance at the University of Texas at Austin. A graduate of Illinois Wesleyan University, she also holds an M.F.A. in Acting from the Yale School of Drama. Her doctoral dissertation, published under the title *Singing for Actors*, was written under the guidance of Lehman Engel, the "dean of American musical theatre conductors." Hampton is a professional actor, singer, director and voice/dialect coach. She is the Immediate Past President of VASTA. She has performed with Highland Park Music Theatre, Oakdale (Connecticut) Music Theatre, The San Francisco Mime Troupe, and the Clarence Brown Company, and has published in the *American Theatre Association Journal* and the *NATS Journal.*

LAURA C. KALO is the Artistic Director of The Belmont Children's Theatre in Boston. She has been working with the Roy Hart Theatre since 1987 and recently began teaching that work. She has written and produced over twenty-five children's musicals. She has been a vocal director and directing consultant for thesis projects at Emerson College and the Berklee College of Music. Kalo was a guest lecturer at Boston College and has been involved with training elementary and secondary teachers to integrate arts into school curriculum. She also teaches improvisation and ballroom dancing.

DUDLEY KNIGHT is Associate Professor and Vice-Chair of Drama in the School of the Arts, University of California–Irvine, and was Head of the Acting Division there for nearly a decade. He is a member of the artistic staff of South Coast Repertory, where he is resident voice, text, and dialect consultant, and is voice consultant at the Center for Voice, Western Medical Center, in southern California. An award-winning actor and director, he has performed extensively in film, television, radio, and voiceover, as well as on stage. He was a founding member of the Long Wharf Theatre in New Haven and the Magic Theatre in San Francisco.

ARTHUR LESSAC teaches voice, speech, singing, and movement and has developed applications of his technique for speech and voice therapy. He is Professor Emeritus at the State University of New York at Binghamton, where for many years he headed the voice program in the theatre department. Lessac studied singing at the Eastman School of Music and spent a year doing a clinical internship at St. Vincent's Hospital in New York. He has coached Broadway productions, worked with the Lincoln Center Training Program, and led many intensive workshops in his approach. Lessac is author of *Body Wisdom: The Use and Training of the Human Body* and *The Use and Training of the Human Voice*, which he has recently updated and revised.

KRISTIN LINKLATER is Head of Voice at Emerson University in Boston. She was born in Scotland and trained as an actress at the London Academy of Music and Dramatic Art, and later returned there to teach voice production as Iris Warren's assistant. In 1963 she came to the United States and established a studio in New York. She has done extensive professional coaching and training and worked with such theatres as the Guthrie, Stratford, Lincoln Center, and the Negro Ensemble Company. She offered her first training program for voice teachers in 1965 and in 1978 founded Shakespeare & Company. Linklater has conducted national and international workshops in her system. She is the author of *Freeing the Natural Voice* and *Freeing Shakespeare's Voice*.

DOROTHY MENNEN is Professor Emerita of Purdue University, where she taught singing and was head of voice for the Department of Theatre. She received an M.A. from Purdue University. She was vocal music supervisor for public schools in West Lafayette, Indiana. She has served as vocal director of productions all over the country. She is founder of the Voice and Speech Trainers Association and was its first President, and has long been recognized as a leader in setting standards in voice training. Mennen wrote *The Speaking Singing Voice, A Vocal Synthesis*.

Eʟɪᴢᴀʙᴇᴛʜ H. Nᴀꜱʜ is Associate Professor of Speech and Singing at the University of Minnesota. She received a B.F.A. from Columbia University and was awarded a two-year Fulbright Grant to study opera in Germany. For ten years she was leading coloratura soprano at Kaiserslautern Pfalztheater, Osnabruck's Theatre am Domhof, Detmold's Landestheater, and Kassel's Hessisches Staatstheatre. She made guest artist appearances at Salzburg, Luxembourg, Strasburg, Nancy, and Lugano. She earned an M.A. at Teachers College Columbia University and a Ph.D. at Indiana University. In 1989 and 1992 she was Visiting Professor at Theatrehochschule Hans Otto, Leipzig, Germany. She is author of *Always First Class: The Career of Geraldine Farrar, The Luminous Ones: A History of the Great Actresses,* and *Pieces of a Rainbow.*

Bᴏɴɴɪᴇ N. Rᴀᴘʜᴀᴇʟ has served as voice, speech, dialects, and text coach for the American Repertory Theatre and as teacher at its Institute for Advanced Theatre Training at Harvard since 1986. In addition to earning a Ph.D. in theatre with a minor concentration in voice pathology, Raphael trained intensively with Kristin Linklater, Arthur Lessac, and members of the Roy Hart Theatre. Raphael has taught at a number of institutions, including the National Theatre Conservatory in Denver, Northwestern University, and the University of Virginia, and has coached close to two hundred productions in regional theatre, Shakespeare festivals, and universities. In addition to participating in a number of experimental studies of actors' and singers' voices, she has served as consultant to performers and public figures.

Pᴀᴛꜱʏ Rᴏᴅᴇɴʙᴜʀɢ is head of the Voice Department at Britain's Royal National Theatre and of voice training at the Guildhall School. She attended London's Central School of Speech and Drama, where she studied with such voice and speech teachers as Joan Washington, Margo Braund, Gwynneth Thurburn, and Helen Winter. After five years of private studio teaching and extensive professional theatre coaching, Rodenburg joined Cicely Berry at the Royal Shakespeare Theatre for nine years. In 1990 she joined the National Theatre. She has given workshops in the UK and all over the world. Rodenburg is author of *The Right to Speak: Working with the Voice* and *The Need for Words.*

LUCILLE SCHUTMAAT RUBIN, Ph.D. is President of Professionally Speaking, a New York City firm offering voice, speech, and presentation coaching to theatre and business professionals. A former university professor, founding member of the Voice and Speech Trainers Association, and past president of the University and College Theatre Association, Rubin teaches at Circle in the Square Theatre School in New York, and is a speaking voice consultant for the otolaryngology departments at Lennox Hill Hospital in New York and Georgetown University Medical Center, Washington, D.C. Author of *The Voice Handbook* and editor of *Movement for the Actor*, Rubin is a frequent workshop and seminar presenter here and abroad.

KATE UFEMA, Voice and Speech Specialist in the Professional Actor Training Program in the Department of Theatre at the University of Minnesota, Duluth, is also an Equity actress and singer, a professional director, musical director, vocal/dialect coach, and a professional voice consultant and trainer. She trains and coaches voices in all the performance media, including contracts with CNN, CBS, NBC, ABC, National Public Radio, and American Public Radio. She has acted and directed across the country and has presented workshops and adjudicated theatre competitions and festivals from Colorado to the East Coast. Ufema is a charter member of the Voice and Speech Trainers Association, and is currently its Treasurer. She holds B.A., M.A., and M.F.A. degrees from Pennsylvania State University.

KATHERINE VERDOLINI is Assistant Professor and Director of Speech Pathology, Joint Center for Otolaryngology at Harvard Medical School. Dr. Verdolini studied voice performance and foreign languages at Indiana, before receiving her first Master's degree in Italian and Music History from the University of Ferrara in Ferrara, Italy. Upon returning to the United States, she completed a second Master's degree in Speech-Language Pathology at Indiana University, and a Ph.D. in Experimental Psychology (Learning and Memory) at Washington University in St. Louis. She served as Assistant Professor of Speech Pathology (1990–1995) and Assistant Professor of Music (1994–1995) at the University of Iowa. Her clinical activities and research have focused on voice and performing voice. Her specific research interests are the pathophysiology of nodule production and treatment, and learning theory in relation to voice training and therapy.

ANDREW WADE is the Head of Voice for the RSC Stratford season. He oversees the voice work in the RSC's three Stratford theatres, their two London theatres, their annual Newcastle season and the company's touring program. Andrew Wade trained at the Rose Bruford College of Speech and Drama in Kent. In 1980 he was appointed Head of the Voice Department at East 15 Acting School in Essex, and in 1985, he became Senior Lecturer at the Arts Educational Schools in London, in charge of the second-year voice programs. He has served as Tutor at the Rose Bruford College in Greenwich and has been involved with the Theatre Center in Islington. He has coached productions in the UK, the United States, Canada, France, Belgium, and the Netherlands and given numerous workshops.

INDEX

SPEAK WITH DISTINCTION
by Edith Skinner

"Speak With Distinction is the **most comprehensive and accessible speech book available** for teachers and students of speech."
>—Joan Washington, RSC, Royal Court & Royal National Theatre

"Edith Skinner's book is the **best book on speech I have ever encountered**. It was my primer in school and it is my reference book now. To the classical actor, or for that matter any actor who wishes to be understood, this method is a sure guide."
>—Kevin Kline

"Speak with Distinction is **the single most important work on the actor's craft** of stage speech. Edith Skinner's work must be an indispensable source book for all who aspire to act."
>—Earle Gister, Yale School of Drama

paper•ISBN 1-155783-047-9

A PERFORMER PREPARES

A GUIDE TO SONG PREPARATION FOR ACTORS, SINGERS AND DANCERS

by David Craig

A PERFORMER PREPARES is a class act magically transformed to the printed page. It's a 13-part Master-class on how to perform, on any stage from bleak rehearsal room to the Palace Theater. The class covers the basic Broadway song numbers, from Show Ballad to Showstopper. With precise, logical steps and dynamic and enteraining dialogues between himself and his students, Craig takes anyone with the desire to shine from an audition to final curtain call. These lessons on the page recreate as closely as possible the unique interpersonal dynamic of Craig's legendary coaching encounters in New York and Los Angeles.

$21.95 cloth
ISBN: 1-55783-133-5

ON SINGING ONSTAGE
New, Completely Revised Edition
by David Craig

"David Craig KNOWS MORE ABOUT SINGING IN THE MUSICAL THEATRE THAN ANYONE IN THIS COUNTRY—which probably means the world. Time and time again his advice and training have resulted in actors moving from non-musical theatre into musicals with ease and expertise. SHORT OF TAKING CLASSES, THIS BOOK IS A MUST."

—Harold Prince

"STUDYING WITH DAVID CRAIG MEANS INFINITELY MORE THAN LEARNING HOW TO PERFORM A SONG. I find myself drawing upon this unique man's totally original techniques in all arenas of my work. If mediocrity ever enters his studio, it is never allowed to depart."

—Lee Remick

"David Craig, through his training has miraculously fused the art of acting and singing. HE HAS PUT THE WINGS OF TALENT ON HIS STUDENTS."

—Stella Adler

paper • ISBN: 1-55783-043-6

THE ACTOR AND THE TEXT
by Cicely Berry

As voice director of the Royal Shakespeare Company, Cicely Berry has worked with actors such as Jeremy Irons, Derek Jacobi, Jonathan Pryce, Sinead Cusack and Antony Sher. *The Actor and The Text* brings Ms. Berry's methods of applying vocal production skills within a text to the general public.

While this book focuses primarily on speaking Shakespeare, Ms. Berry also includes the speaking of some modern playwrights, such as Edward Bond.

As Ms. Berry describes her own volume in the introduction:

" … this book is not simply about making the voice sound more interesting. It is about getting inside the words we use …It is about making the language organic, so that the words act as a spur to the sound …"

paper•ISBN 1-155783-138-6